THE AFRICANS

AN ETHNOLOGICAL ACCOUNT

D0145095

HAROLD K. SCHNEIDER
Indiana University

Prentice-Hall, Inc. Englewood Cliffs, New Jersey 07632

Library of Congress Cataloging in Publication Data

SCHNEIDER, HAROLD K
   The Africans : an ethnological account.

   (Prentice-Hall series in anthropology)
   Bibliography.
   Includes index.
   1. Ethnology—Africa, Sub-Saharan. 2. Africa,
Sub-Saharan—Social life and customs. I. Title.
GN645.S28   967   80-11485
ISBN 0-13-018648-1

PRENTICE-HALL SERIES IN ANTHROPOLOGY
DAVID M. SCHNEIDER, EDITOR

Printed in the United States of America

10 9 8 7 6 5 4 3 2 1

*Editorial/production supervision
and interior design: Jeanne Hoeting
Cover photograph: Stan Wakefield
Cover design: Jerry Pfeifer
Manufacturing Buyer: Edmund W. Leone*

PRENTICE-HALL INTERNATIONAL, INC., *London*
PRENTICE-HALL OF AUSTRALIA PTY. LIMITED, *Sydney*
PRENTICE-HALL OF CANADA, LTD., *Toronto*
PRENTICE-HALL OF INDIA PRIVATE LIMITED, *New Delhi*
PRENTICE-HALL OF JAPAN, INC., *Tokyo*
PRENTICE-HALL OF SOUTHEAST ASIA PTE. LTD., *Singapore*
WHITEHALL BOOKS LIMITED, *Wellington, New Zealand*

For Carol

CONTENTS

PREFACE

THE RECENT SWIFT RISE OF knowledge of Africa in the United States, which correlates with the rapidity with which the world has shrunk since the Second World War, is startling. American interest in Africa extends back to the early days of contact between Africa and the Western World in the sixteenth century, but until the nineteenth century this was primarily directed toward slavery. Even after the abolition of slavery in the United States in 1863, American concerns with Africa were principally commercial, including trade in West Africa for such things as palm oil and in East Africa for cloves. The colonization of Africa, which was essentially completed in 1885, closed the continent to American interests, except in Liberia where there were still strong ties with the United States.

In short, American involvement with Africa depended on the decolonization of the sub-Saharan area which began, for all practical purposes, with the independence of the Gold Coast (Ghana) in 1957. In this country, Melville Herskovits of Northwestern University, because of his long interest in Africa, acted as a kind of center, promoting involvement. (He published his doctoral dissertation on African cattle-oriented societies in 1926 and had done field work among the Fon-speaking people of Dahomey in the 1930s, which helped popularize African culture in America.) However, his efforts bore little return until the tide of independence movements flowed over the continent after 1957.

One of Herskovits' most successful ventures was the impetus he gave to the organization of the African Studies Association, founded in 1958, which acted to disseminate interest in Africa among anthropologists, political scientists, historians, economists, musicians, and others. Today the United States contains a large number of people who can boast of intimate knowledge of various parts of Africa.

During the last 20 years this rise of interest in Africa has led to the publication of a number of ethnologically oriented books, replacing Seligman's *Races of Africa*, a book with which anthropologists were not comfortable because it was based upon a limited amount of data about societies reflecting the situation at the time it was composed.

I have for some time felt the need of a book that combines an adequate treatment of social facts with a treatment of culture history, along with a non-marxist economic approach. As I try to explain in Chapter 1 on economic analysis, I feel we can reach new levels of insight and I hope this book has accomplished this goal.

Because this book attempts to integrate African materials in terms of a social-cultural-economic theory of African society, it does not systematically try to be exhaustive in its treatment of African life. For example, while Pygmies and San (Bushmen) are exotically interesting, they comprise such a small part of sub-Saharan Africa that they are treated rather peripherally. Furthermore, some aspects of social and cultural life are passed over in the interest of economy of length, including art and music. Still, within the canvas I have allowed myself, the reader will find plenty of detail.

In this connection the reader may, in fact, find too much detail in Chapter 5 on kinship, a chapter which the casual reader might prefer to skip because kinship is a rather technical subject. For the more serious reader the chapter is essential. Kinship is a critical part of most Africans' lives because it encompasses such fundamental things as the frequent antagonisms of brothers-in-law, the common friendly relations of grandfathers and grandsons, and the peculiarly close relationship of the mother's brother and the sister's son. From a practical point of view, despite its complexity, it cannot be ignored.

While not representative of all the important things that have been written about African people, the bibliography of this volume gives credit to a large number of students of African societies. Yet there are some who deserve special mention. Herskovits' name as well as Murdock's are among them. I have pleasure in acknowledging my indebtedness to both. Also, a debt is owed to the brilliant group of British social anthropologists whose work remains today the most colossal contribution to understanding African societies, such people as Evans-Pritchard, Forde, Fortes, Gluckman, Gulliver, Richards, Schapera, and Turner. They laid the groundwork for making sense of African life.

The contribution of Africans themselves to the understanding of their own societies and cultures has as yet not been great, compared to European and American scholars because, for the most part, they have not had as much opportunity to get involved in the enterprise. Nevertheless, such people as Onwuejeogwu, Legesse, and Uchendu, whose works are cited in this book, and such people as B.A. Ogot and K. Ndeti, whose works are not cited, are examples of scholars leading the way for many others yet to come. We may all look forward to the fresh insights they will contribue to our subject, as the above mentioned authors already have.

H.K.S.

1

PERSPECTIVES
ON AFRICA

THERE IS NO WAY to describe Africans objectively. By this I do not mean that they cannot be described without conscious manipulation of the data. I mean that people have built into the very core of their being one theory or another about why the world is the way it is and how they see and describe the world is deeply affected by this slant. Later in this book an attempt will be made to describe African philosophy and religion; we shall see that among many Africans, events are inevitably viewed in deeply moral terms and evil is ascribed to the machinations of greedy, selfish people. An African description of America might present America in moral terms.

The Western approach to people tends to a scientific, mechanistic mode, hence the Western view of Africa is not moral but apparently descriptive. Yet there is no truly objective theory. The purpose of this chapter is to elucidate my position by contrasting it with other approaches to the description of Africans.

WHO AFRICANS ARE

A glance at Map 1.1 will help us identify who Africans are. This map of African ethnic units produced by Murdock in his book *Africa* (1959) and commonly referred to as a tribal map, makes the stupendous attempt to indicate every ethnic group in Africa by drawing an approximate line around each of the group's "territories." Students of Africa do not ordinarily consider all these ethnic units to fall properly under the heading of Africa, which they conceive of rather as "Africa South of the Sahara" or "Black Africa" (*Afrique noire* in French terms). This perspective certainly excludes, for example, the Egyptians and Tunisians on the Mediterranean and the lower reaches of the Nile. However, as one moves south across the Sahara and up the Nile Valley, more and more "black" people are encountered, especially when one penetrates the belt of grassy, cultivable land just south of the Sahara running from the Atlantic to the Nile, an area generally categorized as *sudan* (which must be differentiated from the nation Sudan [see Map 1.2]). These black people are considered to be black, not just because of their skin color, which may be no blacker than that of some of the Arabs or Bedouins of the Sahara and North Africa, but because of their mode of life, their culture; it is significantly different from that of the Mediterranean-oriented cultures of these other people. Arab religion and culture have long since penetrated to the western part of the sudan where one may find Africans worshipping Allah or singing in Arab style. These Arabic cultural traits are mixed with traits typical of Africans further south.

Over on the east end of the sub-Saharan area we find the Amhara and Tigre, living high on the Ethiopian plateau, who are often dark colored but whose religion is Coptic Christian, the religion of Egypt until the Arab conquest after the seventh century A.D. These people reject classification with black Africans even though they are surrounded by the Oromo (Galla), and the Afar whom students of sub-Saharan Africa classify as Africans.

The line between North Africa and sub-Saharan Africa is vague and sometimes rather arbitrary. Arabic and Coptic cultures are rejected unless mixed with cultures more typical of sub-Saharan Africa but even then the criteria for inclusion are indecisive. The broken line drawn on Map 1.1 will serve as well as any to separate North and sub-Saharan Africa and will include people with a recognizably distinct cultural complex even though sometimes mixed with traits from the north.

Race

It used to be common in ethnological treatments of African people to include extensive treatment of racial classification. Nilotic physical types, often characterized as tall, were differentiated from Pygmies, depicted as very short, or San (Bushmen) women, who were described as steatopygic (protruding buttocks). However, aside from certain general features, such as kinky hair and dark skin, clear-cut distinctions were never possible. Today physical type is no longer seen as crucial to ethnology. The reason is simply that physical form is of interest only if it relates to behavior—such things as type of marriage, kinds of kinship organization, or styles of dwelling. There is no doubt that the

Alphabetic List of Ethnic Units Indicated on Map 1.1

Abaluyia 31	Kaguru 60	Ovimbundu 75
Abarwanda 43	Karamojong 39	Pokot 34
Abarundi 44	Kikuyu 47	San 88
Acholi 28	Kimbu 58	Sebei 33
Alur 25	Kongo 67	Sonjo 46
Amhara 19	Konkomba 8	Shambaa 56
Arusha 50	Kpelle 3	Shona 81
Ashanti 9	Kru 4	Soga 37
Azande 24	Kuba 70	Somali 23
Baganda 40	Lele 69	Songe 72
Bagarra 18	Lovedu 83	Sotho 87
Barabaig 54	Lozi 77	Suku 68
Bemba 62	Luba 73	Sukuma 45
Bwamba 41	Lugbara 27	Swazi 84
Chewa 66	Lunda 71	Tallensi 7
Chokwe 74	Maasai 48	Teso 36
Dinka 21	Makonde 63	Thonga 82
Dogon 5	Mandari 26	Tiriki 32
Fipa 57	Mende 2	Tiv 16
Fon 10	Mossi 6	Tonga 79
Fur 17	Mongo 42	Tswana 86
Giriama 55	Nandi 35	Turkana 30
Gogo 59	Ndebele 80	Turu 53
Hadza 51	Ndembu 76	Wambugwe 49
Hausa 13	Ngoni 64	Wolof 1
Ibo 14	Nuer 20	Yako 15
Ila 78	Nupe 12	Yao 65
Jie 29	Nyakyusa 61	Yoruba 11
Jimma Abba Jifar 22	Nyamwezi 52	Zulu 85
	Nyoro 38	

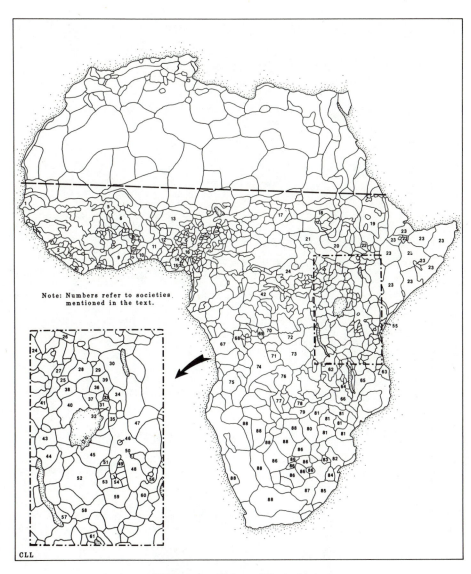

MAP 1.1   African Ethnic Units
(adapted from Murdock, 1959)

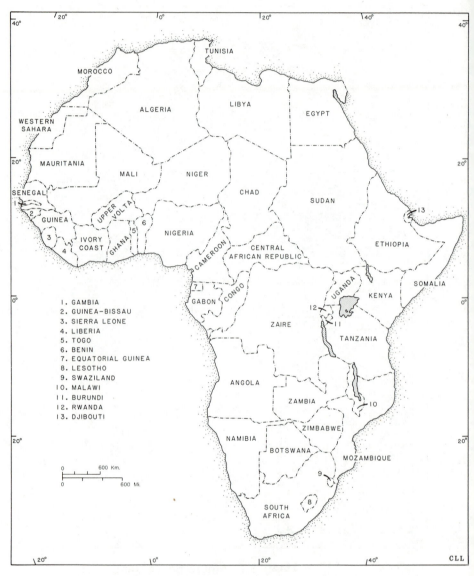

MAP 1.2 Nations of Africa (1979)

1. GAMBIA
2. GUINEA-BISSAU
3. SIERRA LEONE
4. LIBERIA
5. TOGO
6. BENIN
7. EQUATORIAL GUINEA
8. LESOTHO
9. SWAZILAND
10. MALAWI
11. BURUNDI
12. RWANDA
13. DJIBOUTI

An East African family in 1960

same forces which create new language groups (isolation, ingroupness) also create variations in physical type over time so that some Africans have everted lips and others do not, some have very kinky hair and others, straight hair. But there is no clear evidence that the degree of variation is associated with significant behavioral changes. The striking features of African life, such as kinds of descent, marriage, government, ways of classifying good and evil, or artistic talent, crosscut all physical types and respond to causal forces, both economic and natural, that affect the whole human race in a similar fashion. Africans, we now believe, emphasize lineage more than most other people in the world, not because of their special physical form, but because of the unique conjunction of cultural and economic forces that characterize the African continent, which are the subject of this book. Physical form does relate to more or less specific behavior in some instances, but the relationship for Africans is the same as for the human race in general, for example in the tendency to binary classification or the use of speech as a main form of communication. Thus variations in African physical forms are of little relevance to this book.

The Theory of Progress

During the nineteenth century Africa began most steadily to be revealed to the Western world (even though its coasts and parts of the interior, such as the western part of Zaire and Mozambique, had been explored beginning in the middle of the fifteenth century). The Africa which most Westerners saw was colored by what may be called the theory of progress. Since the Enlightenment the idea had grown in Western thought that man was evolving and was in some way following a prescribed, upward course in history. This course was marked by technological innovations whose net effect was considered good. The nineteenth-century anthropologist, L. H. Morgan, divided this course into levels of savagery, barbarism, and civilization. According to his view, Africans would be for the most part barbarians, people who had achieved the level of domestication of plants and animals, which was an advance from savagery, but who lacked, for example, the alphabet, writing, the true arch, the wheel, the plow. These technical accomplishments have distinguished Western and Asian societies since the Bronze Age beginning about 3000 B.C. (and until recently differentiated sub-Saharan Africa from the Africa of the Sahara and Mediterranean coasts).

One of the things about the treatment of African history which sometimes agitates educated Africans is the charge of a lack of progress. Ironically, the concern results from their acceptance of the European evolutionary view that there *is* a preferred course to history which is blazed with technological debris. A former Kenya settler, Christopher Wilson, exemplifies this progressive perspective in *Before the White Man in Kenya:*

It is surprising to know that for many thousands of years before the earliest records of historical time men of advanced physical type, with at least rudiments of culture, lived in Kenya. It is still more surprising to realize that in spite of this early start, those inhabitants of Kenya made almost no further progress towards higher human standards through all the centuries of history. While the rest of the world was being occupied by rapidly developing races of mankind, elaborating from the first rudiments of civilisation their own forms of culture, these Africans advanced hardly at all. The primitive hunters learned to cultivate a few crops and keep domestic animals; they made for themselves huts, instead of living in caves and rock-shelters; they learned to make use of iron instead of stone for weapons. Then progress stopped, and in that state they seem to have been content to remain.

Today, this way of looking at Africans has disappeared, at least in the racist form expounded by Wilson. Anthropologists do not find African behavior to be different because it is tied to African physical type. Nevertheless, some anthropologists continue to hold to a sophisticated form of evolutionism which sees human beings emerging from loose, uncentralized societies, to states and eventually to supergovernments. Typical is the assertion, "the state ranks . . . as a major achievement of human evolution" (Kottack 1979). My own view, which will be presented in detail in Chapter 6, differs from this. I see the state, centralized government, not as a step in evolution, but as one of at least two forms of political organization, the other being headless, or stateless, that may arise in different cultural and economic conditions. There is a self-serving quality about cultural evolutionism similar to the claim of biological evolution that man is the "highest" form of animal, a view which cannot be scientifically defended.

MODERN THEORETICAL VIEWS OF AFRICA

Diffusionism

During the first half of this century, diffusionism challenged the evolutionary view, at least in America, by looking at human behavior in a way that went to another extreme. Diffusionism claimed that most cultural traits are uniquely and accidentally invented; they are dispersed over a wide area from the source of discovery. When applied to Africa, this view appears to derive everything of importance from outside the continent. The Africans I spoke of earlier, who desire to enhance Africa's historical reputation and who denounce evolution for representing Africans as evolutionarily retarded, reject this approach because it finds Africans inventing nothing. To them it seems that whenever the European is writing history, Africans' contributions are neglected.

But the presumption of inherent prejudice in this point of view is an illusion. Any place in the world whose history one choses to study will appear to have acquired almost everything from elsewhere. In 1937 Ralph Linton wrote a widely quoted paper called "One Hundred Per Cent American" in which he made fun of the parochial, isolationist American, who thinks that his way of life is self-generated. Linton took his American step by step from bed to office, indicating along the way the foreign origin of nearly everything the American did, from eating a fried egg (chickens domesticated in Southeast Asia), to reading a paper (paper invented in ancient Egypt), to thanking a Hebrew deity, in an Indo-European tongue that he is a 100 percent American.

The historical illusion in this case derives from the fact that when we value culture traits, we ordinarily focus on those which have prestige or power attached to them, and such techniques are rarely invented. Anthropologists used to make this point by saying that man is really quite uninventive. Instead they should have said that although he is quite inventive, the number of his inventions which have a powerful impact on the world is small. Moreover, the rate of discovery of noteworthy inventions increases with the successful (even though accidental) discovery of any one invention. Those people in the Middle East who stumbled upon agriculture and domestication of animals were favored with an increase in food supply and population as well as with the opportunity to seek out new and sometimes important inventions stemming from the fact that there were more people to find them and more wealth to promote them.

This, of course, is not the whole story. Although the flowering of the Middle East was a case of the rich getting richer, or nothing succeeding like success, their successful traits could have been diffused to Africa, and some were. But, why were not more? There is no certain answer to this question. One suspects that difficulties of communication across the Sahara were an important reason. Just as important may have been the simple problem of cost, which in present-day development programs often proves to be the greatest hindrance to inaugurating new ways of doing things. Tony Hopkins, speculating on the reason why the wheel never established itself in precolonial West Africa, suggests (Hopkins 1973) that even though the people of the Sudan surely knew about the wheel, the cost of making and using wheel-drawn vehicles exceeded the return to be expected relative to donkey or human back transport. People do not embrace new techniques without cost, and for various reasons the cost situation in Africa may have been different from other parts of the world to which post-Neolithic ideas diffused more easily. American Indians took to horses easily, but they were much slower to utilize metal tools of the type requiring smelting. Africans adopted smelting and iron working very quickly, but the plow seems to have been unsuitable for most African soils and economies—even if Africans had known about it.

To say that the Middle East was florescent and favored by past successes does not mean that it, in comparison to Africa, was destined to be perpetually ascendant. The pattern of florescence as indicated by Grahame Clark (1971), is such that areas seem to go into a rocketlike ascendance and then fizzle out. Africa had its first great cultural flowering with the development of lower Paleolithic core tools which accompanied the biological evolution of man into modern human form. However, this thrust lost steam, and cultural expansion (or at least technological cultural expansion) next appeared in Western Europe, as far as the archaeological evidence shows, during the Middle and Upper Paleolithic periods. The center of growth then shifted to the Middle East with the appearance of domestication of plants and animals.

To a diffusionist everything in Africa is explained by history. If cows are not milked in the Ovimbundu Highlands of Angola, that is because they were diffused there before milking was invented. If the pattern of the state system of the Lozi of western Zambia is similar to that of the Ashanti of Ghana and the Baganda of Uganda, at the three corners of Africa, it is because the idea of the state was diffused from one place to the other. If the people in the Central African cultural zone stretching from the mouth of the Congo to Mozambique tend to have matrilineal descent systems, the cultural trait diffused there from West Africa.

While the basic theory of the diffusionists seems to hold up quite well if applied to men's ideational activities (including the material things produced from ideas, such as the idea of how to make an iron axe), it has little validity when fitted to social forms, that is, to the ways men structure relations. Matrilineality, in one sense, is a relationship between people such that they reckon kinship through the mother's side of the family. This kind of relationship seems to arise spontaneously, given the right conditions. It has been remarked, for example, that ". . . the cow is the enemy of matrilineality . . ." (Aberle 1961). Where people have cattle in significant numbers, matrilineality does not usually appear.

Diffusionist explanations can also be questioned for ignoring economic considerations, such as cost. In the case of the neglected Ovimbundu cows, for example, the fact that the number of cows owned by the Ovimbundu is very small is ignored and with it the possibility that maybe they are not milked because it is not worthwhile to do so. Similarly, the Turu of central Tanzania do not make pots, not because they do not know how to make them, but because it is an uneconomical use of time. They raise bulrush millet, cows, sheep and goats and buy their pots from the Nyamwezi and Iramba.

Functionalism

While evolutionism and diffusion have been popular approaches to the anthropological study of Africa, functionalism has been the most widely accepted. This approach, stemming from the teachings of Bronislaw Malinowski and A. R. Radcliffe-Brown, cannot be said to have been in conflict with evolutionism and diffusionism the way those two points of view were in conflict with each other. The functionalists, at least the dominant Radcliffe-Brown group, simply ignored the questions which activated the other approaches and chose instead to view African societies as essentially static. They sought to assess as well as possible the relations of different parts of the social systems to each other and to develop a theory that would explain why societies usually persist in the same form over long periods of time. Where the previous two schools might be thought of in biological terms as phylogenetic, concerned with the history of African societies, the functionalist approach was physiologic, focused on the structure and operation of the organism. Functionalists have been criticized for many things, notably that they have not allowed for change in African societies, and that they have served imperialist interests by seeing African societies as unchanging.

The first of these charges is biased simply because in the nature of scientific investigation it sometimes pays (as in microeconomics) to view a phenomenon in static terms and sometimes in dynamic terms (as in macroeconomics). The two approaches are equally legitimate and conceptually isolable. When a phenomenon is viewed statically, the point of the investigation is to assess the nature of the relations of the variables in the system. (The term functionalism derives from the study of the interactions of the parts of a system.)

A more appropriate criticism of functionalism is that by not sufficiently developing the static model, functionalists were not able to accomplish true static analysis and the conclusions of their studies were too often ad hoc. Functionalists justified that which is in terms of its assumed necessity for maintaining existing society. For example, Gluckman (1950, 192) once made the startling suggestion that the level of divorce in African societies is determined by the needs of the system. To this might be added that in present views, as in economics, a model of society which is dynamic and which allows for change is superior to the static model because it contains within it all the insights that static analysis can produce as well as dynamic insights.

Jacques Maquet specifically charged that colonial governments needed to manipulate African societies for their own ends, and this goal was best served by keeping the societies static rather than by allowing them to change (Maquet 1964, 49). A social anthropology which gave scientific support to the idea that African societies were naturally static was in tune with imperial ambitions.

The difficulty with this half-truth is that it denies any chance of objectivity to the other fellow and reserves all objectivity to oneself. One would think, rather, that all of us are about half objective and half the victims of our aspirations. Thus, Maquet, whose position on African societies falls under the general heading of marxist, could be said to want to see African societies as going through the same dialectical processes that Marx attributed to Western societies based on the competition for power between classes. However, one would be wrong to conclude that insofar as a marxist is ideologically committed to international revolution, his ideas about social dialectics have no validity. There is an important objective truth in the marxist approach which is not revealed by any of the other ways of looking at Africa. This is that control of property has important consequences for the forms that African societies take. It is equal in importance to the truth which functionalism unveiled, that societies can be seen as integrated with the various parts serving to support and complement each other under some circumstances.

Marxism

The marxist approach to Africa, which is increasingly popular in the English-speaking world, but which has always been more nearly taken for granted in the Francophone (French speaking) world, is more difficult to identify than the approaches already discussed. The difficulty arises, not because Marx's ideas were so obscure, but because, as Raymond Aron has said, there are so many competing marxists, each with his idiosyncratic interpretation of the master. A marxist approach to Africa focuses on control of the so-called forces of production (the tools or capital) and the problems inherent in the disparity between the ways things are produced and the way they are owned. With such a view, the marxist Africanist sees a world of conflict and antagonism between disputing sectors of the population ("classes") who differ in the way they relate to the production forces such that one group's property relations conform to an emergent production system while the other's relate to an obsolete system.

In order to import this theory, developed to explain the emergence of industrial capitalist society in Europe, into indigenous Africa, marxists have first had to satisfy themselves that marxism is not just a theory of industrial capitalism. This they seem to have done. Maquet's *Power and Society in Africa* and *Civilizations of Black Africa* implicitly utilize marxist orientations, the latter by typologizing African societies in terms of tools and other features of production (civilizations of the bow, granaries, and spear) and the former by focusing on power relations as nonexchange and exploitative. Claude Meillassoux (1972) explicitly claims the distinction of having adjusted marxism to the nonindustrial nature of African systems. He characterizes the production process in indigenous societies as control of the means of *re*production (that is, men control women). Another marxist, Maurice Godelier, takes a different tack in order to represent a third major element of marxist thought in addition to the organization of production and conflicts between classes. He examines the way that modes of thought adjust to the production system. In his analysis of Bambuti Pygmies of the Ituri Forest of Zaire (Godelier 1977) he sees their consciousness or world view as isomorphic with their hunting and gathering system.

Hence, where functionalists find value in picturing African societies as integrated wholes in which even conflict is a device for supporting and maintaining the system, the marxist approach views these societies as composed of groups in conflict over control of the means of production and as essentially emergent and changing.

THE AUTHOR'S VIEW

At this point, it would be easy for me to shift into the role of arbiter and proclaim that I am an eclectic who will draw upon what is good and true in each of these approaches while standing above partisanship. But I don't think this is possible. Just as functionalism and marxism, or evolutionism and diffusionism are mixtures of objective and subjective attitudes, so is my point of view. The only justification for combining elements from each of these approaches is my belief that knowledge and understanding do grow in history, and that they grow by the same dialectical process which so engaged Marx. New theoretical syntheses emerge from the struggle between opposing views.

On the other hand, a view of Africa which makes sense cannot simply be a patchwork of other views but must be welded into an integrated system. Hence, I add certain things to these other approaches which accomplish that integration. I attempt to discover a fit between reality and a logical model of history and society from which deductions can be made. My view is essentially deductive. This approach utilizes assumptions which fill gaps in the unknown and thus allows us to go on to explore possibilities that would be closed to us if we were unwilling for some reason to speculate about reality. The deductive mode is not so much concerned to account for every fact as it is to obtain some tentative hypotheses. One, which will be explored later, is that before cattle were introduced into Africa from the Middle East, a far greater proportion of African societies possessed matrilineal descent than since that event.

Society and Culture

This deductive approach is served by making a clear distinction between society and culture, a division, which while well established in functionalist social anthropology, is not simple to make. In fact, I have not as yet come up with a fully operational definition. I do not regard this as crippling any more than it is in some other branches of science. Linguistics had to proceed for a long time with only a primitive notion of the difference between a phoneme and the actual sounds people make. It would have suffered unnecessarily by insistence that all work stop until the problem of what is general and what is idiosyncratic in the speech sounds in a speech community was resolved. *Culture,* as opposed to society, refers to ideas, modes of behavior, and artifacts that are products of these ideas. They are created and persist in a manner analogous to genes in contrast to modes of behavior, or social actions, which are generated by the situation. The model for culture is language. If the question is put to an anthropologist: "What conclusion would you draw if you were apparently the first person to penetrate the interior of the Kalahari Desert of southern Africa and found a San hunter carrying a rifle labeled Winchester?" the answer would be: "I would know that I was not the first person of the Western world to make contact with these people." That is, the gun and the name for it would have had to come from the Western world.

Behind this innocent conclusion is a profound theory about the nature of culture and culture change, a theory which is seldom spelled out by those who use it. In order to explain this theory I will make reference to the better known genetic theory of biology which it closely parallels.

When Darwin took his famous voyage around the world on the *Beagle* in the last century, he collected information about different species of animals and plants because, one must suspect, he was beginning to be convinced that there was a way to explain the facts of speciation without recourse to the idea that each species was separately and divinely created. The facts of speciation are simple: At any given moment around the world, one may find n number of species of plants and animals, each marked by the fact that the members of the species are more like each other than they are like members of other species, and by the fact that they can interbreed with each other but cannot breed with other species. (We will ignore the question of marginal groups, like horses and donkeys, which can interbreed but produce infertile offspring, mules). Darwin's explanation for this phenomenon, augmented later by Mendel's discovery of genetics, was essentially that mutations, unique rearrangements of genetic material, occur in individual animals (not in groups as a whole) and spread to other members of the species if the mutations are adaptive, so as to give the species an advantage for survival. Thus, species change over time as they adapt. When species split into two or more groups, each of which moves into isolation from the other, they begin to evolve along separate lines and eventually become discrete, unable to interbreed, by virtue of the continuing process of mutation at the individual level. An important fact which is implied by all this is that mutations, even though they survive only because they in some sense give an advantage to the mutated animals (or at least don't work against its survival), are essentially chance occurrences, fortuitous in effect, and unique in form. A mutation occuring in one individual cannot appear independently in another individual. Therefore, different, independent groups of people cannot independently evolve to look like each other. Rather, because the same mutations cannot occur independently, different biological groups must become more and more unlike each other (must diverge) over time.

The essential features of this theory of species, shorn of certain philosophical biases (such as the idea that mutations occur in order to make adaptations whereas in truth one can only say that at best they may work for adaptation) are three: mutation, selection, and inbreeding. That is to say, speciation is explained by the fact that given n number of isolated, inbreeding populations, mutations occur by chance and uniquely so that no two groups receive the same mutation. A mutation will be judged by the environment (selected) and if allowed to survive, will be inbred so that the group as a whole will take on the trait. For example, the cormorants of the Galpagos no longer fly, whereas cormorants in other places do. A genetic change occurring randomly and uniquely among cormorants happened to a cormorant isolated on the Galpagos which led to selection for not flying and through inbreeding became characteristic of that group. The Galpagos cormorants are not now a different species from others, with whom they can still interbreed, but since they have no opportunity to breed with them, in time they will be divergent enough from the other group to be counted a species.

A Darwin interested in culture rather than species might apply this genetic model so that mutations would become equivalent to inventions or discoveries, selection could be viewed as social selection, while inbreeding would be analogous to social standardization. Accordingly, the world is composed at any given time of n number of isolable groups called ethnic groups. That the members of a society share the same cultural traits is due to the fact that a social system is composed of interacting people who work to insure conformity of behavior. New cultural traits, when they appear either by invention or diffusion from some other group, are selected by social as well as other groups and if they are found compatible or advantageous in some sense, they are standardized or made in some way characteristic of the group. A case in point would be a style of dress, such as the peculiar hair style of the Tutsi of Rwanda. Where it once was innovative, and probably also suspect because it was not standard, it became accepted and characteristic of that elite group. Another case is the style of mask used by the Yoruba of Nigeria, which is so distinctive that anyone who knows the Yoruba can immediately identify its source.

Thus, we are led by this increasingly widely held view of culture (Schneider 1977) to a rather surprising conclusion, surprising because it implies that some cultural traits, like the wheel, were not destined to appear in the Middle East and might have never appeared except by luck. On the other hand, it implies that there are untold ideas in this universe that as yet are undiscovered.

Startling as it may be, therefore, this theory includes the idea or assumption of the uniqueness of cultural inventions as the best way to explain most cultural occurrences. Possibly Africa did not possess the wheel because the cost of utilizing it was too high. More likely (in this case), it was absent because its appearance was not to be expected. Without communication with those people who did invent it, Africans were unlikely to invent it, which is similar to the fact that those who invented it did so by luck. By the same token, the core tools invented or discovered by the earliest Africans, the Australopithecines, must be assumed to have made their way to Europe by diffusion rather than by independent invention there.

I can think of no anthropologist who would dispute the answer of the person who was asked to state the implications of an apparently untouched San having a Winchester rifle, that he must have had contact with Western culture in some way. Yet there are times when independent, parallel invention is invoked to explain facts like the rise of civilization in Middle America. These days there are an increasing number of people who dispute this and argue that diffusion of culture across the oceans must have occurred in prehistoric times, as it surely did between southeast Asia and the east African coast via the Indian Ocean. For the most part, this is not the accepted view. The debate stems in part from the common social process of trying to explain one's origins as unique. Those people involved personally in the growth of modern Latin American or African countries find offensive the idea that basic cultural traits might have diffused into their countries from the outside, just as Americans often like to believe that we invented the auto, electricity, and other important techniques without any outside help.

Summary of Theory of Culture

The way I look at African culture may be summarized as follows:

(1) Where a culture trait, such as true weaving, occurs both in Africa and elsewhere or in two or more African countries, the trait is assumed to have traveled from one of the areas to the other. (The theory does not and cannot say whether the trait moved from or to Africa, although this fact can sometimes be established with archaeological or other evidence.)

(2) Standardization of culture in African societies, such as the use of the distinctive cap masks of the Yoruba, is due to the process of social dynamics which seeks to establish cultural uniformity as part of the required minimal uniformity of society. Cultural elements, in other words, don't form a system except through social dynamics, one element of culture having no necessary connection with another except in certain limited senses.

(3) Each African ethnic group will have a cultural array somewhat distinct from any other because of the fact that human beings are inventive, and certain cultural items, like the particular shape of a spear, may be important to a group even if not to other groups. These locally invented traits, when standardized by social dynamics, give the group its special cultural character.

An important additional dimension of this theory, which will facilitate discussion of culture patterns in Africa, deserves attention. I refer to the fact that different kinds of culture seem to have different patterns of development and diffusion. Language, to begin with, follows the laws of cultural change in such a way that given a group of societies living close together and derived from the same prehistoric group, the languages they speak will vary directly, in words and to some degree in grammar, as a function of the distance in time from each other. Individual words will be diffused from one group to another more easily than the language system as a whole (that is, ability to speak the language). As a result of this, anthropologists ordinarily take the language system of a people as an index to historical connections arguing, for example, that the Yoruba are more clearly related to Fon speakers (in next door Benin) than either is to the Hausa because the languages of the first two are more alike than either is to Hausa.

Contrast this with the pattern of cultural development in the sphere of plastic art. Within a given society there is, as expected, standardization of art, so much so that a person trained in African plastic art on viewing an example can often say what its source is, whether a Bambara carving or a Makonde bust. But two societies living cheek by jowl, having only slightly different dialects of the same language family, may have carving styles that are extremely different.

Technology is probably the most readily diffusible cultural trait when the particular technological skill has a distinct advantage in control of the habitat for the production of wealth. Once Africans were introduced to iron working (starting in the upper Nile about 500 B.C.), they seem to have grasped for it in a way which caused it to spread like wildfire so that every society in Africa became acquainted with it in a relatively short time. It leapt social boundaries in a way that language and art styles seldom if ever do.

The result of these different patterns is that any given African society is likely to have a language which resembles that of its neighbors, an art style which is distinctive of it, and a technological kit which it shares with large numbers of other Africans over a vast area, the way the Nguni of southern Africa (the Zulu) share Zebu cattle with the Nuer of the Sudan 3000 miles to the north.

Nature (Sociocultural Biology)

To further complicate matters, however, there is an important qualifier to the concept of culture. Just as modern linguistics has established the probability that human beings have a biological propensity for speech (some even arguing that if children are not taught a particular language, they will invent one of their own, even if only a simple one), certain apparently pure cultural traits in African life seem to be based importantly on biological structure. The most obvious of these, which will be discussed in Chapter 8, are the propensity to associate stability and peace with the right side of the body and unrest with the left, and the tendency for people, when under stress, to form revitalization groups (communes). These forms of behavior, apparently universal among human beings, nevertheless take on locally distinctive forms. It is an interesting, if not altogether explainable, fact that the most specific forms of biologically based behavior fall in the area of what we think of as religion. Man is often defined as a tool maker and user, but the specific tools he uses cannot be explained by his genetic structure. We have no gene for using plows. Plows are true results of intellectual processes combined with luck. Human beings everywhere have similar binary classification systems, associating the right side of the body, for example, with goodness of various sorts, sometimes in very specific parallels (men are apparently always on the right in opposition to women). Similarly, as we shall see, when under stress, people often band together into what Turner calls *communitas,* antistructure groups, like hippie communes, in order to fight the cause of the stress. Behavior in such movements is often quite specifically parallel among different human groups, including letting the hair grow long or going about naked.

Society

To the cultural and natural parts of this theory must be added society. The term *society,* taken in its most general sense, refers to systems of interaction or exchange between people. The essential form of society is two or more persons engaged in some relationship of mutual dependence in which they agree to abide by certain rules, a contract if you will, governing the exchange. This much the marxists and people like Fredrick Barth (1966, 1967), whose theory closely resembles mine, would probably accept. For example, the functionalists insist that societies are integrated, which is to say that all people in a society are connected by their interlinking exchanges so that a change in relationship in one place has ramifications for other linkages. These agreements must relate to each other in such a way as to avoid contradiction. For example, only frustration and breakdown in the social order can result from a disagreement between a man and his brother-in-law over who should control the man's sons. For one thing, the question of who shall inherit from whom is at issue here. If the means for obtaining control of one's son, through control of one's wife, should become generally possible in a society through changed economic circumstances, this emergent patrilineality will affect other, sometimes remote, relationships, such as the relationship of a man and his father's sister, as discussed in Chapter 6.

Added to this is an idea taken from the marxists that within any society there are groups and individuals who compete for power, which usually means the main productive assets and the exchange of those assets. Thus politics, defined as competition for power, is endemic in any society, including all African societies. A counterpart of this conflict is ideologies and myths which define the competing groups and justify claims to ascendance. I once heard a government-appointed Turu chief justify his claim to the position of paramount chief by arguing that the chief of the society should be the senior man defined in terms of patrilineal descent from the founder of the society, Munyaturu. As the senior man of the Kahiu clan, he felt that he deserved this position because his was the only Turu clan which was based on legitimate descent, all the others deriving either from female ancestors or immigrants!

To the dimensions of rules governing actions and competition for power may be added an idea derived from economics and game theory, an idea that human beings strive in their games for utilities (of which power is only one) by seeking to make intelligent moves among the alternatives open to them in the structure of the society. In other words, the actors are decision makers seeking to achieve general utilitarian goals. This may be the most underrated and traditionally least acceptable idea about Africans. Social anthropologists have often described African behavior as following prescribed courses which exclude the need for economic and political decision making. But studies like that of Judith Heyer on the Kamba of Kenya (Heyer 1971), have brought this view seriously into question. Heyer found that the Kamba farmer must consider at least 200 different combinations of variables relating to farming before he or she can get down to the business of producing a crop.

In sum, African societies may be viewed as systems of interaction, governed by rules or contracts in which the actors seek to obtain utility while competing with each other. Fundamental to this process is stress on production and exchange and the control of means of production and means of exchange as paths to obtaining social power. Usually this competition is confined within the rule structure as the actors seek advantage, utilizing legitimate strategies which do not threaten the system even though following the rules may have bizarre consequences. I once witnessed a court case in which one group of Turu demanded compensation for the death of one of their sister's sons. They successfully upheld their claim, even though they were admittedly in part responsible for their sister's son's death. They claimed that they would not have had the opportunity to shorten the man's life if the brothers of the sister's son had done their duty and kept him home with them. At other times this competition takes the form of what amounts to an attack on the rules of the game as the players seek to devise more equitable arrangements. Illustrative of this kind of competition is the famous case of the abolition of "sister" exchange marriage among the Tiv of Nigeria in 1927 by the colonial government (Mead 1955, 96ff). This change in the rules had profound consequences for the social structure of the Tiv because it raised the power of the young men and demeaned that of the old men. The example substantiates my point even though the rule change was imposed by colonial authorities because after its implementation, the young men supported it enthusiastically. In other words, the structure of the rules of a social game tend to favor some groups (notably the rich and powerful) over others with the consequence that there is usually some strain for rule change in any society at any time.

Revolution

In addition to the focus on the struggle for economic and political power, marxist thought contains another element which may be the most overlooked in the treatment of African societies, revolution, which is, in one degree or another, a rejection of the old contract system for a new one. The functionalist emphasis on statics has been unsuitable, not only for detecting ordinary conflict, but also for seeing the cyclical and sometimes revolutionary changes that mark social systems in in the normal course of events. In the nature of society, activities like levels of production and magnitudes of wealth tend to go through cycles, sometimes due to dynamic feedback processes in the system itself, sometimes because of the impingement of external forces, like the rinderpest epidemic of 1895 in East Africa. This outbreak eliminated large numbers of livestock and reduced millions of Africans to poverty, but it was then followed by more than seventy-five years of economic growth as previous levels of cattle ownership were restored. These cycles are like our business cycles or shifts of political emphasis between liberals and conservatives.

More dramatically, African societies are subject to revolutionary or revitalizing shifts, just as are other societies outside Africa. During these periods, the rationality that marks the game-playing stage declines or is entirely replaced by irrational, emotional action. These major shifts come about as a result of crippling contradictions in the socioeconomic structure. While marxists see revolution as the natural end result of the thesis-antithesis competition between classes or groups in a society which vie for control of the production system, such conflicts do not necessarily have to lead to revolt. Cyclical shifts can be contained by the normal operation of conciliation methods which fine tune the system. A revolt or a revitalization movement seems rather to rise when some segment of the society perceives a blockage in its rational course of action aimed at achieving the rewards of the system while at the same time it sees no reasonable method of removing the blockage. The frustration attendant on this generates the revitalization process. Anthony

F.C. Wallace (1956, 163) feels that every established religion has within it the remnants of its revitalization origin. One must wonder whether the heroic Kintu of the Interlacustrine Bantu legend or the Shilluk's Nyikang were not revolutionary leaders in their time. In the historic present, we have been witness to many examples of revitalization movements stimulated by interference in the social system from outside, usually colonial forces: Mau Mau, Dini ya Msambwa, Gounzism, the Maji Maji Rebellion and many movements that never even received a name, like an uprising of Nyaturu against German occupation forces in northern Singida about 1910 which was led by a woman. Like economic and political cycles, revitalization and revolution need not be stimulated by outside forces. They can arise from the operation of positive feedback within a social system (as Legesse [1973] described for the Borana Galla *gada* system), which in some cases leads to breakdowns in the social order, insoluble by any other means than massive ritual movements of people. According to Victor Turner (1969) this is the explanation for various "ceremonial" activities in African societies, such as rites of passage, like circumcision. Circumcision activities contain many of the elements of revitalization processes and seem stimulated in the first place by conflicts between the senior generation, who have control of property and of the lives of the uninitiated, and the juniors, who want to become active members of the adult class.

These social games played by Africans also seem to vary in the degree to which they are institutionalized. Some societies, such as the Baganda, seemed to be marked by a much higher degree of structuring of the rules and more elaborate strategies than, for example, the "tribes without rulers" (Middleton and Tait 1958), the so-called segmentary and age-oriented societies which are so common in Africa. Between major segments of these societies Mair believes there were no rules of conduct except the very general one that in conflicts between members of the large segments, an injured party has a "right to redress for wrongs" (Mair 1977b).

The position I take on the nature of society has sometimes been called formalist economic anthropology or, as I prefer, analytical economic anthropology. The theory derives from analytical economics and is designed to explain behavior in terms of the hypothesis that human beings everywhere seek to shape their actions in order to increase their individual utility (profit in a very general sense). This view is increasingly being accepted as appropriate to understanding the lives of Africans and other nonindustrialized people, as in Polly Hill's studies of the rural Hausa in northern Nigeria (Hill 1972). This approach contrasts with a more popular view developed most fully in Bohannan and Dalton's *Markets in Africa* (1962). It disavows the notion that Africans are economic men and insists instead that until they came into contact with colonialists, they were not profit-oriented but oriented to the support of society. This position, in fact, is a species of functionalism.

THE THEORY

If we put together the cultural, social, and natural portions of this theory i order to see how they relate, we note that the structure of society, meanin the patterns of interaction that can develop, and the complexity of the rol system of the actors is dependent to a large degree on the kind of cultural base available to it. Ideas, such as algebra, give power for manipulating the real world which is lacking without them. Agriculture, as Forde (1963) has pointed out, ordinarily is necessary as a foundation for the segmentary lineage system that occurs in Africa. Without agriculture, small-scale social systems of the San or Pygmy type are all that can be built.

Granting this, it should be noted that a particular type of social system, for example, a segmentary system, does not exist in a one-to-one relationship with a particular cultural kit. State systems in Africa occur in conjunction with livestock as a main element in the production system, but also with exclusive dependence on savannah horticulture or rain-forest root cropping. A social system seems to relate more nearly to the economy, taken as a system of production, exchange and consumption, rather than to a particular type of technology. It is therefore possible for an agricultural people to produce at such a low level that they are able to support only a relatively small-scale social system while a hunting and gathering people, under some circumstances, can be highly productive and support a complex system. In Africa, one of the main social divisions, that between the centralized and uncentralized societies, seems to be based on the quality and quantity of production rather than on particular types of production, even though the difference seems on the surface to be accounted for by different types of production.

The cultural kit which a people possess, however they got it, thus becomes a constraint (rather than a determinant) on the specific form their society can take. But, unlike culture, social structures can be and are independently invented, given the nature of the culture and other parametric elements. Where two African societies possess states, we cannot infer a historical connection between them as we could if they possessed common cultural traits. Similarly, the distribution of matrilineal descent systems in Africa, which concentrate in the Central African belt, is best explained as situationally determined rather than diffused.

As for nature, those forms of behavior which can be related very closely to all human beings, such as communitas and binary classification, transcend systems and appear everywhere in similar form but with local coloring. Revitalization movements are universal under the right circumstances. Hence male and female rites of passage to adulthood, often including circumcision and clitoridectomy (acts which are themselves inventions, not instinctive), occur

widely, but not universally, and represent variations in the degree of tension between generations.

Determinism

The way I will describe African life seems inevitably destined to be charged with economic determinism. Although I have made it plain that I consider culture to be a principal constraint and a powerful causal force on social behavior, and although I have stressed that important parts of behavior are caused by biological forces, I will tend to approach most topics from the point of view of how levels of production and kinds and degrees of exchange cause the phenomena.

My excuse for this is simply that the approach is revealing of social dynamics in ways that other approaches are not, and social dynamics is the focus of this book. When we try to explain why marriage takes different forms, we discover that the different forms are importantly linked to the amount and kind of goods available. Economics is a proven good strategy in accomplishing explanation.

Yet we should keep in mind that it does not explain everything. Africans did not raise cattle only because this was profitable. If cattle had not been invented and diffused to Africa, there could have been no economic use for them. Furthermore, people apparently do not hold to incest taboos for economic reasons. In addition, while I primarily pay attention to the rational, economizing behavior of Africans, I think I have made it plain that during periods of social unrest, when revitalization processes are ascendant, I recognize that rationality is put aside to one degree or another.

Economics is a way of looking at social behavior that is fruitful. That is reason enough for emphasizing it, despite the obvious fact that other causal forces are working.

CONCLUSION

I would like to conclude this theoretical overview by turning to a question that, given the times we live in, must inevitably arise. The current stress on relevance translates in this context to the questions: "How does this theory of African life relate to current African aspirations? What does the theory specifically have to say about how changes can be achieved?" Maquet's rejection of structural-functional theory as static was due as much as anything else, one might guess, to the feeling that there are human problems in Africa which demand solution and static theory, designed as it is to show how a workable and

satisfying system operates, is not suitable to this task. The marxist treatment of this problem, on the other hand, identifies an exploiting class and works with the assumption of inherent structural failures in any of the social systems. It is too doctrinaire.

The theory I have presented suggests that change in African societies may occur in the following ways. It can sometimes be accomplished by the introduction of new ideas. In the nature of culture, powerful new ideas are not easily invented. They must usually come from the outside. And since Africans, as I have stressed, are not tradition bound, new ideas can be accepted. But this possibility must be set off against the fact that whether new ideas will be utilized depends on other things than a mere wish to change. Specifically, an economic decision must be made. Is the innovation acceptable in view of the cost of utilizing it? In many, if not most, cases, it will be found that powerful new ideas cost too much to put into practice.

It follows also from the theory that if cultural innovation is accomplished, this may have consequences for the social and ideational system. In some cases the consequences may be massive social disruption stemming from social contradictions consequent on the interactional implications of the innovation. I am reminded of the introduction of dwarf wheat, one of the so-called miracle crops, into the Punjab which, in the opinion of many, has had the unforeseen effect of generating violent class divisions due to the fact that only wealthy Punjabis were able to exploit the innovation, thus casting the less wealthy into a state of comparative poverty. It is now recognized that this kind of polarization of wealth is a common effect of development strategies, as for example in present day Ivory Coast (Stryker MS).

Thus concentration on abstract theory, as in this chapter, is not an irrelevant exercise. In our survey of Africa, it will point the way to practical considerations, some of which I shall discuss toward the end of this book.

PURPOSE OF THE BOOK

As we turn to a survey of African culture and society, we must be clear about what it is I am going to describe. I am not going to describe a static, unchanging, "traditional" Africa that existed before modern development forces intruded. African groups, like all groups, have always been changing and developing, a point I have stressed in this chapter. My purpose is to describe the nature of nonindustrial and non-Arab African society and culture, both as they existed immediately preceding the impact of colonialism and Arabism and insofar as they continue to exist. To do so is sufficient reason unto itself. In addition, this will be a useful background for an examination of the course of modern events, which are heavily affected by the conditions of the immediate past.

A BRIEF HISTORY OF SUB-SAHARAN AFRICA

OUR KNOWLEDGE OF THE PREHISTORY of Africa has grown rapidly with the rising interest in Africa beginning in the late 50s and with increasing sophistication in anthropological theory. Thirty years ago anthropologists were not even sure where the ancient Africans came from, and most had no inkling of the present generally accepted idea that they in fact grew up from primitive human forms right in Africa itself, the apparent birthplace of mankind. Even today there is much that is poorly understood about African prehistory, but the picture is far clearer, especially since Murdock's *tour de force* attempt to delineate it in his 1959 book *Africa*.

ANCIENT MAN AND CULTURE

It was Leakey's uncovering of Olduvai man in association with tools, which was reported in 1958, that acted as the key to African, and for that matter, human, prehistory (J. D. Clark 1970). Olduvai man was a man only in the sense that he was a culture carrier. That is to say, Olduvai man, or Australopithecus, meaning the "Southern Ape" because he was first discovered in south Africa, was small in stature and brain even though he was, unlike his cousins, the gorillas and chimpanzees, perfectly upright walking. However, the fact that he made tools, even though they were very simple so-called pebble tools, indicates that he could create and hold ideas in his head and pass them on from generation to generation. This is the core idea associated with the concept of culture in anthropology. A tool is a material representation of an invented idea, but the idea is no different in its essential cultural status from the idea of God. In fact, some people even create statues attempting to represent God. Australopithecus was apparently the forerunner of all modern humans who lived, invented, and passed on their culture in the early part of the geological period stretching back over the three million years prior to the present, the period known as the Pleistocene or Paleolithic, during which the glaciers successively came and went.

Throughout the Pleistocene, humans gradually developed physical abilities and culture, mainly through the expansion of the brain although the differentiation of mankind into the present races was one of the minor biological sideshows of evolution during the latter part of the Pleistocene. As human cranial capacity grew from the approximately 400 cc of the Australopithecus to the average 1300 or 1400 cc of modern man, the ability to invent and carry more and more complex culture apparently grew also.

After the Pleistocene, the people of Africa, who with their core tools had led the way in technological developments in the Lower Pleistocene, became a technological backwater to Europe and the Middle East. The invention of agriculture and domestic animals about 8000 years ago gave the people of Europe and the Middle East as well as others who got the ideas from them power so great that it has to this day never been overcome by Africans.

The picture of what happened in Africa in the later part of the Pleistocene, when technological ideas were flowing into that continent from the new dynamic centers outside Africa, is still rather unclear. In any case, that period is too remote from the subject of this book to concern us much. We will be content to pick up the story about the time of the introduction into Africa of domestication of plants (agriculture) and domestication of animals (herding) which replaced the traditional hunting and gathering system of production.

AFRICAN LANGUAGE FAMILIES

I mentioned earlier that in 1959 G.P. Murdock revolutionized the study of African history by attempting a bold synthesis of existing knowledge (Murdock 1959). Murdock's history has since been widely challenged and a more accurate picture of what happened is gradually evolving, in good part due to the stimulus of his attempt. However, it will be useful to look at Murdock's account while noting corrections in it.

If we observe a linguistic map of Africa (Map 2.1), we will notice that the majority of Africans speak languages in one of two main groups. Congo-Kordofanian or Nilo-Saharan (names invented by Joseph Greenberg [1963] who is responsible for the most widely accepted present classification of African languages). There are in fact two other families of languages, but they are of minor consequence. One, the Click, is spoken by diminishing small numbers of San in southern Africa, and the other, Afro-Asiatic, is spoken mainly by peoples of the Mediterranean littoral but also by the rulers of Ethiopia, the Amhara, and some people of the Horn and northeast part of Africa, such as the Somalis and Oromo.

Since, as explained in Chapter 1, language families develop in a "genetic" way, the logic of the genetic process tells us that at one time there had to be one group of people from whom all later diverse languages in that family grew. Thus, there had to be a proto-Congo-Kordofanian and a proto-Nilo-Saharan. These were probably insignificant groups who by some chance survived while other speakers of related languages, divergent survivors from some earlier age, disappeared, the way that Gothic as a Germanic language has been forgotten in Europe in the last 1000 years. These groups probably lived in the sudanic savannah or Sahara (Map 2.2) from which they subsequently expanded to fill up the rest of Africa after the introduction of agriculture and herding.

THE INTRODUCTION OF AGRICULTURE

Murdock felt that about 6000 to 7000 years ago (that is, about 4000 to 5000 B.C.) the proto-Congo-Kordofanian-speaking people independently invented agriculture in the western sudan. Today most scholars feel that the idea must have been diffused into this area from the Middle East. It is difficult to believe that these people would have had to invent agriculture separately since the idea had about 3000 years to travel from the valley of the Euphrates diagonally across the Sahara (which during much of this time was not the extreme desert we know today, but more or less savannah grassland).

Murdock apparently felt that agriculture was a separate invention be-

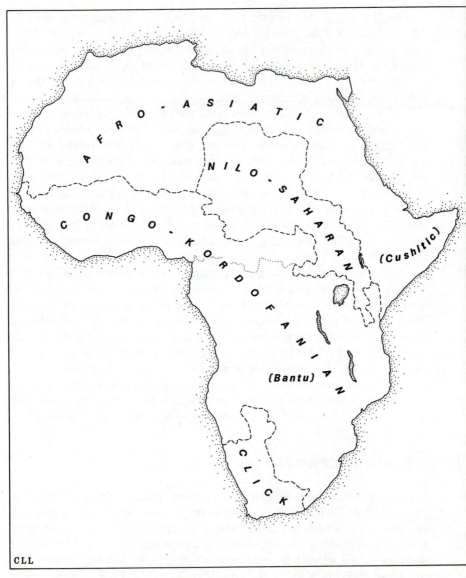

MAP 2.1   Major Language Groups of Africa

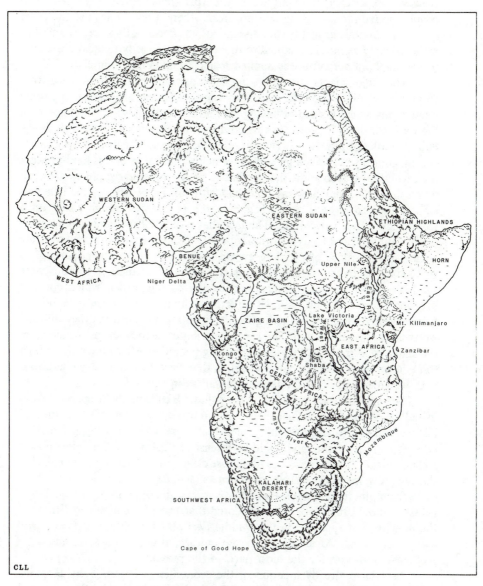

MAP 2.2 Topography and Points of Historical Interest

cause of the relatively long list of new crops which these people developed. However, experience in other parts of the world tells us that very often when people receive the idea of agriculture from others, they do not use the exact crops and animals grown by the disseminators. Because these crops and animals probably cannot be adapted to the new zone as easily as local ones, only the principle of agriculture is applied to local plants and animals.

The major plants characterizing early agriculture in West Africa were sorghum (which in the field resembles maize, or corn, to which it is closely related, but which instead of having ears on the stalk, has a head of seeds on the top—sorghum is grown in this country for molasses and as cattle feed); bulrush millet or *pennisetum* (which resembles sorghum in some ways); fonio; cotton; guinea yams; oil palm; and watermelon. The effect of this food-producing revolution was to allow the population of the sudanic regions to grow, so much so that we may now say that the historical rise of Africa from insignificant groups to large societies began in the sudanic savannah based on a technology of hoe agriculture. The fact that today the two language families of Nilo-Saharan and Congo-Kordofanian are distinct argues that two separate ancient main groups of people grew up utilizing this advantage, perhaps in small enclaves in the western and eastern sudan. That these new crops were available to both groups is suggested by the current belief, which corrects Murdock, that sorghum, bulrush millet, and finger millet (*eleusine*) did not rise in West Africa, but in the highlands of Ethiopia from when they diffused westward across the sudan. The special attributes of these crops, which form the staple food for most savannah-dwelling people in Africa today (although some have replaced them with maize), is that they do well in dry conditions with irregular and compact annual rainfall as in the sudan.

The agricultural revolution in the Middle East is really inseparable from invention of the plow, which harnessed animal power for the first time in history and led to the possibility of a really great rise in crop production because so much more land could be intensively cultivated. The plow makes it economical to pull stumps and otherwise clear and fertilize plots by replacing the nonplow method of slash-and-burn or swidden, hoe agriculture which shifts from plot to plot and leaves stumps, rocks and other impediments in the fields. It should therefore be underscored that except for highland Ethiopia, the plow, which appeared in the Middle East about 3000 B.C. or 5000 years ago, never came to Africa where hoe agriculture, usually using slash-and-burn methods continued, for the most part, to the present.

As I have already mentioned, the economic historian, Tony Hopkins (1973), and the anthropologist, Jack Goody (1973), have recently suggested that Africans, at least in the early days of agriculture, knew about the plow but did not employ it because it was not economic to do so. That any people could see the plow as nonprofitable compared to hoe agriculture seems absurd, but we must remember that Africans, like ourselves, have to face the realities of economic life and use those tools and employ their time in ways that accord with what seems reasonable to them. There are conditions in which using the plow might also seem to make no sense to us, such as if we had no cattle or horses to pull them. In Africa, Hopkins has suggested, the problem was more complicated. Africans, at that time (and up to modern times), had plenty of land and few people. The need was to employ their resources in a way that would bring the best relative return. Since land and tools were easily obtainable compared to labor, it made sense to use what labor there was in the most efficient way, which meant, in this case, employing hoes, not plows, and slash-and-burn agriculture, rather than intensive methods of land utilization. Or, put another way, in order to obtain the tools which would lead to increased production, tools like the plow, wheeled wagons, and roads, the cost to relatively poor economies would have been so high (the opportunity costs) that the people could not afford them. Hence they made the best use of the combination of resources which they had. Thus swidden, or slash-and-burn, agriculture came to characterize people in the savannah of Africa (the situation became somewhat different when they moved into the rain forests further south) and eventually, no doubt, they became committed to this form of production with the result that one of the reasons Africa today may be classified as "underdeveloped" is this historical movement along a nonplow path. Since, for various reasons, it is now economical to economize capital more than labor, Africans must radically alter their basic ways of life because, as we shall see, social structure is intimately related to modes of production.

While Hopkins' ideas about the economic sensibility of swidden are undoubtedly relevant to agricultural production in Africa, we should also be aware that for those people living in the rain forests and even in some of the savannah grasslands, a more important constraint was the tsetse fly. Where the tsetse fly exists, cattle and horses cannot. Without them plowing is impossible.

THE INTRODUCTION OF IRON

Another important innovation leading to increase in production, population, and general cultural and social complexity was iron. Iron was not invented in the Eurasian area until about 1500 B.C. Plows could be and were made of wood although iron plows were more efficient than wooden ones. In Africa, the effect of the appearance of iron beginning in the upper Nile somewhere about 500 B.C., was not to make plows economical, but to stimulate a move out of the western sudan into the rain forests typical of most of the West African coast. Bohannan and Curtin (1971) felt Africans with iron axes could more easily cut down the trees and control the luxurious vegetation. Whether this is true or not, the introduction of iron into the sudan occurred in conjunction with a move to the coast and the rise of a new method of production, tropical cropping. Sorghum and other grain crops do not do well in such a climate with the result that the people turned to root crops, including yams and palm trees whose oil was used for food and wine. To these were added such things as okra, a vegetable.

One of the most controversial chapters in Murdock's history of Africa is the next, the contact between the people of Africa and those of Southeast Asia around the time of Christ or just before. That this contact occurred is undoubted. To this day, the basic culture of the people of Madagascar, the huge island off the east coast of southern Africa, is Southeast Asian, as much as the basic culture of Australia is that of England, an island halfway around the world from it. (That is why Madagascar is ignored in this book.) For Africans, this culture contained such important items as bananas and plan-tains, a type of banana, (which are the staple foods of the people of Buganda —the great state that was situated on the north shore of Lake Victoria) and chickens, as well as such other things as bark cloth and xylophones. Murdock felt that these elements of Southeast Asian culture were communicated to the east coast of Africa, perhaps from Madagascar, and then diffused across the tropical parts of Africa, to which bananas were adapted, into West Africa. Others feel that the Southeast Asians, as great seafarers, were capable of carrying these items around Africa by boat.

In any case, to the indigenously developed elements of West African coastal culture and those diffused from the north, such as cattle, sheep, goats, and iron were added the important bananas, chickens, and some types of yams.

THE RISE OF THE BANTU

Subsequent to these technological developments, there occurred one of the greatest movements of people in history, a movement which today we deduce largely from linguistic evidence (Greenberg 1963; Phillipson 1977). This was the rise and spread of the Bantu people.

Bantu is a term derived from a word common to Bantu languages, -*ntu*, meaning "man" and a common prefix, *ba-*, which is a plural prefix. Thus *bantu*, in some dialects, means "men" or "people" as opposed to *mu-ntu*, the same root with a singular prefix, which would mean "a man" or "a person." The fact is that the prefix indicating number varies in Bantu languages so one might find the equivalent of bantu being *a-ntu*, *aba-ntu*, *ovi-ntu*, or even *wa-tu*, as in Swahili. The belief now is that the ancestors of the modern Bantu speakers, who are part of the Congo-Kordofanian language family, lived in the area of the Benue River (Map 2.2) of Nigeria. This conclusion is based on comparison of the structures of the Benue area languages with Bantu. Further-more, that this migration was fairly recent (beginning around 2000 years ago) can be deduced both from archaeological evidence and from the fact that despite the Bantu languages being separated by vast distances (for example, between Cameroon on the one hand and South Africa on the other), the forms of the languages are much alike. They did not have time to diverge greatly.

What appears to have happened is that the ancestors of the Bantu found the area to the south of the Benue congenial, especially after they acquired control of production methods suited to the rain forests. They moved southeast into the jungles of the Cameroons and the Zaire or Congo Basin, pioneers separating off from settled groups and by their new isolation steadily developing new varieties of the Bantu language and new societies. However, it is also increasingly apparent that the movement was given impetus by the florescence of Bantu speakers who settled in the Shaba area of southern Zaire as well as in certain other secondary dispersal centers (Phillipson 1977). Here some kind of social revitalization sent new waves of migration into eastern and southern Africa. The result is that when Europeans first began to have extensive contacts with peoples in the interior of Bantu Africa, they found signs everywhere of continuing spread and growth as Bantu populations pressed further into the southern tip of Africa and moved out to fill up the open lands that remained. Thus Bantu Africa is sparsely populated for its size.

THE SPREAD OF THE PASTORALISTS

Another important migration that occurred, although not as impressive as the Bantu movement, is that of the pastoral peoples of the Sahara and northeast Africa. While comprising smaller numbers of people and societies, it was economically perhaps even more significant. Traditional ideas about Africa have not prepared us to understand that outside the rain forests of Africa, which consist mainly of a thin stretch of the West African coast and the Zaire Basin, most Africans are grain farmers who combine this form of agriculture with the husbanding of cattle, sheep, and goats. A reverse misconception is that those Africans who raise cattle do so to the exclusion of agriculture. In modern times only a few African societies such as Maasai, Somali, Barabaig, Samburu, and Turkana were nearly exclusively pastoral, and some, like the Somalis, nearly exclusively camel raisers. All the rest mix the two means of production to one degree or another, although there is always a tendency to move in the direction of increasing the production of livestock at the expense of grain, if necessary. This indicates the historical importance of livestock, especially as wealth, a subject we will explore in more detail in the next chapter.

We know less about the appearance of cattle in Africa than of domestication of crops, because its prehistoric remnants are rarer. Camels, on the other hand, are a relatively recent introduction though less popular than cattle because they are confined to the desert margins. While Africans domesticated for themselves or borrowed from Asia a number of crops which differentiated their type of agriculture from that which originated in the Middle East (where barley, wheat and oats were the staples), no African animals were domesticated. All of the domesticated varieties had been tamed in the Middle East. In other words, Africans ultimately took cattle, sheep, goats, and camels from the Middle East or Asia. There seems little doubt that as these animals moved into Africa, they were immediately seen as a popular alternative to agriculture. However, as already noted, an important limiting feature to the raising of cattle, the most valued of the livestock outside the camel areas, is the presence of the tsetse fly, which causes encephalitis or sleeping sickness.

Probably because they occupied superior grazing land, originally the Sahara Desert itself until it became inhospitable to most grazing by about 2000 B.C., certain African people became notably specialized in cattle raising. These included both Afro-Asiatic speakers of the Cushitic subtype (the present Somalis and Galla of the Horn of Africa for example) and Nilo-Saharan speakers such as inhabit most of the southern half of the country of Sudan and the upper reaches of the Nile. By A.D. 1 Cushitic speakers with cattle had moved into East Africa as far south as Tanzania, where some of their descendants, such as the Iraqw and Burungi still live. The Bantu were also coming into this area in sufficient numbers so that acquaintance with livestock husbandry spread to all the Bantu who did not inhabit tsetse zones. Then about A.D. 1000, following the Afro-Asiatic speakers, the Nilo-Saharan-speaking ancestors of the present Maasai, Nandi, Turkana, and others, arrived to replace these Cushites, who continued, however, to hold the Horn, giving us the distribution we see now on the linguistic map (Map 2.1).

The Importance of Cattle and Camels

While a full discussion of the significance of cattle and camels must await later chapters, it seems useful at this point to say a word about why they are so important. The traditional opinion is that they provide a backup to agriculture, a way to supplement the diet when there is crop failure, as so often happens in the savannah zones. However, this interpretation is simplistic. Africans do eat cattle, but the chief importance of these animals derives from an economic role they play, a role which is as important as food. Cattle are the main repositories of value, and therefore they make it possible for an African producer to create and preserve wealth in a way he could not do if he had to depend only on crops. Africa without cattle would be like the Western world without gold. You will find that it is a mistake to assume that any food products raised by Africans are produced simply to satisfy hunger. The mistake becomes doubly misleading when livestock are the subject. The error is as fundamental as if a stranger to Western culture assumed that the passion we have for gold is due to its value for filling teeth.

In sum, throughout history Africans have been subjected to some powerful forces from the outside in addition to those they were responsible for creating themselves, such as their indigenous cereal crops. They have felt the effects of domestic crops and animals as well as iron from the Middle East and Asia, and they have felt the impact from Southeast Asia of bananas and chickens (not to mention the effects on their artistic life through the introduction of such instruments as the xylophone).

EUROPEAN CONTACT

The external force about which we know most is that of Europeans beginning in the fifteenth century when the Portuguese, under the rule of Henry the Navigator, began to explore the West African coast. Although Anselme Isalguier of Toulouse reputedly crossed the Sahara from Tunis to Niger in 1402, he was merely repeating what must have been a very long history of trade and contact across the Sahara going back to at least 1000 B.C. The first known penetration of the coastal areas began when the Portuguese reached the Madeira Islands in 1418, but it took them until 1471 to reach Ghana after which there was an explosive penetration reaching the Cape of Good Hope at the southern end of the continent in 1498 (Vasco da Gama). Coming quickly up the whole east coast, among other things, they built Fort Jesus at the site of the present Mombasa. Except for some gold in West Africa (until independence, Ghana was called the Gold Coast), Africans did not have much to offer the Europeans in trade with the unfortunate exception of human beings and ivory, so that almost immediately after contact with the West African coast, where the largest populations in Africa were concentrated, the slave trade started. The Portuguese hauled slaves to Portugal for plantation work during the fifteenth century even before they discovered the New World in 1492. As soon as they did reach the Western Hemisphere, slaves were sent to Brazil, mainly to Bahia where blacks even today are most heavily concentrated. Slaves soon found their way to every nook and cranny of the New World, from Buenos Aires and Brazil to all the Caribbean islands, the United States, Mexico City and even down the west coast of South America to Chile. For over 250 years, the main interest Europeans, including Portuguese, Spanish, English, Dutch, Danes, and Americans, had in Africa was obtaining slaves. While slaves were taken from all the coastal areas of Africa, the main source of supply was the proximate and populous West African coast, principally the areas of modern Nigeria, Benin, and Ghana, and they traded at the mouth of the Congo as well. Despite this fact, there was some minor penetration of the continent.

One of the most interesting events was the development in what is now northern Angola, among the Kongo people, of extensive contacts with Europeans which led for a while to an exchange of ambassadors between the Kongo kingdom and both Portugal and the Vatican while the Kongo officially became a Christian nation until relations deteriorated and finally, about 1525, disappeared.

Around 1650, 150 years after its discovery, the Cape of Good Hope was colonized by the Dutch, who by then were extensively engaged in trade in the Far East and wanted a provisioning station for their fleet. This was the beginning of the modern Afrikaans people who dominate the Republic of South Africa and who moved to their present main areas of settlement in the east part of South Africa during the nineteenth century to escape the rule of the British who had taken over control of South Africa beginning in the early 1800s.

ARAB PENETRATION

This history of European contact with the East Coast is not particularly complex. While the Portuguese had forts and maintained contact in such areas as Mombasa and Mozambique, their hold was weak, and no other European powers were much interested in the area. Arabs, on the other hand, were quite interested. Arab penetration of Africa was mainly across the Sahara and through the sudan, rather than on the coast, the East Coast being the exception. After the rise of Muhammed, Arab culture, infused with Islam, overran the entire sudan zone of west Africa and continued to penetrate south to the whole African coast even up to modern times, overlaying indigenous African cultural systems with an Islamic veneer. Arab interest also extended to the Horn of Africa, affecting the Somalis and coastal northeast African people. The Arabs and Persians had traded with the East African coastal areas by at least the tenth century but in the late eighteenth and early nineteenth centuries, they began to move inland in East Africa. Accompanied by or following the Swahili, an Arabized coastal Bantu pariah group, they crossed what is now southern Tanzania and reached all the way to southern Zaire in the Shaba region, making important contacts with Bantu people, such as the Fipa on Lake Tanganyika, along the way. In the middle nineteenth century, they crossed central Tanzania to establish one of the most famous slave and ivory routes, to Tabora and Ujiji on Lake Tanganyika, where Stanley had his famous meeting with Livingstone in 1871. Trade in East Africa also included slaves, but ivory was added and continued as a much desired commodity even after the slave trade was abolished. Unlike west African slaves, slaves in East Africa were taken mostly to Arab countries.

THE RISE OF COLONIALISM

After the abolition of slavery, Africa had so little that was desired by Europeans, one must wonder why Europeans rushed to occupy all African lands in the wake of the Berlin Conference of 1885. Indeed, when Britain took over control of Uganda about 1900, there was widespread debate over whether she should burden herself with that country. The answer is complex, including elements of global power politics among European nations and visions of wealth derived from developing African populations as markets for European goods. Whatever the reason, after 1885, colonial rule began in earnest in Africa. The country which took control over the most territory was the most powerful global nation of the time, Britain. In West Africa she acquired the minute country of Gambia (merely a long enclave along the Gambia River surrounded by French-controlled Senegal), Sierra Leone, Ghana, and Nigeria. Putting down the Afrikaans, Britain administered all of South Africa, as well as Botswana (then Bechuanaland), Lesotho (then Basutoland), Swaziland, Zimbabwe-Rhodesia, Zambia, and Malawi. In East Africa she grabbed Kenya and Uganda and part of Somaliland as well as the country now called Sudan. The French, the second largest European power, took the second largest bite: most of West Africa became a French colony, including all the sudanic regions below the Sahara, and the coastal regions of Senegal, Ivory Coast (Cote d'Ivoire), Dahomey (now called Benin), and Gabon. The latter was combined with the present Zaire and Central African Republic to constitute French Equatorial Africa, while the areas to the west were all combined into French West Africa. As for other regions, the French had only a small piece of Somaliland, Djibouti, on the Gulf of Aden. Through all this, the Portuguese managed to hold on to Portuguese Guinea in West Africa, Angola, and Mozambique. Germany took Togo and Cameroon in West Africa, Southwest Africa (Namibia), and Tanganyika, in East Africa, all of which were lost after the First World War. Then the territories were turned over to the British as mandates, except for Cameroon, which went mostly to the French, and Rwanda and Burundi, which the Belgians acquired and attached to their one colony in Africa, the former Belgian Congo, now Zaire.

Control of these African territories continued up to 1958 when the first of the modern independent African nations, Ghana, appeared. Liberia, established by Americans in the early 1800s, had been independent all along (or rather, colonized by black Americans). Today the independence movement has been nearly completed; the only disputed area still existing is Southwest Africa, or Namibia. The future of South Africa, which has an African population dwarfing its four million whites, the largest concentration of whites in any country in Africa, is still in doubt.

The Governor of Tanganyika and other colonial officials greeting Africans during a visit to a rural community

THE CHARACTER OF AFRICAN NATIONS

It is useful to keep in mind, as this survey of Africa continues, that the rise of independent nations in Africa is not usually to be taken as the emergence into control of surpressed political units. They are not like the American colonies emerging from British rule, or even the reemergence of an India from the status of a British colony. Few African people had any political units corresponding to the present states, which were created by the colonial powers and are now staffed and ruled for the most part by Western-trained, Europeanized Africans. Nigeria is a good example. When Lord Lugard acquired Nigeria for the British, the boundaries he established were sometimes made by simply rushing to take as much territory as he could until he ran up against the French. The result is that three great ethnic groups who were often mortal enemies, the Hausa, Yoruba, and Ibo, were pulled into it. In addition, the western boundary cut some Yoruba off from their kinsmen and included them in French Dahomey. Some of the Hausa, likewise, were relegated to French rule. It is as if a pair of colonial powers had invaded Europe and cut it up in such a way that Italy, southern France, and southern England were held by one county and northern England and Scotland, northern France, and Germany were held by another. The natural desire of these ethnic units to reunite would, upon independence, be defeated by the fact that the rulers of the new

nations had little ethnic identity with their subjects. Rather, these rulers identify with the powerful former colonial powers, despite the fact that they were
of mixed cultural background. In fact, today the largest proportion of these
African nations use the language of their former colonial masters as official
languages because there is no linguistic unity within the countries. Other than
this, the power that comes from possession of territory in the modern world
has overridden ethnic identity.

MATERIAL
ECONOMICS

AFRICANS PRODUCE AND EXCHANGE THINGS,
like all other people. This is usually the subject matter of economics so the
production and exchange of *things* could be called African economics. However, I wish to treat economics in a broader sense, as the exchange of not only
material things, but behavior, such as the activities of a wife in relation to her
husband, or of a client in relation to his lord. This kind of *social exchange*
includes the transfer of both things for behavior and behavior for behavior and
is the basis for the kinds of social structure that will be discussed in succeeding
chapters.

Material economics must be differentiated at the outset from culture.
The kinds of economies Africans had or have depended, as all economies do,
on the kind of knowledge or culture they had, a point I stressed in the first
chapter. However, this knowledge, strictly speaking, is not economics. Eco-

nomics concerns itself with how much to produce and whether to exchange. Sometimes, as perhaps in the case of the plow or wheel, knowledge is available but will not be used because the products it can generate are not worth the cost. Sometimes the cost of implementing the knowledge is beyond the means of the producer.

So in this chapter we will concern ourselves with Africans' practices with respect to the questions of whether and under what conditions to produce and exchange material things, even though material economics, as we shall see, is not strictly separable from the total economic system which includes social exchanges.

AFRICANS AS ECONOMIC MEN

A debate among Africanist economic anthropologists centers on the question of whether Africans make decisions about production and exchange in terms of self-interest, as economic men, so I must be clear at the outset as to why I think they do at least as much as we do. If one thinks of African economies as "subsistence," or without economic orientation as just defined, they are imagined to be basically different from our own in that they are oriented toward provisioning, rather than toward utility or profit in a very general sense. It is probably for this reason that it has become customary to focus on the production of "staple" foods. As I shall try to explain, it is a mistake to think of Africans as engaged only in provisioning and, correspondingly, a mistake to think of even the edibles they produce as raised solely to eat. Some important goods raised by Africans are not edible—cotton, kola nuts, or tobacco are examples, and some edibles, like cattle, are not intended primarily for food.

This point can by made another way be referring to a quotation from an account of the Igbo or Ibo people of southeast Nigeria by Victor Uchendu, himself an Igbo. Although the Igbo are admittedly unusually intensely commercial in their attitudes their basic profit orientation cannot be taken as unique for Africa by any means (Uchendu 1965, 15):

> If you ask the Igbo why he believes that the world should be manipulated, he will reply "The world is a marketplace and it is subject to bargain." In his view, neither the world of man alone nor the world of spirits is a permanent home. The two worlds together constitute a home. Each world is peopled with "interested" individuals and groups and much buying and selling goes on in each. People go to the marketplace for different reasons, but the common motivation is the desire to make a profit. Although the profit motive is the guiding factor, there are occasional losses. From the Igbo point of view, a person does not abandon trading because he suffers losses. It would be cowardly to do

so, but he cannot carry on indefinitely if he does not balance his losses with gains. The Igbo would advise the perennially unsuccessful trader to change his line of merchandise. Instead of trading in yams, he should try pepper; eventually he will find his line. But if all else fails, magic will not. This description of life in the idiom of market exchange is not a mere theoretical formulation of mine; it is the Igbo way and is manifested in their everyday behavior.

While most Africans do not express their orientation toward obtaining utility in quite such direct terms, we shall see plenty of evidence throughout this book that such aspirations are there, as they are among all people.

In this chapter we shall first examine African production and then exchange in economic terms, beginning with farming as a production system.

AFRICAN AGRICULTURE

Farming Complexity

The most fundamental fact about African farming is that it is complex, requiring skills and knowledge about a wide variety of things in order to be successful. As Marvin Miracle (1967), an agricultural economist, has said, although African agriculture is less productive than American, it is more intricate. For example, all Africans raise mixes of crops, rather than single crops; the various mixes and extent of mixing is dependent on such things as habitat and climate, as well as profitability in terms of traditional notions of value. Coffee, which is a modern cash crop in many parts of Africa, is often grown among banana trees. Calabashes may be grown among the millets, as are beans. This diversity of cropping is explained as a function of the need to spread labor requirements over different times (Miracle 1967) to make the most of the available labor supply, or to extend harvest time so that new crops become available over a longer range of time. In that way hunger is reduced as are the periods during which prices of food are high, as they always are before harvest time. In addition, interplanting may also be beneficial to the plants themselves. It has been observed that interplanting of rice and cassava (manioc) leads to a lower yield for each than could be obtained individually but that the aggregate yield from this practice, with appropriate successions of crops, is higher than might otherwise be the case. A study of Zambian farming (Schultz 1976) shows a typical example of mixing in a sample of farms with an average of 5.4 acres under cultivation, 1.4 acres of which were in maize, 1.8 in cassava, 0.8 in finger millet, 0.15 in beans, 0.15 in peanuts, and the balance in miscellaneous crops. This is a simple case. It is reported that in Zaire in some places as many as sixty crops may be planted simultaneously, many of them interplanted.

The complexity of farming is increased further by the common practice of sequencing crops, somewhat as our farmers do when they rotate them to get the best combination. One example is maize, which draws nitrogen out of the soil, being followed by a crop which puts it back. Miracle records that in Zaire forests, bananas are usually planted first, followed by other appropriate crops, terminating with cassava, which grows well in the soil depleted by the preceding crops. In the savannah of Zaire, there is no pattern which can be detected. This suggests that the farmers are freer to use more complex patterns and usually do.

Swidden

For Americans, used to intensive farming on large plots by machines, the usual African method of extensive farming is strange indeed. Most Africans use some form of swidden, or long fallowing. Basically, this system requires farmers to select a plot of forest or thick bush on the basis of its fertility, as shown by the kinds of grasses and other plants growing on it, and to cut the trees and shrubs, piling them on the plot to be tilled. The ash from their burning adds

An African woman tilling the soil in a field prepared by means of swidden technique

to the fertility of the soil. When the land so selected is tilled, the tree stumps, or trees from which branches have been lopped, and the rocks and other imperfections in the soil are not removed because this would be a wasteful expenditure of labor since the plot will only be used for a year or so and then abandoned for a new plot. The time required for a plot to recover its fertility and be available for new planting varies from place to place. The Bisa and Lala of Zambia do not use the plot for more than one year whereas in some places it may be used, if sequenced, for three or four years. After being abandoned, the land may recover its fertility in a few years or it may take so long that the land is in effect abandoned forever. As the reader may imagine, the swidden method of crop production may require huge expanses of empty, unused land. The fundamentally important economic fact about this method of farming is that it economizes on labor. Where there is plenty of land, as in much of old Africa, it is cheaper to produce crops this way than to intensively cultivate a single plot with all the expenses of stumping and clearing it and producing fertilizer for it, as well as purchasing and maintaining machinery (which Africans did not have anyway or cannot afford today). To put it in economic terms, given the available conditions, supply of labor, supply of land and tools, combined with the high cost of shifting to more productive tools, it makes more sense in most cases when seeking to obtain the best return, to try to make labor go as far as possible.

Swidden agriculture has been employed by Africans for a very long time. We know that the Zaire River Basin rain forests are all second growth (Allan 1965, 220), the original forest having been cut over successively by swidden farmers for hundreds of years. Since it has been around for such a long time, the system is complex. A study of swidden in the Zaire River Basin has shown that there are at least twelve different kinds of swidden, and I suggest that the number is even greater since the classification into twelve types was made on the basis of the various ways the operations of cutting, burning, cleaning, hoeing and planting are combined. This set of operations theoretically could be combined twenty-five different ways. Sometimes it makes sense to cut the trees and shrubs on the plot first, then to plant the crop, and finally to burn the dried wood on top of it. It makes cleaning the plot unnecessary and hoeing for weeds comes later. This way of proceeding is proper in the forest where manioc or bananas are to be grown since burning the dried debris does not injure the buried tubers. In other cases, where seeds could be injured, cutting and burning precedes planting. This would be true where millet seeds are to be spread among the ashes and hoed in.

While swidden is therefore a labor-conserving method of crop production, the amount of labor cost which has to be assumed differs from place to place; probably the most costly swidden system is that practiced in Central Africa, known as *chitemene*. In Zambia, for example, soils are exceptionally poor, and the more common type of swidden does not produce sufficient fertilizer. In chitemene, branches are cut off trees in a circle much wider than the plot that will actually be cultivated; the branches are then hauled to the site for burning. There are varieties of chitemene, including small circle and large circle, the former more laborious than the latter.

Some Central Africans also resort to cutting the sod, and removing dried grass to be mounded, dirt covered, and burned for fertilizer, also a costly labor method. The Haya on the southwest shore of Lake Victoria have created the fertile soil necessary for banana production by laboriously bringing all degradable material, including manure, to the banana plots. The Jos Plateau of Nigeria is well known for the labor-intensive methods used in agriculture, as is the Island of Ukara in the southeastern part of Lake Victoria where along the shores the people actually dig pits which reach down to the water table. The grass grows better in the pits and thereby provides grazing for their cattle during the dry season. Finally, the Chagga of Mt. Kilimanjaro in East Africa used to keep their cattle in underground shelters, protected against raids by Maasai from the foot of the mountain. Therefore they had to cut and carry the fodder necessary for cattle feed. Africans, then, will use more labor-demanding methods of production if the situation warrants. In all these cases we must assume that the added labor expense is for one reason or another acceptable relative to the return to be expected. This is another way of saying that the probable reduced profit from such activities compared to the usual swidden was not so great as to make the enterprise unworth the time expended.

Dominant Crops

Of all the various kinds of foods raised by Africans, certain ones stand out because of the much greater amount of time and space given to their production. Their distribution is summarized in Map 3.1. First among these are certain native African crops mentioned earlier—sorghum, bulrush millet, and finger millet—and also fonio *(digitaria)* and *teff,* grown only in the highlands of Ethiopia. All of these crops except teff have the special ability to go dormant and begin growing again after spells of drought, and all have a short growing season of up to eighty days. Thus they are well suited to the African savannahs with their erratic and short rainy seasons. Today some New-World-derived crops, notably maize and cassava, challenge these ancient African crops, but the African crops persist in large areas because nothing else can take their place.

Sorghum resembles maize except that it has a fist of large seeds at the top, rather than ears on the stalk. Bulrush millet also looks like maize, but as its name implies, the seeds at the top look like a bulrush, a dark brown rod

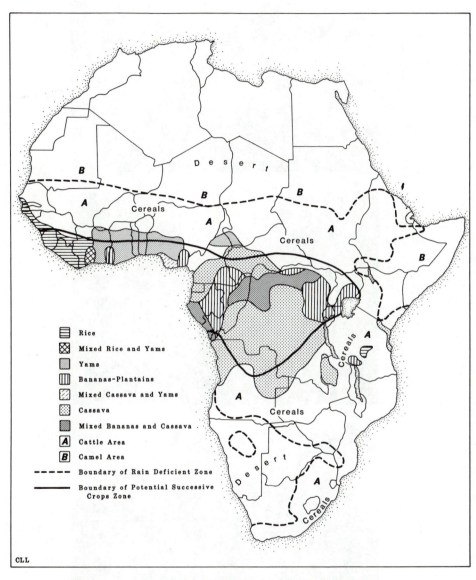

MAP 3.1   Distribution of Staples and of Dominant Livestock
(adapted from Bennett, 1962)

Three of the African cereal grains: (beginning top photo) bulrush millet, sorghum, finger millet consisting of small seeds tightly packed together. Finger millet is a short plant looking like grass with a cluster of seeds at the top which resemble a set of fingers. The first two of these cereal plants is found throughout Africa's savannah zones from the western and eastern sudan down through East Africa, across Central Africa, and into southern Africa, in other words, everywhere outside the rain forests and their borders, which are wet enough to support other crops of better yield. However, they are excluded from the desert and semidesert zones because they are not immune to drought, only highly resistant. Eleusine and fonio are mutually exclusive; fonio is grown in most of savannah West Africa while eleusine exists in the rest of savannah Africa wherever conditions would be such as to favor fonio too.

These various cereals have combinations of characteristics which make one or the other a better main choice for different circumstances; the pattern of their distribution is therefore complex. However, it seems generally true that they vary in their drought resistance sufficiently to say that bulrush millet is favored under the driest conditions that will support cereal agriculture, sorghum is next, and finger millet is the most demanding, although it will still grow under conditions too dry for maize. It is for this reason that in the better cattle areas of Africa, which happen also to be the driest, bulrush millet is common where any agriculture is possible at all.

Maize, another great cereal crop, imported from the New World, is preferred over the African cereals wherever it can grow (for reasons which will become apparent later in the chapter), but since it requires more rainfall than is usual for the African cereals (a minimum of 30 inches a year), its distribution is limited. Since it is tolerant of moisture, it appears in West Africa on the rain forest borders, has been grown extensively in the northern Zaire Basin, where yams also are staples, and is cultivated extensively in the moister areas of southern Africa, where the African cereals used to dominate.

Rice is the last cereal we need to consider. There are two kinds of rice grown in Africa, wet, or paddy, rice and upland (*oryza glaberrima*) rice. Only the latter is indigenous to Africa and it would not even concern us because of its limited distribution except for the fact that its production dominates agriculture in an appreciable chunk of the western part of West Africa (see Map 3.1). This cereal requires a good deal of moisture, which is why it appears in the rain forest zone, and it makes possible a reasonably productive crop in an area which for various reasons is not as good for yams and cassava. These are staples in the rest of the rain forest of West Africa.

The rain forest areas of Africa, outside the rice area, mainly West Africa and the Zaire River Basin, have as their most important crops yams and cassava, although plantains are also important in some places, as are cocoyams and sweet potatoes. Since all of these except yams proper are imports from outside Africa—plantains from southeast Asia, cocoyams from the Pacific, and cassava from the New World—it can be appreciated how important yams once were in Africa (Coursey 1977), an importance which has yielded, especially in Zaire, to these imports.

Yams, like sweet potatoes, are tubers, grown in mounds. The most widely cultivated is *Dioscorea alata*, the "water yam," probably because of its high yields; tubers sometimes reach a hundred pounds. But, *D. rotundata*, the "white yam," although producing tubers up to only six pounds, has a preferred quality, as do *D. cayanensis*, or "yellow yam," and *D. esculenta*, "lesser yam," (up to only two pounds). Yams are very demanding of soil (as are bananas), preferring sandy loam for the best yields. Therefore farmers usually reserve their best land for them.

Cassava is the more common root crop. It is prepared by removing the bark and pulping the stringy interior, and it can be stored by grinding it into a flour or meal. Cassava meal is most common in West Africa, and manioc flour, in Zaire. Yams are best stored in the ground until they are needed, since they are as perishable as bananas. Therefore cassava, among its other favorable characteristics, has the ability to be transported when made into flour or meal. Paradoxically, despite their perishable nature, root crops are cheaper to store so that except for yams, the cost of crops increases as we move from root crops to maize to the African cereals, which must be put in granaries, facts which show up in calculations of the general cost of raising these various crops.

The term *staple* implies that a people depend on the crop nearly exclusively. While it is true that one crop, such as bulrush millet, might occupy the vast majority of tilled land, in some societies the commonest crop may occupy only 35 percent of the tilled land while another occupies, say, 33 percent. While yams are a staple in much of West Africa, they face heavy competition from bananas and cassava where these can be grown. In Zambia maize is grown almost everywhere in varying amounts, sometimes competing heavily with the African cereals, especially at the boundary between root crops and African cereals as shown in Map. 3.1. In the southwestern Zaire-Zambezi confluence, cassava and maize compete for dominance, and in southern Africa maize and African cereals compete. While rice has no competitor in the West African tropical rice region, it competes with African cereals in northern Guinea. Rice and plantains are both important in lower Guinea. Plantains are important along with root crops in southern Ghana, and rice and root crops, in northern Zaire.

Other Crops

Other than these fundamentally important crops, Africans grow a great variety of things. One of the most important is kola nuts, a kind of stimulant similar to caffeine which is a common trade item over much of West Africa, the indigenous African Coca-Cola. Another is palm oil trees which are especially important for cooking oil and for palm wine, a favored drink in the rain forest areas, as beer made from African cereals is in the savannah regions. Indigenously developed crops in Africa include sesame, pumpkins, watermelons, sweet melons, calabashes (used for utensils and musical instruments), cowpeas, Bengal beans, horse-eye beans, winged beans, velvet beans, okra, black pepper, guinea pepper, indigo (for dyes), henna (narcotic), and spinach. Plants introduced from various places include Asian yams, sweet potatoes, cocoyams, peanuts, onions, lima beans, butter beans, soy beans, pigeon peas, tomatoes, pineapples, ginger, turmeric, cotton, sugar cane, tobacco, bush greens, and Indian spinach (Morgan and Pugh 1973). Cotton is especially interesting. Although listed here as an import, there is some dispute about whether it was domesticated in Africa. In traditional Africa, cotton cloth was unknown except in West Africa where the true loom had also been introduced from the Mediterranean in prehistoric times. There are two basic kinds of cloth woven in West Africa, long narrow strips, by men, and wider, shorter sheets, by women. Hence, African dress outside of West Africa consisted of woven palm cloth, bark cloth, or leather in the areas of domestic animals where goats were the source of most clothing.

Africans as Planners

The complexity of African agriculture, as seen in the large number of crops from which farmers must choose, the need for mixing them in the field, the need for sequenced planting and the type of swidden or intensive agriculture to use, strongly suggests that these farmers had to be planners; they had to be choice makers who could not produce acceptable results simply by acting in a customary manner. A striking verification of this is the way dominant crops have altered in Zaire over the last 500 years. The evidence is that African farmers have reacted to new opportunities to improve their productive performance. The dominant crops in northern Zaire before contact with Portuguese were African cereals and yams. The whole Zaire River Basin was interlaced with trade routes (Vansina 1968) along which word of the introduction of maize from America probably passed. Maize replaced the original crops, probably for reasons of lower production cost relative to return (as I shall show shortly), and held sway for a long time until within the last hundred years when cassava moved in to replace maize, also probably because of lower production costs.

The list of imported crops also supports the claim that Africans have always reacted to new opportunities, rather than simply relying on tradition. A remarkable study of a region of the former Belgian Congo by Drachoussoff

(1947) makes this point dramatically. He indicates that the following list of plants had been accepted into that region within living memory: bitter cassava, sweet cassava, tomatoes, bananas, yams, taro, peanuts, beans, maize, tobacco and sesame. Furthermore, Johnston (1958) has also established that in Zaire the current pattern of crop production has been startlingly affected by the appearance of cheap transport and new markets in the rising cities. Maize fields, for example, have grown up along the right of way of the railroads, as is also true in Zambia, maize being the cereal most in demand in the cities. This naturally raises the question of why, like the northern Zairians, Zaire farmers did not take to maize earlier. The answer, one may guess, is that the opportunity costs were too high in the past, since raising maize in those areas required special expensive machinery and fertilizer. However, the returns from sales in the new urban centers would have been high enough to overcome these costs, costs which were alleviated by proximity to cheap transportation, the railroad.

Labor-Conserving Crops

If we are agreed that Africans can and do alter traditional patterns of production as new opportunities arise, we must realize that they probably do so in terms of some goal they wish to achieve and can achieve better with the new method. Many different kinds of ends could be responsible for change, for example, taste. Some kinds of crops are considered to be better tasting than others. Many Africans prefer finger millet for making beer. New bulrush millet is tastier than old bulrush millet, much as fresh sweet corn is tastier to us than older sweet corn in which the sugar has turned to starch. The taste of low-producing yams is favored over high-producing ones. The evidence, however, is that over the long haul, the most fundamental consideration in choice of crops to produce has been labor relative to caloric output, as Hopkins found to be true in West Africa. A fact which may account for the generally heavy emphasis in Africa on starchy foods is that they are also the cheapest in terms of labor to produce. This is a surprising conclusion when put alongside the old myth about tropical parts of the world which picture the people as living shiftless lives depending on nature to produce bountifully for them without effort. It is in fact true that during much of the year, African men have free time; but during the crop production season, there are climax events such as weeding, threshing, or harvesting when labor is immensely important because the task must be accomplished quickly or part of the crop will be lost. In fact, it will be argued that the most pervasive social structure in Africa, the lineage, is a product, in part, of the need to mobilize labor on a large scale for short periods. African women are always busy at all times of the year and are nearly everywhere the mainstay in the production of staple foods.

The Kuba of southern Zaire probably cannot be taken as a measure of the amount of labor actually expended in African societies because they seem to be unusually hard working. Nevertheless, it is instructive to review Vansina's (1962) table of work hours by people in a compound in the Bushong area in the spring of 1954, which is one of the few tabulations of labor expended to be found in the African literature (Table 3.1). This was compiled during the harvest season, when more agricultural labor was required than during most of the year, but it should be noted that one-third of the labor was devoted to production of trade goods. It should also be noticed that the average number of hours worked per day, 7.34, is a very respectable number by any standards.

Looking at the whole of Africa, and not just West Africa as Hopkins did, we can expand his thesis and show that while labor was the critical cost factor

TABLE 3.1   Bushong Labor—Work Hours of Fifteen People in a Compound—Nsheng (Spring 1951)

PEOPLE	NUMBER OF DAYS	WORK HOURS	AVERAGE PER DAY	HOURS DEVOTED TO PRODUCING FOR MARKET OR TRADE
Girl	10	77.35	7.45	42
Woman	11	92.55	8.26	21.55
Woman	12	90.45	7.33	18.50
Woman with two babies	12	71.45	5.59	29.55
Girl	10	82.30	8.19	21.05
Women (all)	13	92.50	7.08	47.00
Tailor	8	46.40	5.40	31.50
Woman	8	57.30	7.11	28.45
Woman	14	116.20	8.18	20.25
Young girl	13	94.30	7.16	16.20
Woman	7	63.50	9.07	10.20
Woman	15	127.00	8.28	34.05
Old man	13	86.40	6.40	64.25
Woodcarver	11	90.25	8.13	84.20
Chief of the compound (smith)	11	80.30	7.19	36.10
Totals	168	1,271.45	7.34	507.25 (= approx. 1/3 of total work-hours)

in crop production, the cost of labor relative to number of calories produced varied from place to place, and this variation had important social consequences, as we shall see in the next chapter. In other words, wherever we look in Africa, we find that among the crops they know, people mainly seem to choose to grow those which under their local circumstances are cheapest in terms of labor. This conclusion is based on the work of Johnston (1958, 144) whose examination of African agriculture makes possible the following model of cost of production, from highest to lowest:

↑ Yams

Rice

Millet

COST Sorghum

Maize

Cassava

Plantains

Some interesting deductions are possible from this model. For one thing, plantains are the most economic crop to grow, but since they need much more moisture and better soil than cassava and other crops, they can be grown in only a few places. Map 3.1, adapted from Bennett (1962), indicates the main areas (southern Uganda, northern Zaire Basin, southeast Nigeria, and southwest Ghana) in which they are grown. They seem to be cultivated wherever they can be. However, cassava seems to be the most economic crop in the tropical rain forest within what Bennett calls the "successive crop zone," the zone within which crop successioning is economic. This map, in fact, is somewhat deceptive because although yams are extremely important in West Africa, cassava may be more important there since Bascom (1977) says of Yoruba that yams are a luxury. Perhaps because of generally high productivity, the West Africans can afford to grow yams because they prefer their taste, but the matter is in question. In Map 3.1 the "boundary of potential successive crops" is a boundary of generally high tropical rainfall. Where cassava or yams, for example, go outside it into the lower rainfall areas, yields decline. This border also straddles the zone where maize is likely to appear since it is partially adapted to both lower rainfall rain forest and higher rainfall savannah. However, maize also appears in other areas, such as Zambia and southeast Africa in the higher rainfall savannah. Within Bennett's "rain deficient zone," we get cattle only in north Namibia, in a pocket of higher rainfall. Other than these, the whole of Africa between the two zone boundaries is dominated by

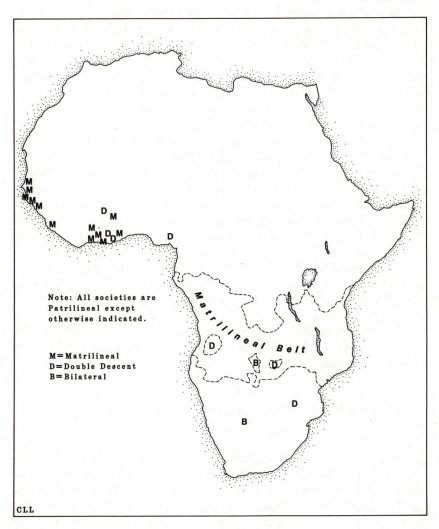

Note: All societies are
Patrilineal except
otherwise indicated.

M=Matrilineal
D=Double Descent
B=Bilateral

Matrilineal Belt

CLL

MAP 4.1   Descent Systems

Other than these, societies with matrilineal descent groups are scattered around the continent. For example, there are a few in the Nigerian plateau and in the Cameroon Highlands.

In addition to the societies which have either matrilineal or patrilineal descent groups exclusively, there are some, such as the Yako of southern Nigeria (Forde 1964) or the Wambugwe, who are described as having double descent groups. In these societies both types of descent groups exist, each with a different purpose. For example, title to a political office may descend through the father, and title to land, through the mother. Among the Wambugwe (Gray N.D.), a man inherits political position from his father even though he also belongs to a matrilineal clan. Both real property and political title descend through the mother in the case of the Ashanti (Lystad 1958), but a man's soul is derived from his father, making him a member of an important patrilineal ritual group. Therefore this makes the Ashanti, in a sense, a double-descent society, rather than a simple matrilineal one.

To complicate matters further, in some instances, such as among the Shambaa of northeast Tanzania, the descent system is mixed in a way called *ambilineal* (Winans 1962). In this instance a man belongs to only one descent group at a time, but it may be reckoned through his mother or father depending on circumstances. Groups constituted this way, where descent may be reckoned alternately between the mother's and father's side, are called *ramages,* whereas those in which it is constant on one side or the other are called *lineages.* While lineage systems are very common in Africa, ramages are very rare. However, it should also be recognized that scholars sometimes dispute about groups like the Yako and Shambaa because they are unsure whether to describe them as double-descent or ramage systems.

Unilineal Descent and Rights in People

Thus, the terms matrilineal and patrilineal usually refer to the types of descent groups possessed by African societies. However, the terms are also used to refer to rights a man possesses in other persons as when there are signs that a mother's brother may still have some control over his sister's son even though the sister's son is classified in the society as a member of father's descent group or lineage. This suggests an important fact about African societies; namely, that when a man trades off rights in his sister to a man of another lineage who becomes her husband, he does not necessarily trade off all his rights and may retain some rights in her offspring and in other valuables, such as the crops she possesses.

The Turu of central Tanzania illustrate the concept of "lingering matrilineality" (Schneider 1970). Turu society may be classified as having patrilineal descent groups. When a man marries, he brings his wife to live with him in the village of his father (that is, the patrilineage is localized, residence being patrilocal or with the father). His sons inherit his rights to the land and his other possessions. However, if the son should die, a kind of settlement meeting, called *mupanda,* is held at the father's village, in which representatives of the mother's group debate with members of the father's group how much compensation the father's group should pay for the death of "our son." (It is necessary to know that these people do not have the idea of "natural death." All deaths are somebody's responsibility. Since the boy was a member of his father's group, the father's group is responsible for him.) The settlement conference is identical to the one which is held when a man's wife dies. It appears, therefore, that while this society has only patrilineal descent groups, rights to the dead man are divided between the mother's and the father's side.

Matrilineality and patrilineality, interpreted as rights in people rather than as membership in descent groups, is hardly ever absolute so that one may speak of a society as having one degree or another of patrilineality or matrilineality. No matter how patrilineal a society is reckoned in terms of descent, there continues to be some matrilineality in the sense of rights retained by the mother's group in the offspring of their women. Similarly, even where there are matrilineal descent groups, men feel some sense of right in and identity with their sons so that although they may be legally obligated to pass their property to their sister's son, they may secretly hold some out and give it to their own sons. In the Wambugwe case mentioned earlier, while officially there are matrilineal groups, fathers quite openly pass their property—titles and cattle—to their sons. In such a case, one suspects, the society is on the verge of shifting to patrilineal descent groups.

Bridewealth

The determinant of whether and to what degree an African society will be patrilineal or matrilineal (or one of the other forms) is generally how much a husband is able to pay for his wife. If he can manage it, a husband ordinarily desires to pay bridewealth or brideprice and thus obtain exclusive rights in his wife, or if he cannot afford exclusive rights, whatever degree of rights he can. In most societies, if the economic base produces valuable movable wealth, bridewealth will be paid, and some rights in the wife obtained. However, there is one important exception to this. As one might expect, the amount of rights a man receives varies with the value of the woman relative to what is given for her. Some women are more valuable than others so that more must be given for them. Among the Nupe of Nigeria (Nadel 1942), for example, most men obtain rights in their wives by paying a brideprice. However, the daughters of rich and powerful men are more valuable than are other women because by marrying them, their husbands obtain important contacts with their powerful fathers. The fathers, in turn, obtain young political allies. In such instances, little or no brideprice is paid. Instead, the son-in-law pays with allegiance, and the marriage is essentially matrilineal. Conversely, Yao society in Mozambique is essentially matrilineal (Mitchell 1951), so much so that a woman does not even go to live with her husband but remains with her brothers, and the husband must come to visit with her. However, this extreme form of matrilineality, called matrilocal residence, is not followed by the chief of the village. Because of the power he has, from which his wife's family may benefit, he is allowed to take his wife to live with him. This is called virilocal residence (going to live at husband's home). In other words, power and allegiance are valuable commodities and sometimes enter into marriage transactions along with or in place of movable material wealth.

Bridewealth consists, when it is material, of valuables sufficient to accomplish the transfer of rights. Sometimes a society is spoken of as having no bridewealth, for only nominal gifts are paid. Nominal gifts are simply valuables of too little worth to obtain many rights. Cattle and camels are valuables par excellence, and nearly everywhere that people raise them in sufficient numbers, they are demanded as part or all of the brideprice. But the various African moneys also serve: iron goods, brass rods, cowry shells, cloth, or salt. In the Zaire Basin, where patrilineality is general, brideprice includes goats, slaves, dogs, chickens and sheep. In East Africa a cow will ordinarily serve to allow a man to remove a woman from her mother's residence to his own, give him exclusive sexual rights to her, and permit him to place his sons in his descent group. However, twenty head of cattle will accomplish much more, tying the woman so firmly to him that often divorce becomes essentially impossible.

Such high brideprices are rare, but good examples of societies which pay them are the neighboring Jie of northeast Uganda and the Turkana of northwest Kenya. Philip Gulliver (1955), who studied both these people, gives an example of bridewealth from each society as well as an indication of the source from whom the groom borrowed the animals. (In most African societies where bridewealth is paid, a young man when marrying for the first time must borrow the animals which he subsequently repays.)

In the Jie case, Gulliver records one bridewealth totaling fifty head of cattle of which the groom provided twenty-one himself (probably inherited from his father, who was dead) and got the others as follows:

Half brother	3
Full cousin I	4
Full cousin II	2
Father's half brother I	5
Father's half brother II	3
Half cousin I	1

Half cousin II	2
Half cousin III	2
2 clansmen (1 head each)	2
Mother's half brother	1
4 bond friends (1 head each)	4

From the Turkana Gulliver provides an example of the way the bride-price was composed in a case in which it was the second marriage for the groom. The total number of animals given for the bride was fifty-two.

Groom	22 cattle and 4 camels
Full brother	3 cattle and 1 camel
Half brother	1 cow and 1 camel
Father's full brother	4 cattle and 1 camel
Father's half brother	2 cattle
Half cousin	1 camel
Mother's brother	2 cattle
Wife's full brother I	2 cattle
Wife's full brother II	1 ox
Sister's husband	1 camel
6 bond friends (1 each)	6 cattle

Few African people are as rich as the Jie and Turkana so that bride-wealth is typically much lower than this. The Turu, for example, have a high rate of divorce, and a woman's brother, as we have seen, retains many rights in her after marriage. The bridewealth paid over the life of a marriage that lasts a lifetime may be about seven head of cattle. But the ratio of cattle to people in Turu society is less than two to one whereas in Turkana society it is more than ten to one.

Where movable material wealth sufficient to constitute a bridewealth is lacking, it is possible to effect a marriage by an exchange of women, sometimes mistakenly called *sister-exchange* marriage. This is a misnomer because a man does not necessarily give one of his sisters for another man's. He gives a woman who is a member of his agnatic (patrilineal) group. Suppose he has no sister, not even someone classified as a sister (because she is of the same generation as his actual sister would be), he might obtain the right from another man of his lineage to use that man's sister or daughter. In return, he gives that person rights in a woman he will control in the future, such as a daughter from the marriage, or he may take the woman as repayment for rights he gave in the past. The important thing to be aware of in such a marriage system is that men who are patrilineally grouped, and who have special credit relations with each other, make deals allowing any one of them to transfer rights in a woman of his patrilineage to a man of another patrilineage for rights in one of their women. Woman-exchange marriage is comparatively rare. There is no explanation for this. In the absence of cattle, camels, slaves, or other high valued movable goods, one would think woman exchange would be a common solution to the problem of gaining rights in a wife. But this is not the case in Africa. In both bridewealth and woman-exchange situations, the payment should not usually be thought of as a purchase price, but rather as a loan of capital or labor in return for use of the woman, thus balancing an equation. If either party loses control of the wealth he receives in the exchange, the other must replace it or give up his part of the exchange. If a man's wife dies before she is old and worn out, the bridewealth must usually be returned or a woman sent to replace her (called the *sororate,* also a misnomer since the replacement may not actually be a sister of the deceased but simply a woman of the deceased's lineage). In the case of the Turu, and among many other Africans, the bridewealth cattle are returned at the death of a wife, but the death conference described earlier (mupanda) will decide how many will be deducted by her kinsmen for depreciation.

In other words, then, when bridewealth (including woman exchange) is given for a woman, the two parties are exchanging valuable and productive capital which each values and can use to make more wealth. A man desires to get rid of his sister because he cannot marry her. According to the laws of exogamy it is usually prescribed that he must marry outside his clan or lineage. She is of great value to a man of a different lineage or clan who can marry her without violating this law. On the other hand, the wealth which the controller of a bride gets is always of value to him since it is usually in the form of a repository of value which gives him leverage in the market system to invest in eligible women for himself or to do other things. One reason cattle are so valued for bridewealth is that they produce calves and because of this, and because of the other products they provide—milk, manure—their economic function parallels closely that of women (as well as slaves) who are valued for children as well as for the food they produce.

Bloodwealth

This should be constrasted with bridewealth. The payment of blood money was very widespread and probably nearly universal in Africa, but far less is known about it than bridewealth, to which it bears a resemblance (I.M.Lewis' [1961] writings on Somalis are notable exceptions.) Bloodwealth is payment to a person or his kin for inflicting injury or death on a person. Typically it was comparatively high (for example, as many as a hundred cattle among the Turkana). Lesser amounts were paid for injury. Unlike bridewealth, the money paid was completely lost to the payers, just as the dead person was completely lost to his people, or his person was permanently diminished by the assault. Because this payment was not loaned, the amount paid tended to vary with relationship; payment for injury to a close relation was less than that for a distant relation or tribesman. (No payment would be made for killing a member of a different tribe.) The reason for this seems to be that the economic affairs of kinsmen are increasingly intermingled the closer they are related, and charging a close kinsman a high fine would have economic ramifications that would feed back on the receivers of the bloodwealth. Because of this, among the Turu, no bloodwealth would be charged a man for killing his full brother. The tenuous position of slaves can be fully appreciated when we understand that as "persons without clans," they had no one to make claims for them if they were injured or killed. They were socially dead in that respect.

While there are few instances where rights in women are sold outright, the Sonjo of north central Tanzania seem to be a case to the contrary. Robert Gray (1963) reports that when a Sonjo man pays about a hundred goats for a wife, she is his absolutely, so much so that if he wants to get rid of her, no divorce is possible. He must simply find another man to buy her.

If no bridewealth arrangement can be made, it is possible to resort to brideservice. As we saw in the last chapter, labor is a valuable commodity, and it is therefore possible for a man to acquire some rights in his wife through a labor-exchange arrangement. When Richards studied the Bemba of northeast Zambia in the 1930s (Richards 1939), she found that in return for giving five years brideservice, a man acquired the right to take his wife from her brother's home to his own. However, he did not obtain the right to ally his sons and daughters to his own lineage. Instead, they returned after puberty to live with their mother's brother, a type of arrangement called avunculocal residence, common in African matrilineal societies.

Wherever brideservice is not possible, a man may, for a few nominal gifts, obtain exclusive sexual rights to a woman, thereby becoming her husband. However, she does not leave her home. This practice of matrilocal residence is followed by the Hadza hunters of Tanzania (Woodburn 1970) and the Yao and Chewa of eastern Zambia and Mozambique, to name only three. How few rights a Chewa man has in his wife in such societies is illustrated by Richards who says (1950, 233–234) that:

> ...unsuitable husbands are dismissed with compensation and sent away...the husbands of the women of a village are often away visiting and are definitely not reckoned as members of the community. Stannus states that a widower is usually given a present with the suggestion that he go elsewhere since he no longer has any standing in his wife's village. Marwick (1965) indicates that Chewa marriage ties sit loose and speaks of a man and his sister and "her current husband." ...The Chewa talk of the father as a stranger. "He is a beggar; he has simply followed his wife." At divorce he leaves his wife's village with

A bridegroom performing brideservice by harvesting bulrush millet for his mother-in-law

his hoe, his axe and his sleeping-mat and has no right to any of the children of the marriage, even if he may have begotten as many as seven children.

Because of the insecure position of the father (unless he is a headman or a man of power), some Central African people have worked out ingenious compromises. Among the Kuba of southern Zaire (Vansina 1954), intermarrying lineages live in villages consisting of two lines of houses divided by a street. While it is therefore true to say of Kuba that a man must go to his wife's locale to be with her, in this case that means simply crossing the street!

Unlike this latter instance, where there is no bridewealth or brideservice of importance, the balancing of the equation of exchanged wealth is central to marriage in most African societies. This involves certain other elements that I want to mention before leaving the subject. In many African societies one finds the customs of sororate and levirate. Where in the sororate another woman is procured to maintain the equation of marriage if a wife dies, the levirate is the procuring for the women of a substitute husband if her husband dies. In the Turu case, for example, if the husband dies, or goes away and does not return, she will be taken in (at her choosing) by her husband's heir, usually his brother. This man now continues to work with her in the management of her house and fathers her subsequent children, but legally the establishment and the children continue to belong to the dead or missing man. Needless to say, whether sororate or levirate is ever invoked depends on the worth of the marriage. A woman who has little wealth and no children is far more likely to return to her parents at the death of her husband than a woman who has wealth and children, all of which she would lose by a divorce.

Social Transformations.   Much of what I have been saying can be summarized by reference to Figure 4.1 on a comparative study of bridewealth (Schneider 1964b). We note that as the amount of bridewealth increases (woman exchange is considered to be a high bridewealth), divorce is common until payments become very high, signifying, perhaps, that very high payments convey nearly absolute rights. On the other hand, residence at marriage is matrilocal and avunculocal only at very low levels of payment and shifts quickly to patrilocal (or virilocal) when significant payments begin, indicating that removal of wife to husband's home is comparatively cheap. When the husband dies or disappears, the likelihood that a wife will return home seems to continue to about the middle of the scale after which there is much greater likelihood of the levirate's being involved, suggesting that leviritic marriage is not worthwhile until payments become significant. When divorce occurs, there is no return of the gifts at the lower level because, no doubt, of the fact that

FIGURE 4.1   Social transformations relative to the amount of bridewealth

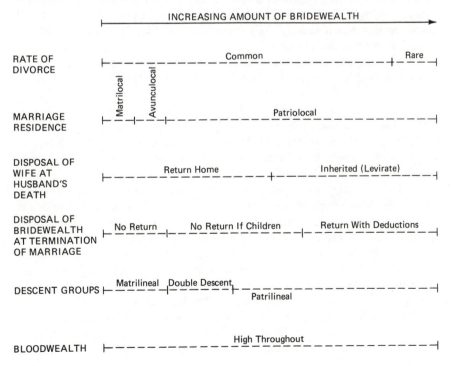

the wealth is token. When the amount paid becomes significant, either there is no return of the bridewealth if the heirs of the dead man keep the children, or the bridewealth is returned with deductions against what the woman has produced for her husband. Finally, matrilineality occurs only at the lower end of the scale; systems shift very rapidly to patrilineal at the first sign of significant bridewealth. Double-descent systems occur as alternatives (for unknown reasons) at the lower ends of the patrilineal scale.

One other fact about this diagram is important. It will be noticed that bloodwealth paid for killing another person is high over the whole scale. Less may be paid for killing a woman than for killing a man, but in both cases the amount is high, reckoned in terms of amounts paid for bridewealth. A society in which bridewealth payments are small will still charge a high fine for murder, as much as would be charged in a society paying significant numbers of cattle. This fact is important as supporting evidence for the idea that in all these societies, a woman (or a man) is considered to be very valuable. The range in amounts of bridewealth paid is due to the varying ability to get together enough wealth to obtain rights. If a man wished to take full charge of his wife, he would have to pay a good deal for her just as he would if he killed her, even where wealth is scarce. The question naturally arises how such bloodwealth payments can be assembled in the poor societies. Payment for killing a person may consist of a slave or another human being, ordinarily a woman, all rights to the woman being abrogated by the giver. Among pastoral societies, this is unnecessary, for cattle act as payment in all cases of blood-wealth as well as bridewealth.

These results, with some other additions, can be stated somewhat differently based on another study of bridewealth (Schneider 1969). The average amount of livestock given over as bridewealth correlates highly with the ratio of livestock to people in a society. What this seems to mean is that people will always pay as much as they can for a bride in order, presumably, to get as many rights as possible. Secondly, matrilineality correlates very highly with lack of payment of any significant bridewealth. Thirdly, there is a tendency for property to be inherited laterally in matrilineal systems and lineally in patrilineal ones. The meaning of this seems to be that matrilineal systems have wealth principally in the form of nonmobile goods, especially land, while patrilineal societies have movable wealth as well as land. This is why they are patrilineal. Since land is the principal asset of matrilineal systems, it is more likely to be controlled by a group in the sense that when a person dies or leaves the piece of land, it reverts to the group and the elders who manage it. This process continues until all the older generation are dead after which it passes to the new generation of corporate managers. The land passes as a unit from the mother's brothers who have managed it to the new generation of sister's sons.

Continuing the summary of this study, the incidence of rules of residence other than patrilocal or virilocal is very insignificant, more so than the rule of matrilineal descent, since many matrilineal people nevertheless follow the practice of patrilocal residence.

Variability of Descent

At one time it was felt that the type of descent system found in a particular society was inherent in it, a cultural trait passed on from generation to generation, changing only gradually over a long time and in response to certain progressive forces in history. Today evidence increasingly supports the conclusion that it is merely a response to this basic problem of exchanging rights in women. Consequently, the type of descent found in a particular society can change as economic fortunes change. This is substantiated by looking back at Map 4.1 on the distribution of types of descent in Africa. In the far northeast section of Central Africa, the coastal region of Tanzania, the so-called Eastern Tanzania Matrilineal people, such as the Kaguru and Luguru, are today not really matrilineal anymore (Beidelman 1967). Strong patrilineal tendencies have asserted themselves, apparently in response to an increase in wealth as a result of the colonial encounter. Similarly, the Nyamwezi (Abrahams 1967) and the Kimbu (Shorter 1972) of western Tanzania, the Sukuma (Malcolm 1953) south of Lake Victoria, as well as the Rangi of central Tanzania and the Bemba of northeast Zambia have been undergoing a patrilineal transformation with the rise of wealth as a result of encounters beginning with Arab traders in the eighteenth century. Along the southeast border of the Central African belt are people like the Tonga (Colson 1962) and the Ila (Fielder 1973) whose fortunes have changed over the last hundred years, as cattle husbandry became increasingly possible and who display mixed patrilineal and matrilineal features. Paradoxically, matrilineality seems to be asserting itself in parts of the cattle-rich Tswana society of southern Africa where a recent study shows a 100 percent increase in the number of unmarried women of marriageable age since 1934 (Schapera and Roberts 1975). The reason may be that with the rise of plow agriculture and other forms of investment, men no longer consider women to be a good investment.

This is not to say that Africans do not treat a particular descent pattern as a custom or law. It is common in East Africa, for example, for patrilineal people to act as if patrilineal descent is a rule and to exclude persons from land on the grounds that they did not come by it through their fathers. It is simply that such laws cannot for long resist the economic facts, and all these systems are susceptible to change.

Sometimes, perhaps in most cases, marriage is not even consistent within a single society. In patrilineal systems it may be common for a man whose prospects among his patrilineage are poor to ask his wife's brother to allow him to live with him and to receive a piece of land to farm. In such cases the localized patrilineage is augmented by the occasional, hang-on brother-in-law, which constitutes a kind of matrilocality, even combined with matrilineality if the mother's brother allows the husband's children to have land. Alternatively, in some societies, like the Nyamwezi, descent in the chiefly line may be matrilineal whereas it is patrilineal among commoners, signifying, no doubt, that bridewealth for a princess is too high for anyone to pay or that, as in the Nupe case, the chief does not choose to release his sister.

Although the predominant marriage pattern in a society may be designated as patrilineal-patrilocal or matrilineal-avunculocal, individual circumstances may give rise to deviation. At base this depends on the nature of the economy and the ability of people, in general or as individuals, to put together the capital necessary to arrange a marriage. A consistent or variable pattern is also, to some degree, a measure of the state of the economy. Probably the most complex system of variation yet described in Africa is the one found among the Fon or Dahomean people of West Africa studied by M.J. Herskovits (1938).

The Fon considered themselves to be patrilineal yet this did not stop them from resorting to alternative practices where profitable. In the most usual type of marriage, the husband gained control of his wife and her children, removing them to a patrilocal residence, through a complex series of payments, including (in the 1930s) (1) an initial, nominal payment of a sack of millet, five and a half francs, some tobacco, matches, and so on; (2) brideservice in which firewood was provided for the future mother-in-law, field work for the future father-in-law, and the like; (3) death articles consisting mainly of cloth and some money, if a member of his future affinal (in-law) family died during the period of negotiations; and (4) the main bridewealth which generally consisted of 720 cowry shells, a large man's cloth, one women's cloth, a sack of salt and a ten-year-old castrated goat. (Note that all of these items are money in some African societies.)

A number of variations could be played upon this basic form. For example, since the Fon had a centralized kingdom with a despotic king, the king could order a common man to marry a princess, thereby taking away from both the father of the bride and the groom any choice in the matter. However, for both, such a marriage would be profitable; the father would be pleasing the king, and the groom would be establishing connections with the king. (This benefit was often bestowed on men the king wanted to favor.) The resulting marriage constituted a kind of matrilineality.

Another variant was for a man to sponsor his poor friend's wedding and to pay all the costs over the life of the marriage until the time came when the man's wife had a daughter who would be given in payment to the sponsor. (This sounds like a good investment for some.) Furthermore, there is the case of the man and woman who became lovers, officially unmarried, who could make the relationship permanent after the birth of a daughter by giving rights in the daughter to the father-in-law. This tactic was probably resorted to by an infatuated man too poor to pay the bridewealth. Women-exchange marriage also occurred and in this context appears to be a variant of the preceding cases in which a daughter is used to pay for the marriage. It is noteworthy that in Dahomey, as in Africa in general, it seems that woman exchange is practiced only among the poorer people.

Then there are instances, usually among the wealthy, in which a woman contracts a regular marriage with a woman (she being married herself), who is called "husband" by her wife, and who provides her wife with a lover to beget children; the lover, however, has no rights in the children. Similarly, there is matrilineal-matrilocal marriage in which a father-in-law, in return for allowing his son-in-law to keep some of the children (on a ratio of three to one or two in favor of father-in-law), makes a deal with the son-in-law to father children with his daughter. The children he keeps then become members of the father's lineage and thereby help to augment it. (Take note that to children in this position, the descent system looks ambilineal.) In this type of marriage the son-in-law is specifically forbidden to pay the bridewealth. Women who have married women may also use this technique for augmenting their own lineages.

Herskovits is explicit that in all these marriages very careful cost accounting is the rule. For instance, if a woman to whom a man is betrothed runs off with another, her husband may pay back to the original suitor all his costs, of which the suitor will have kept a clear record. These include not only goods given to the wife's family, but time spent in brideservice.

In summary, it is interesting to see that in Fon society the types of ways that marriage can be arranged seem to include, to one degree or another, every form found in Africa as a whole from patrilineal through mixed to matrilineal.

Descent and Economic Regions

It is possible to characterize our various production regions (Map 3.4) with respect to their prevailing forms of descent. The West Sudan is characteristically patrilineal. This seems to be due to the fact that cattle can be raised there and that even a small number will insure transfer of rights in children. However there are certain exceptions. The western coastal region has produced a group of matrilineal societies, as has the area just north of the rain forest portions of Ghana and the Cameroon Mountains, to the east of Nigeria. These, it can confidently be predicted, have little or no livestock for one reason or another or any other forms of mobile wealth to substitute for them. They can be contrasted with the West Africa zone. While the western part has a massive matrilineal enclave (with some double descent), the eastern part is solidly patrilineal, bridewealth being paid in brass rods, cowries, and other monies. For some reason, this eastern matrilineal area is not able to generate mobile wealth in the manner of the west. The rice region is also patrilineal, with a few exceptions. The livestock-raising areas outside the Western Sudan, including East and Southeast Africa are solidly patrilineal too. However, the Zaire Basin manages patrilineality without significant livestock. Central Africa, of course, has no livestock or other movable material in significant amounts and is matrilineal. Southwest Africa and the southeast fringe of the matrilineal belt have sufficient cattle to shift to double descent. Why they have not become strictly patrilineal is not clear.

All this again demonstrates a basic economic principle noted at the end of the last chapter, that the wealth of an area is not directly correlated with the kind of basic "staple" products it produces. This point can be best illustrated from Central Africa. We have already seen that in that area, five basic types of food are produced. What seems to make this area matrilineal, despite this variability, is the lack of cattle or other exchangeable repositories of value in significant amounts. In addition the high cost of crop production, due to poor soil, raises the price of labor. In modern terms we could call this matrilineal belt a depressed, economically deprived area, not necessarily because the people do not have enough to eat, but because their poverty of resources stifles economic growth. Unfortunately, while this thesis can be asserted with great confidence based on what data are available, it must be admitted that in all these areas the kind of information that has been gathered in the past does not allow us to determine just what the variations in movable wealth consist of. The fundamental problem is lack of data on quantities of goods produced as well as other quantitative measures. It is as if we knew that America and England both have silver and gold as movable repositories of wealth without knowing how much each has and how much each produces. A basic fact about industrial economies in the modern world is the balance of payments, which relates to the varying quantities of gold they control. This in turn affects intensities of exchanges and therefore has an impact on the social structure, including for example, political structure. Similarly, varying amounts of the products affect descent systems in Africa.

To summarize, in Africa, societies have matrilineages, groups composed of women with their children who are under the control of the women's brothers, or patrilineages, groups composed of women and their children who are under the control of their husbands, or double-descent and mixed systems. These societies may also vary in the degree to which a woman is controlled by her brother and her husband, independently of the existence of matrilineages and patrilineages. Such control depends on the extent of the bridewealth a man can compose to give a woman's brother.

The Status of Women

The status of women in African societies is a complex subject about which only a few words can be said here, mainly because it has not been systematically studied. For the most part, it may truly be said that women are simply chattels controlled by men. They ordinarily have no legal status and are equal to children in this respect. A man treated like an African woman would probably be classified by a Western observer as a slave or serf, the former in a state of servitude lacking any rights, and the latter in a position more moderate but still subordinate. African wives may or may not be betrothed to a man voluntarily, and their rights may vary. Where the demand for wives is very great, women may be promised to men, engaged so to speak, when they are still infants, or are prepubescent ten-year-olds as among the Turu. Often it is said that they need to be beaten to keep them in line. Affection has little public place in the marriage arrangement because it interferes with the man's need to keep his wife's nose to the grindstone. Old men say of young men that they should not be given too much leeway in deciding whom they will marry because they are foolish and let their feelings interfere with businesslike estimates of the value of a potential wife.

Yet despite this legal subservience, women's positions are not totally inferior. They have various ways of asserting de facto power. Besides the fact that a woman does have family to look out for her interests, probably the greatest power she has is the leverage she acquires against her husband based on the fact that whatever wealth her house produces eventually must go only to her sons, not to the sons of her husband's other wives. This makes her sons, if she is lucky enough to have any, her grateful benefactors and allies against her husband. In patrilineal societies, a married woman is given her own fields, house, and livestock, if there are any. As a matter of fact, in many cases, like the Turu, the total livestock a man possesses must become part of the house of his first wife. This can create serious problems for him if he wants to get married again since he must either cheat the house and secretly hold cattle at a friend's house, or he must persuade his first wife somehow to cooperate with him in a second marriage. She may do so because she expects to use the second wife as her servant or, as in one case I know of, to help him produce sons if she has none so that the wealth she produces will at least stay in her household and not pass to a parallel line.

In matrilineal societies the wealth still passes to a woman's sons, but the sons are controlled by her brother, not her husband. This underscores the fact that whatever the legal situation with regard to women's status, they have de facto rights in what they produce.

In those parts of traditional Africa where economies were more complex and affluent with regard to manufactures and crops, and in modern situations

An old senior wife by her house in the Singida District

where opportunities to make money outside the home present themselves, women are sometimes able to assert even more power. In the last chapter we saw how active Yoruba women were in the marketplace. Women seem to be involved in all the market systems. A recent study of the Kpelle of Liberia concludes (Bledsoe 1976, 386):

> In traditional Kpelle society labor, and political loyalty constitute the bases of power and status. Women are placed under the legal control of men, who need rights in female productive and reproductive capacities to increase their own status and power *vis-a-vis* other men. In modern areas, however, cash gives women more freedom from moral and legal ties. Here, women with access to cash through marketing or lovers can pay for goods and services without having to rely on a husband. Consequently, in modern areas such as Haindii and Dobli Island, marriage rates fall and divorce rates rise, especially among young and middle-aged women, those ordinarily most dependent on marital ties for economic security.

Women often were organized secretly to cooperate in protecting each other's interests against the men, and men often thought of women as witches because they understood that they worked against the interests of the men. Probably the most exotic example of assertions of power by women, other than the role of Queen Mother which was so prominent in African kingdoms, was the fact, seen among the Fon, that occasionally women of wealth managed to engage in marriage themselves. What they were doing, of course, is not engaging in lesbianism, since the emotional dimension of Western marriage was lacking, but, like men, creating production units by using wealth to obtain the labor service of other women.

We may summarize women's status by comparing them with slaves. When we say that they have no legal rights to property, we are saying that they, unlike adult males, can be and are controlled (owned?) by others (usually men, but sometimes other women). Unlike slaves, they "have a clan," and so their husbands have to borrow them in exchange for capital and cannot mistreat them with impunity. Like slaves, the husband technically has complete rights to command his wife; however, he cannot expect her to work efficiently unless she is willing. So he must treat her with consideration. This, paradoxically, allows her, over time and in varying degrees, to assert independence just as do slaves.

Structure of Homestead

While African homesteads varied greatly in general form and in the quality of construction, wherever women were set up as semi-independent economic units, as they were in most of Africa outside the strongly Moslem areas, the homesteads had analogous form. The Yako (Forde 1964) are a good example of a rather complex kind of house construction (Figure 4.2a) and form. As this and Figure 4.2b indicate, each compound is notable for the distinctiveness of the individual houses of the wives. Each wife has her own fields, separate from the man, and each jealously guards rights to her yams (the main crop). She gives some to the husband only in return for appropriate compensation. This pattern of extreme separation of the husband's and the wife's produce is symptomatic of the fact that the Yako have a double-descent system, in which matrilineal and patrilineal principles are still in strong contention.

If we move to East Africa, among a transhumant (that is, seminomadic) people, the Jie (Gulliver 1955), we see (Figure 4.3) a more extreme patrilineal structure in that the men have no houses. They sleep with different wives at different times, and the individual yards, houses, and granaries belong to individual wives. Being pastoralists, the Jie have to have a corral in which to keep the animals, which, though communally herded, belong to the individual houses. Jie houses are of far more impermanent construction, beehives in fact, because the people must make frequent moves. In some East African areas, where a more settled life is possible despite the possession of large numbers of cattle, more permanent structures, circular huts with grass roofs and mud and wattle walls, or rectangular huts with mud roofs and mud and wattle walls, are possible.

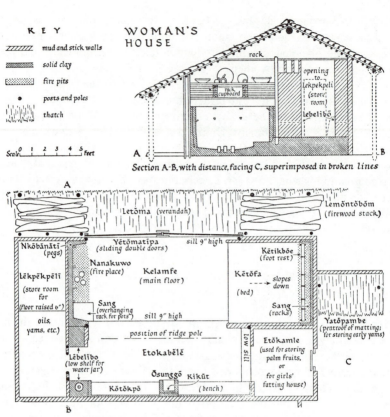

FIGURE 4.2a Yako house arrangement

FIGURE 4.2b Yako compound arrangement
(both from Forde, 1964)

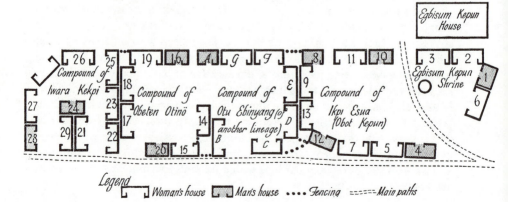

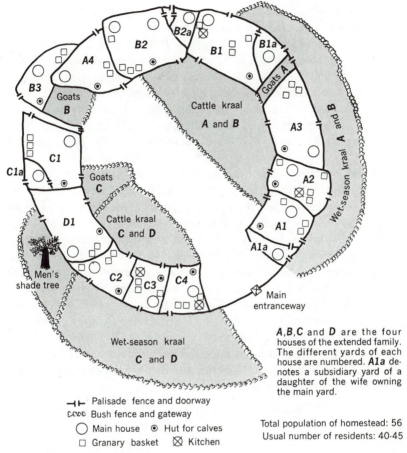

FIGURE 4.3 A Jie homestead
from Peoples of Africa *edited by James L. Gibbs, Jr. Copyright © 1965 by Holt, Rinehart and Winston, Inc. Reprinted by permission of Holt, Rinehart and Winston)*

Labels within figure:

B2a
B2
B1
B1a
A4
Goats A
B3
Goats B
Cattle kraal A and B
A3
C1
C1a
Goats C
A2
Wet-season kraal A and B
D1
Cattle kraal C and D
A1
A1a
Men's shade tree
C2
C3
C4
Main entranceway
Wet-season kraal C and D

A,B,C and D are the four houses of the extended family. The different yards of each house are numbered. A1a denotes a subsidiary yard of a daughter of the wife owning the main yard.

—ᛁ⊢ Palisade fence and doorway
ᘓᘓᘓ Bush fence and gateway
◯ Main house   ◉ Hut for calves
▢ Granary basket   ⊗ Kitchen

Total population of homestead: 56
Usual number of residents: 40-45

Affines

Before leaving marriage and turning to the subject of lineage, a word must be said about a common pattern in the relations of men and their affines (in-laws). When a man sets out to marry, the kind of relationship he will have with the family of his wife will depend importantly on the nature of the economy. Among the Turkana of Kenya, for example, a husband is friendly with his affines. Patrilineal relations are not so important for the Turkana and other very nomadic people (although they are for the Somalis [I. M. Lewis 1961]). Because the maximization of return from cattle raising depends on the extreme mobility of individual families, they must, therefore, depend on arranging ad hoc relations with others as necessary. A most important way to do this is with affines so Turkana affines are, of necessity, friendly and cooperative.

The more usual pattern in Africa, where lineage continues to be important, is quite different. There is hostility between the parties, mitigated by varying circumstances. For example, most Africans have respect for seniority and will avoid insulting or antagonizing older people. The most extreme distance is between a man and his mother-in-law. This is due to the fact that the marriage contract is primarily with the house of the wife's mother. She sees her son-in-law as an economic competitor from whom she must try to extract as much as possible in return for her daughter. As a result, we find hostility combined with difference in generation manifesting itself as mother-in-law avoidance. This custom has varying magnitudes. In some places in Zaire, when a man approaches a village, he first inquires whether his mother-in-law is present, and if she is, he skirts the village. In other instances, this practice shows up merely as avoidance of sitting in the same room with her, even when they are conversing, which they do by shouting through the wall or door.

With affines of his own generation, brother and sister-in-law, hostility shows up as "joking," as it is usually called. Brothers-in-law insult each other in ways men otherwise never would, and brother and sister-in-law often utter obscene remarks to each other.

As a marriage progresses and the years reduce uncertainty over the equality of the exchange equation, this hostility may decline so that in time affines become more friendly.

LINEAGE

It has been said that lineage is more important among African people than among any other people on earth. Some have even tried to argue that it is very important to all Africans. No doubt the first generalization is true; the latter is not. To some Africans, as we shall see, lineage is of minor importance but to most, it has great importance and to nearly all it has some importance. Thus, we will now fill in the details of our earlier discussion of this subject.

A lineage, as I said earlier, is a group of people who use as the criterion for determining who belongs to the group the rule of unilineal descent. The rejected line is usually, but not always, excluded from consideration in some way. For example, Africans customarily utilize a binary system for classifying things in the universe, to which is assigned an evaluative tone. If the society is patrilineal, father's kin may be thought of as being on the right hand and mother's kin on the left hand, at the same time that the right hand is associated with friends and the left with enemies.

Put another way, unlike a bilateral rule, adoption of a rule of unilineal descent, whether patrilineal or matrilineal, leads to the creation of *discrete* groupings of people. Suppose that in America we were to define our kin as anyone up to second cousin. My second cousin would be my father's father's brother's son's son. However, my father's second cousin would be my third cousin once removed (father's father's father's brother's son's son). Hence, my father's kin group would not be the same as mine even though my father and I were kin. This cannot happen with unilineal-descent groups. A lineage is formed by choosing some ancestor to designate as founder, a so-called apical ancestor. Any living person descended from that ancestor reckoned through the father is related to all the same persons as any other descendant through a father, as is illustrated in Figure 4.4. The rule of unilineal descent with a designated apical ancestor can therefore be seen as a device used by Africans (and other people) to constitute the basic discrete cooperative groups in society.

At the very start of this subject, it is important to recognize that while genealogies are necessary for deciding who your kinsmen are and who they are not, genealogies can be and are manipulated, so that people may be included in a lineage who are not in fact biological relatives, simply because they are desirable. This is precisely like our own custom of making into a kinsman a person described as a stepmother or a stepchild. It is true that the word *step* qualifies the term, but can it be doubted that in all legal ways and perhaps also in emotional ways the persons become kinsmen? As a matter of fact, is it not true that it is a wise person who knows his own father?

Lineages, when they are most important, are usually localized. That is

FIGURE 4.4   Discrete patrilineage

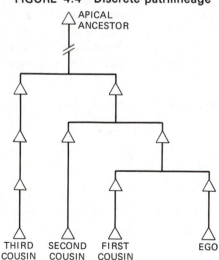

to say, persons who belong to the same patrilineage or matrilineage live together. Their group may be diluted with affinal relatives or even strangers, but unilineal kinsmen dominate the community.

Lineage Nesting

Lineages usually exist in a nesting pattern, such that smaller lineages occur within larger lineages. Middleton (1965) illustrates this for the Lugbara of west central Uganda in Figure 4.5. Important things about the social structures of people are not always obvious. It therefore seems strange now to remember that until E. E. Evans-Pritchard first detected this nesting, or *segmentary lineage,* structure among the Nuer of the Sudan (Evans-Pritchard 1940) it was not recognized. Evans-Pritchard illustrated the nesting, or branching, lineage structure as a tree, in Figure 4-6. Figure 4-7 says the same thing in more formal terms, resembling the Lugbara scheme. Jinaca are a clan composed of Rumjok, Gaaliek, and Gaatbal lineages; the Gaatbal lineage is made up of Nyarkwac and Leng lineages, and so on, down to the lowest level composed of such lineages as Diel and Kwoth.

Figure 4.8 of Turu lineages says essentially the same thing as the foregoing diagrams but represents the nesting lineages spatially. Level I consists of a group of adult brothers living together. Level II consists of a group of Level I lineages, all purportedly descended from a common ancestor. This unit is encompassed by a broken line in the diagram of Figure 4-8 to indicate that it is also the village of a spatially isolated complex of homesteads. Contained in this village is one Level II lineage. The depth of a Level II lineage—that is, the number of generations between the present adult group and the founding ancestor—is about five. Level III consists of a number of Level II village lineages. In fact, there may be more than the two indicated in this diagram for the sake of simplicity. The actual number varies, with some containing as many

FIGURE 4.5 Lugbara nesting lineages

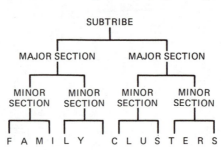

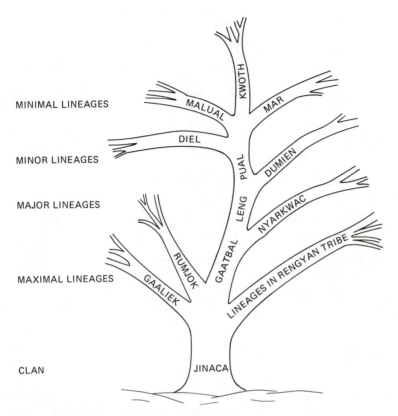

MINIMAL LINEAGES

MINOR LINEAGES

MAJOR LINEAGES

MAXIMAL LINEAGES

CLAN

KWOTH

MALUAL

MAR

DIEL

PUAL

DUMIEN

LENG

NYARKWAC

GAATBAL

RUMJOK

LINEAGES IN RENGYAN TRIBE

GAALIEK

JINACA

FIGURE 4.6 Nuer nesting lineages—tree diagram
(from Evans-Pritchard, 1940)

as thirteen. While the Level III segments balance off structurally, so that there seem to be four in each Level IV, they do not necessarily balance in actual numbers of people or villages. The depth of this Level III lineage is about ten generations. Level IV is coincident with the clan of the People of Kahiu, the second largest clan in the Wahi subtribe. It is composed of four Level III lineages, located in the areas of Wijue, Nyakulu, Ghumpi, and Weeya. All the people of these lineages are said to be descendants of Senge, who is reputed to have been directly descended from the founder of the clan, Mukahiu. In comparison, the largest clan in Wahi subtribe is that of the People of Nyahati, which has two Level IV lineages, making the clan coincident with a fifth level of lineage, one higher than Kahiu. The eastern section at Damankia is one Level IV and the western section at Mpumbui is another. All these people claim descent from the founder of the clan, Munyahati.

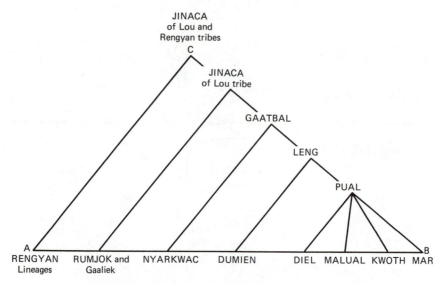

FIGURE 4.7 Nuer nesting lineages—formal model
(from Evans - Pritchard, 1940)

Lineage Functions

Corresponding to the different levels of lineage in these segmentary lineage societies are varying functions. For example, the major section of the Lugbara is the largest group within which disagreements are settled by negotiation and agreement. Its members are regarded as too closely related by kinship to use force against each other. But between major sections within the clan, force may be exercised. In the Turu system the Level III lineages, generally equivalent to Middleton's major sections, also feud while disputes within the third Level are settled in indigenous courts, called *mwandu*, named from the baobab tree under which the disputants sat in the shade to hold their discussions. More will be said about feuding shortly.

FIGURE 4.8 Model of Turu lineages

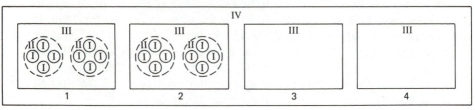

In the Turu system, again, the lowest Level, I, the group of brothers of the same father, is the group of most intensive sharing. While men in this group do not give cattle to each other without thought of repayment, credit is extended on an open-ended basis. Between men of the same village, Level II, cattle are given with clear understanding of when they have to be returned. Among members of Level III, there is little lending of cattle.

Clan

Lineage must be distinguished from clan. A *clan* is best thought of as a kind of subtribe or subethnic unit, whose members feel some special relationship, often having a label and totems, as in this list of common clan names among the Plateau Tonga (Colson 1962): Bahyamba—hyena, rhinoceros, pig; Batenda—elephant; Baleya—goat, tortoise, vulture; Bansaka—leopard, bee. By contrast, Turu clan names—Kahiu, Nyahati and so forth—are thought of as the names of founders of the clans, whatever the literal meaning of the names might be, and there are no totems attached to them.

Clans can be very irregular in size, and societies vary greatly in the number of clans they have. Lugbara have sixty or so, the Turu, perhaps fifty altogether, while the Pokot and the neighboring Sebei (Goldschmidt 1976), as well as many others, have a very large number of very small clans, so many that no one has been able to count them. What makes the clan distinctive is that it is ordinarily the unit used to reckon exogamy. *Clan exogamy,* which is extremely common, means that a man may marry no woman within his clan, no matter how large it is. However, clan or lineage endogamy, marrying within the clan or lineage, occurs on occasion. The aristocrats in Tswana society sometimes do this (Schapera 1953), by marrying father's brother's daughter, as do the Bagarra or Cattle Arabs of the Sudan (Cunnison 1966), or some of the strongly Moslem people of the Western Sudan. Clan endogamy, in other words, is particularly characteristic of Moslem people, but it does occur occasionally in non-Moslem, or non-Arab, African societies. The reason for this will be examined when we come to discussion of kinship classification.

Clan and lineage seem to be different principles of organization, sometimes in competition. There are societies in which the clan principle is almost overrun by lineage. In those circumstances, clans become merely large lineages, incorporated into a genealogical system that encompasses the whole society. On the other hand, sometimes clans exist with hardly any trace of lineage structure within them. The members of the clan know they are related but they do not know how. It is as if lineage were an important and regular way to structure relations among people while clan is an arbitrarily arrived at collection of kinsmen. Analogously, a democracy is a kind of political structure within a society whose size is arbitrarily determined; no two democracies are the same size, but they all have the same internal structure. Lineages are more regular in size because they serve important economic functions related closely to the particular types of production going on in the society. Hence, when a lineage gets too small to carry out these functions, it tends to aggregate to itself other small lineages, thereby reconstituting itself. When it gets too large, it segments, breaking into smaller, more efficient units. Clans do not so apparently aggregate or segment; rather they grow and decline irregularly like small tribes or ethnic groups. They may, in fact, be treated as a structure medial between the ethnic group or tribe and the lineage, having some features of both.

Genealogy

Where the principle of lineage is operating, it is extremely important for individuals to know just how they are related to others because the kind and degree of relationship is related to rights. For example, if a man can show that he is related to another in a patrilineage in such a way as to make him a member of that man's minor section, he can make demands on that man which are of more value than if they are of the same major section but of different minor sections. Alternatively, if a stranger coming into a village can prove he is the grandson of a man whose brother's offspring have died out, he can claim the land of that deceased line.

Hence people in such societies have an extensive knowledge of geneology. However, the knowledge is specific to the function it serves. It might be important to know the specific names and relationships of men in an individual's direct patriline going back ten generations and the names of all the brothers of such men. (Incidentally, it is conventional to call the person in terms of whom kinship relations are calculated Ego. I shall follow this convention henceforth when convenient.) On the other hand, knowledge of the specific descendants of all the brothers of any men outside Ego's direct line, at least beyond, for example, the great-grandfather or grandfather might be unnecessary. As a matter of fact, because the importance of relationship declines with distance, it is common for the genealogies to become more and more mythical, the farther back they go. Ask a Turu who was the original founding ancestor of the Turu people, and he will say "Munyaturu," that is, "The Turu," much as a Westerner might say "Adam." However if you ask him who his grandfather was, he will give a specific name, for example Nkuwe, son of Lisu, and so on.

Genealogies are not necessarily remembered with accuracy. The important thing is that in negotiations involving genealogy, the parties agree on the genealogy, even if they make it up, as they sometimes do. In the Turu case again, lines sometimes pass through women, which makes them illegitimate. Thus a female ancestor is transformed into a male. As long as other segments of the society agree to this, there can be no dispute. However it gives rise to the amusing fact that often persons outside the lineage in which such an agreement has been made will describe a segment as descended from a woman (that is, illegitimate) while within the lineage, the people will deny it.

Lineage Stability

Although lineages are continually reforming, their members speak of them as if they are static and unchanging. This, no doubt, is due to the fact that important rights are defined in terms of lineage, for example, rights to land. If it were admitted that lineages are liable to split, rights to property might be threatened. Commonly it is believed that pioneered land belongs in perpetuity to the person who opened it up and his unilineal descendants, despite the fact that none of the founder's lineage members still live on it. Among the Turu, when rain-making ceremonies are held, a descendant of the head of the lineage who pioneered the land threatened with drought will be invited to officiate in the ceremony. So land does not necessarily stay in perpetuity in a certain family or lineage. It may be abandoned to others, or sold, or given to strangers to settle a debt. There are many ways for effective, legally defensible control to be transferred. However, at any given moment, where right to land is based upon descent, claim to the land is supported by reference to genealogy based upon an apical ancestor. If a lineage splits, this amounts to creation of a new set of apical ancestors to define the new lineages, and the matter of land ownership is liable therefore to come into question.

Aggregation of Collateral Lines

Members of the same lower level lineages often use terms to classify each other which in effect project the relations of the immediate family on to the whole group. As we saw, Ego not only refers to the other sons and daughters of his mother as sibling (*muuna*) in Kinyaturu, but all other persons in his lineage who are of the same generation as he, determined by reckoning from the founding ancestor of the lineage, are siblings. Similarly, all persons of the same generation as his father and mother are called father and mother, and so on for grandfathers and grandmothers, children and grandchildren. How far this will continue laterally varies. Using the Lugbara as our example again, perhaps only members of the same family cluster will speak of each other as father, siblings, and so on. On the other hand, the practice might extend out to members of the same minor section. However, at some point within the clan, the practice will stop, and other members of the same clan will simply be called clansmen or "relatives" (*ndughu*), as the Turu say.

An African may not in fact address a distant classificatory sibling as "sibling," but by some name. Nevertheless, it is important that he know who the person is in the system of classification. Thus, for example, toward fathers one must show deference, and it is even possible that if this classificatory father has no children, Ego as the closest child in line will be the heir to his fortune. Knowing who a person is in the kinship classification scheme and how one relates to him is essential in relations of property. Disputes over inheritance of property are often closely tied to disputes over genealogy.

Segmentary Lineage Systems

In old Africa, some societies were governmentally structured only in terms of lineages, with no chiefs or centralized heads. Even within the lineages, there were often no appointed leaders. These segmentary lineage systems operated in a way described for the Nuer by Evans-Pritchard and for the Tallensi by Fortes (1945). Taking the most extreme case, murder, let us suppose that one person in such a society did in another. For this, compensation or bloodwealth would have to be paid. As I said earlier, it would not matter whether or not the murder was accidental, a condition of which Africans have no conception. The first thing that would have to be determined would be how the two persons were related. Suppose they were brothers of the same mother. In this case it might happen that no compensation would be paid simply because it would come from the mother's estate, which belongs to the survivor and his brothers anyway. No one else in the society would take any interest in settlement of the case, although they might entertain some questions about the moral status of the person who committed the murder.

Suppose, however, that the murdered man was from a different minor section (1 in Figure 4–9) within the same major section (1 plus 2) of the murderer. In this case the two lineages would be distant enough so that property would be distinct, and the survivors of the murdered man could effectively demand compensation without, in effect, taking property out of one pocket and putting it in another. Instead, suppose the defenders of the murderer were to dispute the claim. This would lead to a confrontation, maybe even a clash of arms. However, avoidance of a fight and encouragement to settle peacefully would be promoted by the fact that in such an instance, the lineages would balance off in opposed segments of approximately the same size.

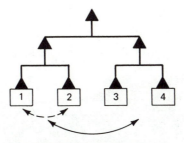

FIGURE 4.9 Pattern of lineage opposition in a segmentary lineage society

All the members of the murderer's minor section would be obliged to support their man, just as all the members of his minor section would be obliged to support the interests of the murdered man. No other minor sections would be involved. However, if the murdered man was from one major section (1 plus 2) and the murderer from another (3 plus 4), this would bring the two major segments into opposition.

Thus the genealogical relations of people are the basis for mobilization of balanced segments of society in opposition to each other, encouraging peaceful settlement of property disputes without the presence of government officials.

Economic Functions of Lineage

Most African societies were not segmentary lineage systems, but even where chiefs existed, the lineage system often persisted and operated for certain types of things even when other things, such as settlement of bloodwealth, were being usurped by political authorities. Perhaps the most common activity based on lineage was the mobilization of labor for highly labor-intensive, short-term projects. Women might also be involved in such activities, but because they were more fully occupied at all times, this activity fell heavily on men, who had the spare time for it. In the last chapter, it was mentioned that weeding the crop rapidly at just the right time is critical for its best success. Men of the same low level lineage, such as the Lugbara family cluster, might do the weeding, circulating through each other's fields, which were planted at different times, and accomplishing this important task. They might also help each other with the threshing of the crops, which must be accomplished rapidly in order to get the grain into storage and away from possible destruction by wild animals or birds. They also joined in the hard task of erecting a new house once the owner had assembled all the parts. In addition, they merged their efforts in sacrifices to the ancestors, calling upon them to relieve the supplicants of miseries unloaded on them by an angry ancestor.

Turu men acting as a cooperative group in apprehension of the alleged
perpetrators of a *mbojo* crime (see chapter 8, p. 218)

In the old days, especially in segmentary lineage societies, they joined together
to repel attackers, and they also joined together to form large-scale military
units in the state systems. Thus they were able to repel strong enemies or to
loot nearby societies which would have been impossible for small bands.

As Middleton indicates for the Lugbara, the degree to which members
of a lineage felt an obligation to help each other varied with the size of the
lineage. Men of the same family cluster felt much stronger obligations to help
get together the bridewealth that would make marriage possible for one of
them than did men whose lineage was only the minor section. The lineage at
its strongest was a group of men who, while maintaining their individuality
and individual property, felt strong obligations, supported by the image of the
family, to extend credit and to support each other. While Africans always have
had some institutions that would accomplish this outside the family; in most
instances, the family and lineage were the most important.

Nevertheless, the intensity of mutual aid varies not only with distance
of relationship but, according to Laughlin (1974), with prevailing economic
conditions, such that as the wealth of the community expands mutual aid
expands, and as it contracts, mutual aid contracts. In fact this thesis fits the
situation of the benighted Ik of northern Uganda, described by Turnbull
(1972), a people who, because of virtual destruction of their production system

as a result of actions by the Uganda government, became for a while the paragons of the evil way people will behave toward each other when pushed to extreme conditions. All mutual aid disappeared, parents would not even give food to their children, and the dying were forsaken.

Variations in Use of the Lineage and Clan Principles

The great variety of ways that the lineage and clan principles show up in African societies can best be demonstrated by reference to actual practices. The general overall pattern is one of movement from full-blown, complex lineages in the sense just described, through weakened lineages and clans, proceeding somewhat independently of each other, to the extreme where lineage as an organization seems extinct to be replaced by associations.

Full scale operation of the lineage principle occurs among stateless people like the Lugbara, whose nesting system was outlined. Other such segmentary lineage systems include the Turu, the Tiv (Bohannan 1968), the Bwamba of western Uganda (Winter 1958), and the Konkomba (Tait 1958) of northern Ghana, to name only some. A study of these societies (Middleton and Tait 1958) shows that they can vary radically in population, from 900,000 among the Dinka (Lienhardt 1961) to 30,000 among the Bwamba. They also vary widely in the complexity of the lineage structure as measured by the number of generations needed in genealogies to describe the whole nesting system, from twelve among the Tiv to six among the Bwamba and the Konkomba. Some of these societies allowed feuding (a kind of modified warfare in which the heaviest weapons were not used) among segments (Tiv and Lugbara) while others did not (Bwamba and Konkomba, who only conducted warfare with other societies).

Information about African societies is not complete so that we cannot say how many societies were of this full-blown lineage type, but an estimate can be made on the basis of Murdock's *Ethnographic Atlas* (1967). It contains a compilation of statistics with respect to societies of the world, which includes approximately 275 African societies (nearly one half of the total number of African societies as Murdock reckons them). This suggests that about 14 percent were segmentary lineage systems of one type or another.

About one half of African societies in the sample, in addition to the segmentary societies, a total of about 65 percent, employ lineage and clan organization in significant ways, far less than all African societies.

It used to be thought that state structures with chiefs were incompatible with lineage and that as the state arose, the lineage declined. Today it is felt that this point was exaggerated. Nevertheless, the rise of headmen or chiefs does dilute the operation of lineage from its full-blown form. For one thing, many disputes are no longer allowed to be settled by opposition of segments; settlement is now the prerogative of the chief.

There is a class of African societies, the next along our continuum, which have nesting lineages but which also have political authorities. The Shona of Rhodesia (Kuper, Hughes and van Velsen 1955) have regional chiefs along with nesting patrilineages, although they also have dispersed matrilineages. That is to say, this is a double-descent system in which the patrilineages are localized due to patrilocal residence and the matrilineages are therefore dispersed. Logically both cannot be localized simultaneously. The Yao also have headmen or local chiefs but nesting matrilineages.

Throughout much of Central Africa lineage continues to be very important, as among the Lele of the lower Zaire Basin (Douglas 1963), but the exceptional value of labor in the production process led in the past to the growth of a system of what Douglas (1964) calls *pawning*, or slavery. Douglas uses this term because the pawns still had rights. In this area it was unusually valuable for lineages to gain adherents so they took to slavery because normal growth through births was not fast enough. This led logically to deemphasis on complex genealogies and the growth of genealogically shallow lineages as lineage segments grew up from slaves. To put it another way, the need for adherents became so great that the lineage principle was seriously challenged by an essentially associational principle of organization that aggregated people by buying rights in them.

Our next point on the continuum is those systems in which localized unilineal groups, lineages or clans, exist but where there is no nesting system. There is only one level of localized lineage. The Afikpo Ibo (Forde and Jones 1950), the Suku of southwest Zaire (Kopytoff 1964), the Somalis, and the pastoral Wodabbe Fulani (Stenning 1959) exemplify these localized one-level patrilineages. This does not mean that there are never any higher units. For example, the Somali local lineages are part of clans, but the higher units are dispersed.

Taking our continuum a step further, the Barabaig of central Tanzania (Klima 1970), who are a mobile pastoral people, retain the concept of nesting lineages within the clan, but all lineages are dispersed, making each community a collection of members of different lineages and clans. Among pastoral people who are nomadic, as we shall see more clearly in the chapter on power and authority, lineage becomes far less useful because people must move around in small units. So lineage tends to become very much reduced in favor of other, associational, principals of organization. Because the Barabaig are not literally nomadic but rather mobile, moving freely from one settled community to another, some sense of lineage can be retained, especially since their territory is relatively small.

By contrast, the Pokot (Schneider 1953), cousins of the Barabaig even though separated from them by more than 500 kilometers, and the Tiriki

(Sangree 1966), one of the Abaluyia Bantu people of western Kenya (Wagner 1956), have only small, nonlocalized clans. Among such people, knowledge of genealogy is very sparse since, so to speak, it is unnecessary. Members of the same clan know they are related because they share the same clan symbols, not because they know the genealogies. Few Pokot know who their great grandfathers were. Thus, while people of this group may conceive of individual localized lineages (or families) as part of a larger clan structure, all but the local unit is dispersed. Perhaps a further decline in the unilineal principle occurs among the Yoruba and the Jie who have localized clans. The Yoruba clans are segments of towns, since they are an urbanized people, and the Jie live in clan hamlets. On the other hand, since both have at least some kind of localized unilineal group, in another sense the Pokot and people like them are further along the continuum of decline of the lineage principle.

Shifting back to Central Africa, in many places, as among the Ngoni (Barnes 1951), an offshoot of the Zulu wars, the Lozi (Gluckman 1951), and the Nyakyusa (Wilson 1951), and also the Hausa (M. G. Smith 1966), the decline of lineage takes a step beyond pawning systems. Communities become organized under political leaders who pull in people from any place they can. Alternatively, communities are organized on the basis of bilateral relationship, applicants for admission being judged on the basis of whether they are related to anyone in the community through either side of the family.

Kinship, especially unilineal kinship, probably never totally loses its meaning for Africans but perhaps it does in the extreme cases, like the Baganda (Fallers 1964), the Swazi (Kuper 1963), and the offshoots of the Zulu, among whom communities were organized regardless of kinship according to the ability of the local chief to recruit a following. In fact, in such kingdoms the leaders tended to see kinship as a competing principle. When the king of Buganda first acquired guns from the Arabs, he used them to attack local chiefs, whose power was somewhat autonomous. The chiefs depended on localized lineages, but the king depended on the chiefs to put together an army. Taking power by force, the king in the end delineagized the kingdom, so to speak.

Essential Principles of Lineage Continuity

Are there any principles governing the strength or weakness of lineage? For one thing, mobility, whether literal nomadism or simply the need for people to be able to move around the ethnic territory in order to pursue their goals, works against lineage. Lineage is strongest where people can stay put and where they have something, usually land, whose exploitation is best achieved through large-scale cooperation. However, as in Central Africa, if the operation of the lineage principle is too cumbersome to cope with unusual problems, in this case the heavy demand for labor or political following, it also comes under challenge. In modern Africa it is being steadily eroded by the rise of economic processes which are more capital intensive and depend less than in the past on labor. In such cases, individuals move to where the opportunities are; they leave lineage behind (along with polygyny, which is also peculiar to labor-intensive activities). On the other hand, even in modern African cities, on occasion, the value of lineage as a large-scale cooperative structure reasserts itself, and strong lineages appear in the cities.

ASSOCIATION

Despite the significance of lineage in African life, interaction based on principles other than kinship is also important. Unfortunately, the great stress placed on lineage during the height of African social anthropology led to neglect of other aspects of life. Against this context, it is useful to make a brief assessment of association, but this and related features will be discussed more thoroughly when we come to politics and authority in Chapter 6.

A most common type of association transcending kinship is the widespread existence of what may be called *associateship.* This is a relationship between two persons who are either not kinsmen or whose kinship ties are so weak as to be negligible. For example, In Rwanda the institution called *ubuhake* (Maquet 1971, 471) consists of one person called *shebuja* who gives some good, such as a cow, to another, and a second person called *garagu* who pays for the good with some other good or service. Since the relationship is meant to persist over a period of time, usually a long time, it constitutes and is perceived by the participants as a kind of quasi-kinship relationship. Turu, who have a similar institution called *uriha,* say of this relationship that one would not create it with a patrikinsman because among such people it already exists by virtue of membership in the patrilineage.

At the other extreme, so to speak, is one of the most famous associational systems in Africa, the Poro and the Sande, secret societies for men and women respectively, which are widespread in Sierra Leone and Liberia among such people as the Mende. The Poro resembles such secret organizations as the American Ku Klux Klan or South African Afrikaans' Bruderbond, pulling almost all men into a cooperative association which transcends kinship and wields political power (K. Little 1960, 204). Such pervasive associational organization is unusual, but the basic principle seems widespread in West Africa, as among the Afikpo Ibo (P. Ottenberg 1965) where the Ogo, a village-based society, performs similar functions. The associational life of people in the tropical parts of eastern West Africa seems especially rich. The Afikpo, for example, also have age sets and grades as well as title societies, composed of elites who obtain membership through financial success so that they can buy the titles.

In Central Africa, association ties appear prominently in the composition of political communities, as already noted (Cunnison 1960). In the wealthier cattle-raising areas of northeast Africa, the value to be found in raising these animals combined with the need for seminomadic movements by individual families work against kinship as a basis for community. Kinship is replaced by voluntary communities supported by age-set societies crosscutting the whole society. Among the members, there were rights and duties sometimes resembling those among kin, such as prohibition of marriage with a woman who is daughter to a member of one's age set, that is, age-set exogamy.

Finally, an intriguing question is how widespread secret or semisecret associational organization may be among women. Since women ordinarily accompany their husbands to their places of residence, women customarily must live among and cooperate with strangers. Turu women act in concert to cope with problems peculiar to them, including keeping the men in line. So well organized are they, under the leadership of the older wives, that Turu men speak of them as having a secret government and express fear of them.

If a generalization can be made about association in Africa encompassing the principles underlying association for the whole continent, it might be this. Descent as the basis of organization was strongest where assured ties of cooperation in the production system were most important. This tied together both some exclusively agricultural people and also some pastoral people, like the Tswana and the Somalis. Where the possibility for individuals to operate freely in circumstances of great opportunity arose, or where association was thrust upon them, people organized on an ad hoc basis. The overwhelming importance of descent as a basis for grouping is therefore an index to the tight economic, usually land-based agricultural, system that prevailed. Paradoxically, it was also in such areas that states tended to arise and came into competition with descent as the basis for organization.

KINSHIP

WE SAW IN THE LAST CHAPTER how Africans arrange marriages and descent. In this chapter we turn to the more complex subject of kinship. Just as every society has a pattern of descent, matrilineal or patrilineal and so forth, each has a kinship system which classifies kin and affines in certain ways. However, there are many more types of kinship classification than types of descent, in fact the six important ones in Africa are Iroquois, Hawaiian, Descriptive, Omaha, Eskimo, and Crow, in that order of frequency, highest to lowest. (From time to time, I shall refer to these different systems by a shorthand code as I, H, D. O, E, and C.) The labels for these types, as can be guessed, derive mostly from studies of kinship classification among North American peoples and have been standardized for use all over the world by G. P. Murdock (1967). As will be seen, the Omaha type occurs in conjunction with patrilineal descent, but so does the Descriptive and sometimes also the Iroquois and the Hawaiian. Crow is usually associated with matrilineality although patrilineality, in fact, is also part of the system in Africa.

In other words, descent is not the same as kinship. People in different societies arrange the people they think of as their relatives in different ways (kinship). Sometimes there is a correlation between kinship and descent, but not always. The best way to think of it is that people first decide what kind of descent system they will have (matrilineal, patrilineal, and so on) and then superimpose on that a kinship system which determines how they will organize their relations within the boundaries of descent. If they "choose" to be patrilineal, they may select Omaha, Descriptive or Iroquois, to name only three. However, they cannot choose Crow because Crow seems also to occur in conjunction with matrilineality, that is, it uses double descent or mixed unilineality. (To be perfectly accurate, though, we must understand that people do not choose a descent system and then a kinship system in that order. The two things evolve together).

ROLE OF KINSHIP CLASSIFICATION

The reasons why people have different types of kinship classification are still obscure although some are understood better than others. Generally speaking, whereas rules of descent determine inheritance and group membership, kinship classification spells out in more complex fashion how kin and affines shall interact. Our own society provides an example which can be easily understood before we plunge into the African varieties. In America, descent, as previously explained, is bilateral, except for the surname, which descends patrilineally (we get our family names from our fathers). Wealth descends from both parents to all their children and is divided equally among them regardless of sex, unless the parents make a will providing otherwise.

Having evolved this bilateral system, we Americans developed a kinship classification system to go with it. As it turns out, bilaterality is rather limited in this respect, the most usual type of kinship classification system accompanying it is Eskimo. However, there are several varieties of Eskimo. All Eskimo systems have in common the isolation of the main group of brothers and sisters, father and mother, and sons and daughters from surrounding relatives. What we do is lump all those surrounding relatives together, either as grandmothers, grandfathers, uncles, aunts, cousins, or nephews (Figure 5.1). Compared to most African systems, such as the Omaha system used by the Soga, it is as if we are saying that peripheral relatives are not unimportant but they are not nearly so important as those persons of an individual's family, his linear (not to be confused with unilineal) relatives. In the Soga system, by contrast,

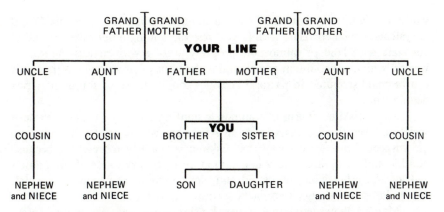

FIGURE 5.1 American kinship classification

all the patrilineally related cousins (father's brothers' children) are called by the same term used for one's brothers and sisters.

The way we classify our relatives is not the only Eskimo way. We could differentiate maternal aunts and uncles from paternal aunts and uncles, as some people do. The reason we do not do this might be because we do not have distinctive relationships with these different sets of uncles and aunts.

In Africa some kinship terminologies are more popular than others. Using a nonrandom sample of 168 African societies (about one-fourth the total number) derived from Murdock's *Ethnographic Atlas* (1967), we find the following frequencies for Africa and then for all the societies of the world:

TABLE 5.1

	% AFRICA	% WORLD
Iroquois	35	25
Hawaiian	26.7	32
Descriptive	14.8	8
Omaha	13.6	10
Eskimo	3.5	16
Crow	2.9	8
Total	96.5%*	99%

*This figure does not equal 100 percent because in the original calculations, some minor systems of classification were included but have been left out of the tabulation.

The reasons for this distribution, as will soon become apparent, seem to reside in the fact that many African people, a greater proportion than in the world as a whole, were wealthy enough in movable goods to generate D and O systems, which correlate with large livestock, among other things. I and H correlate with land or immovable property and/or with maldistribution of wealth, which are common where land is the basis of production, although it can be maldistributed in pastoral societies too, as those of southern Africa demonstrate.

As for Eskimo, it is most common in hunting and gathering and Western societies. Even the few cases found in Africa are widely scattered, and some are suspect. Thus we can say that Eskimo is scantily represented because hunting and gathering is very uncommon as a primary mode of production and, on the other hand, industrial and plow methods of production, which seem related to Eskimo, were lacking until recent times.

Map 5.1 shows how some of these kinship systems are distributed. Information, particularly from Zaire, is insufficient to make a complete map, but as can be seen, large areas can be characterized by type. The main centers of Iroquois terminology are central and southern Africa and the western part of West Africa. While this includes the Central African matrilineal belt, it also contains the cattle-wealthy patrilineal groups of southern Africa and a large part of the patrilineal forest and savannah people of West Africa and the West Sudan. East Africa is characteristically Descriptive and Omaha although Omaha also occurs in an enclave in southeastern Africa. Finally, the eastern part of West Africa is notably Hawaiian. As the map also indicates, the elements that promote a certain type of classification are responsive enough to local conditions to produce a scattering of each type within other areas, as the Omaha Igbo occurs among the generally Hawaiian people of eastern West Africa, or the Hawaiian Lozi appears among the generally Iroquois people of Central Africa.

The main conclusion that may be drawn by perusing this map is that while there are subtle correlations between the production areas dealt with in Chapter 3, such that the cattle-rich people of eastern Africa are Omaha and Descriptive, the association is not one-to-one. Just as we noted that the wealth of a people is not simply a function of their production system, so their kinship system is not just a function of the production system. Rather, as we shall see, the indications are that kinship and economy correlate, moving together somewhat independently of production system.

IROQUOIS

We will begin our survey of the various types of kinship classification systems by examining the Iroquois. (Incidentally, I shall use another shorthand code from time to time to refer to these various relations: B = brother, Z (sic) = sister, F = father, M = mother, MB = mother's brother, and so on).

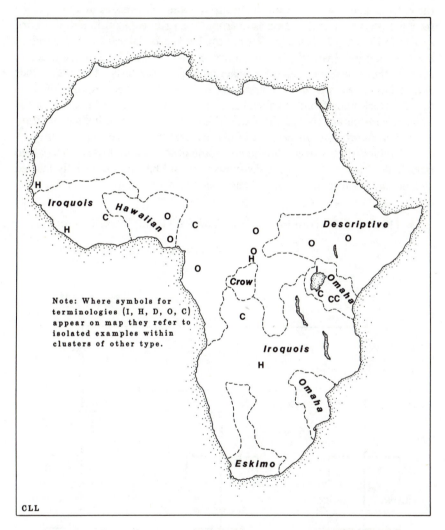

Note: Where symbols for terminologies (I, H, D, O, C) appear on map they refer to isolated examples within clusters of other type.

MAP 5.1   General Distribution of Kinship Terminologies in Africa

There are several interesting features of Iroquois which contrast strikingly with our own system but which, however, are not found only in Iroquois. If we look at Figure 5.2, which illustrates how relatives are classified *within* the patrilineage, that is, within the group of close relatives, as in a village, we see a pattern which is the same as in Iroquois patrilineages although the Turu system in Figure 5.2 is Omaha. Within the lineage, collateral (that is, parallel) lines are merged. Instead of calling a first cousin "cousin," he or she is called *muuna*, the same term as used for an actual sibling. Similarly a father's brother is also father, as is a father's first cousin. The rule governing all this is as follows: Reckoning from the apical ancestor of the lineage, all persons of the same generation are classed the same. Thus all persons of father's generation are father *(tata),* and all persons of GF generation are GF, and so on.

Iroquois differs from Omaha and some other terminologies when we go outside the lineage. Iroquois is distinctive for and becomes especially labeled as Iroquois because of the way it classifies the whole range of cousins, com-

FIGURE 5.2 Turu internal patrilineage kinship classification

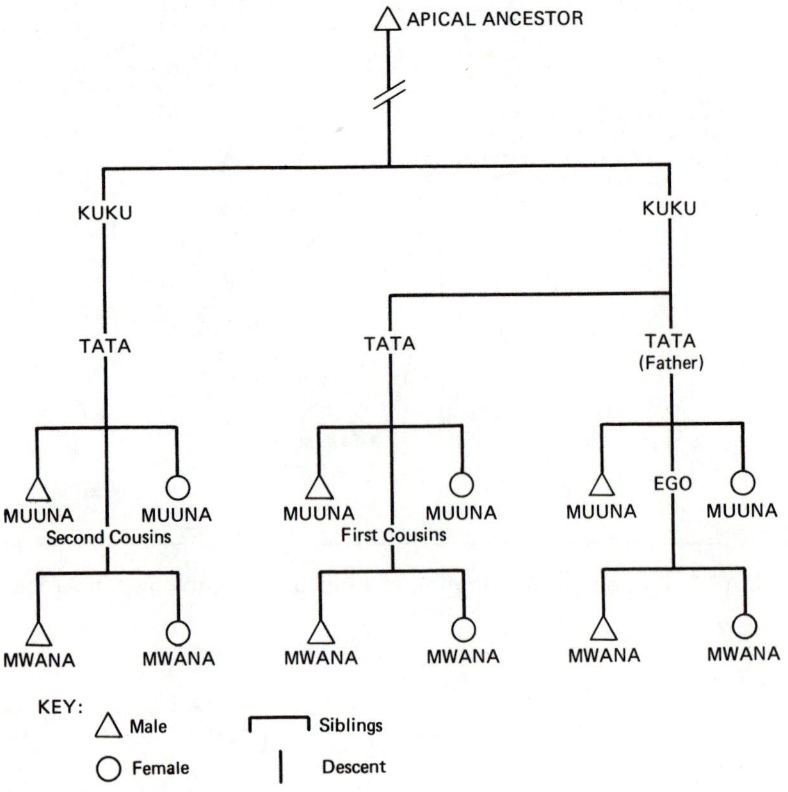

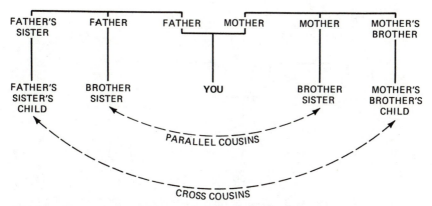

FIGURE 5.3   Cross and parallel cousins in Iroquois kinship terminology

pared to other systems. It distinguishes *cross* from *parallel* cousins (Figure 5.3).

The logic dictating who are cross or parallel cousins can be clearly seen in this diagram. Cross cousins should be called "cross-parent cousins" because it is the crossing of sex in the parental generation that is the determinant. Ego's cross cousin is either his-her father's sister's child or mother's brother's child. Conversely, Ego's father's brother's child or mother's sister's child are parallel cousins.

The rationale behind Iroquois terminology seems to be the prevalence of cross-cousin marriage as an economic strategy (or political strategy, if you wish) to which Iroquois classification is adapted. In none of the other terminological systems is cross-cousin marriage important, and none of them single out cross cousins terminologically. Murdock's sample of African societies shows about 74 percent of all Iroquois systems using some form of cross-cousin marriage, and it probably occurs also among at least some of the remaining 26 percent.

Marriage to cross cousins can occur, theoretically, in three forms. One may marry MBD, FZD, or the two of them simultaneously in those instances where they are one and the same person. Since this latter type, popular among Australian aborigines, is almost nonexistent in Africa we shall ignore it and pass on to the other two types.

What is behind the practice of marrying MBD or FZD? The answer will be suggested by examining two examples of such types of marriage from different parts of the Iroquois zone, the matrilineal Kaguru of eastern Tanzania (Beidelman 1971), who are part of the Central African production region, and the patrilineal Batswana of the southeast region. The Kaguru, as we saw earlier, depend for their wealth on cultivating land since they live in

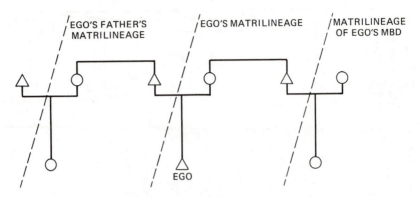

FIGURE 5.4 Matrilineal descent

a tsetse fly zone and cannot raise many cattle. Thus the owners of the land have much power. These powerful men play games with each other in which the young men are pawns (other than in the slave sense), as Beidelman explains (1971, 65–66). The Kaguru have dispersed matrilineages, a factor which makes the cousin marriage system seem more complicated to us than if it were simply patrilineal. This system is diagrammed in Figure 5.4. Beidelman says that about 25 percent of Kaguru marriages are arranged between cousins by elders. A man (Ego in Figure 5.4) may not marry a woman of his own matrilineage (MZD) because that would violate the rule of clan exogamy. He does not marry FBD for reasons not explained, although this person could be an eligible spouse since in the Kaguru system she is not a member of one's lineage and therefore marriage to her would not violate exogamy. Ego is required to marry either MBD (matrilateral cross cousin) or FZD (patrilateral cross cousin). It will be noticed that MB is a member of Ego's lineage, but since this is a matrilineal system, MBD is not of Ego's lineage. Similarly, FZD is a member of F's lineage but not of Ego's.

In Kaguru society it appears that residence is patrilocal, despite matrilineality. Thus Ego ordinarily lives with his F because his M does. However, if he marries MBD (who also lives with *her* father), he seems to be under great pressure to live with his MB; residence for him then becomes matrilocal. What all this means is that such a marriage is a kind of political act. MB, while retaining control of his own daughter and son, manages to draw into his group his son-in-law as well, probably in return for allowing the marriage without bridewealth or with little bridewealth, and thus he builds up his following and power.

Marriage to FZD is not simply the reverse of a matrilateral cross-cousin marriage since the F does not gain any special advantage in expanding the size of his following through such a marriage. The son already lives with his father, and any woman the son marries, FZD or a stranger, would ordinarily come to live with him. Why F should want his son to marry his sister's daughter is not explained by Beidelman, but one possibility that in fact occurs in some societies is that this is reciprocation by father's sister's daughter's family for FZ, who was provided as a wife for Ego's father in the previous generation.

As Beidelman explains, cross-cousin marriage is not prescribed or universal in Kaguru society. It is a strategy facilitated by the system of classification (or whose utilization generates the system of classification as an epiphenomenon). Furthermore, the choice of MBD or FZD is not random. Each relates to a different set of circumstances, dependent on the fact that the two forms are not symmetrical or reversals of each other. What they apparently do have in common is the facilitation of marriage exchanges in the absence of large amounts of mobile wealth which would work against the need for such exchanges.

While Iroquois terminology with its apparent ability to encourage cross-cousin marriage is the preferred mode among the Central Africans, it does not only occur where economies are least productive of mobile wealth. Its presence in southern Africa among the cattle-rich people testifies that cousin marriage can be a valuable strategy for wealthier people. However, when we survey how the Batswana utilize cousin marriage we come upon a new element. The Tswana do not confine themselves to cross-cousin marriage, as one might anticipate, considering how commonly Africans expect marriage to conform to the rule of clan exogamy (Schapera 1950). They, like the aristocratic Bito clan of Butoro in Uganda, allow marriage with parallel cousins too, most importantly with FBD. The Tswana are divided into two classes, the nobles, who are members of royal lineages, and the commoners, who are not. Among the nobles all four forms of cousin marriage are practiced in this order of frequency, from highest to lowest: FBD, MBD, FZD, MZD. Among commoners the frequency is: MBD, FBD, MZD, FZD (A. Kuper 1975, 129). That is to say, nobles most frequently marry a parallel cousin, FBD, and since they are a patrilineal people, this means marrying within one's patrilineage. Commoners most frequently marry out, to the daughter of mother's brother and hence into the lineage from which the mother came. Kuper's explanation for this is as follows (A. Kuper 1975, 131):

> Senior nobles wish to transform competitive power relations into supportive relations. They therefore marry brother's daughters, father's brother's daughters and other close agnates (patrilineal kin). More junior nobles, those more distantly descended from a ruling chief, will make some marriages of this kind, but will be more concerned to create closer relationships with the really powerful men—and so they will make marriage alliances, where possible, with senior royals. This will be most easily accomplished if their fathers or father's fathers were related by marriage to such royals—and so they will often be marrying cross-cousins.

Put in the terms discussed earlier, senior nobles marry FBD (or BD) in order to protect their seniority from dilution by keeping it in the lineage. However, junior nobles create useful alliances by giving subordination for a wife and for a hold on powerful men (thus MBD marriage). Furthermore, as we have seen, FZD marriage does something similar to FBD marriage, although the supportive relations are between lineages, rather than within the lineage. The effect of marriage to MZD is unclear, but since it is relatively unpopular we may guess that it fails to achieve the ends just described as well as the other alternatives.

The preference shown by commoners for MBD marriage is explained in a way similar to that for the Kaguru. They utilize MBD marriage to make links with powerful men. However, they also use the FBD alternative, seeking no doubt to protect what they have if they cannot arrange the preferred MBD forms or, if they are rich commoners, simply seeking to protect their wealth unless they can tie it to a noble family of high stature.

To summarize, among both the relatively poor Kaguru and the wealthy Tswana, in both matrilineal and patrilineal societies, Iroquois terminology has come to serve the interests of people who find it strategically useful to marry cross cousins, that is, to marry inward or intensively. The strong tendency of the Tswana to marry endogamously confuses the pattern most typical of Africa, where such behavior is rare, but it does underscore that cousin marriage of all kinds can serve the same end.

OMAHA

The frequency of Iroquois terminology in Africa and in the world suggests that if there is a characteristic type of nonindustrial society, it is the Iroquois type in which the nature of the production and holding of wealth is such that it is maldistributed, and access to it is uneven. This causes men to make marriage alliances which have a political dimension. However, not all nonindustrial people have such economies. I chose to examine the Omaha system next, not because it is the next most common, but because it contrasts so vividly with the Iroquois and thereby helps us grasp the meaning of Iroquois and, at the same time, the meaning of Omaha. Omaha terminology seems to rise where there is wealth like cattle and camels and where there is wide access to it, but where fixed property still remains. Like Iroquois, Omaha terminology ordinarily occurs in conjunction with unilineal descent, but Omaha is always patrilineal, whereas, as we have seen, Iroquois may go both ways. Omaha systems all over the world are also of several types. One African variety, found among the Turu and the Soga on the northeast shore of Lake Victoria, takes the form seen in Figure 5.5.

The most distinctive feature of Ohama is the way men of lineages from

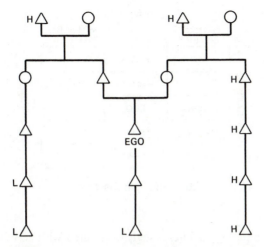

FIGURE 5.5   Soga Omaha kinship terminology
(adapted from Fallers, 1965, 1967)

which Ego's lineage get wives or to whom Ego's lineage gives wives are lumped under a single term which ignores generational differences between them. In this Soga system, for example, note how a male Ego refers to maternal males —GF, MB, MBS, and MBSS—by the same term (designated by the letter H). If we analyze this type of Omaha into its essential structure, it looks like Figure 5.6, the Turu system.

Not all East African Omaha systems equate grandparents with MB and his offspring as the Soga and Turu do. For example, in the Nandi system maternal and paternal grandparents are *akui,* as are grandchildren, whereas MB and MBS are *mama* (Huntingford 1953, 25). Furthermore, among the Maasai, while MB and MBS are *apu* relatives (an abbreviation of the full designation), maternal and paternal grandfathers, as in Nandi, are *akwi.* Thus, while the first class of Omaha types carries terms for kin and affines across lineage lines by equating a mother's brother with his own father (maternal grandfather) and with Ego's paternal GF, the second type does it by equating maternal and paternal grandparents and allowing generation to cut across lineage lines.

Omaha terminology has been explained in various ways. The most popular explanation suggests that it is designed to fit societies in which the principle of patrilineage is most fully developed. Ignoring differences in generation and aggregating inlaws of different generations, both on the wifegiver and wifetaker sides seems to be a way of expressing the extreme solidarity of those lineages in relation to Ego and his kin. However, this explanation has been challenged and is suspect because we have seen that some of the terms used to designate affines are also used for patrilineal relatives.

LINEAGES

	FATHER'S SISTER'S	EGO'S	MOTHER'S BROTHER'S
		KUKU	KUKU
		FATHER	KUKU
GENERATIONS	MWIPWA	EGO	KUKU
	MWIPWA	SON	KUKU
	MWIPWA	MWIPWA	

FIGURE 5.6   Turu Omaha terminology

Omaha terminology is interestingly correlated with certain relations of alliance and opposition that occur in societies using this type of terminology. In East Africa, the relations among men become cooperative and competitive over control of livestock, especially between father and son and between brothers-in-law. A father spends his life manipulating cattle to acquire the largest herd he can. However, a son, when he reaches adulthood, begins to pressure his father to pass on to him the share of the herd which belongs to his mother's house. This conflict is manifest in many ways, sometimes through accusations of witchcraft, but always in the rites of passage into manhood.

On the other hand, a man is continually in competition with his wife's brother over the amount of bridewealth. When he marries, a man may have to deal with his father-in-law, but his relationship is essentially with his wife's brother, who is the rightful heir to the estate of his mother's house, which includes the bridewealth obtained from the marriage of his sister. He wishes to get from the sister's husband the maximum bridewealth, and the husband wishes to keep it to a minumum. While the tension between these two, appearing, for example, in the joking relationship spoken of in the last chapter, declines with the length of the marriage, it may continue for many years. Visits from the wife's brother are a time of anxiety because he may insist on further remuneration with the threat of dissolving the marriage, and therefore the wife's brother is lavishly entertained in order to keep this threat to a minimum.

Taking these two forms of competition into account, we now note another feature of the system that derives from these primary relationships. On the one hand, grandson and grandfather have something in common, their mutual opposition to a man who is father to one and son to the other. The grandfather resents his son who is trying to reduce his herd, and the son resents his father's resisting giving him his inheritance. In addition, the son also has in common with the mother's brother (father's brother-in-law) opposition to

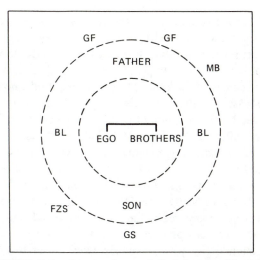

FIGURE 5.7   Economic model of Omaha kinship

the father, in this case because both identify with the interests of the mother's house against the father.

In the 1920s the brilliant kinship analyst Radcliffe-Brown (1952) produced a paper called "The Mother's Brother in South Africa," in which he pointed out that among the Thonga (who also use Omaha terms) of South Africa and Mozambique, the sister's son has a peculiarly open relationship with MB, what he called "privileged familiarity." The sister's son can visit with MB when he wishes, ask for gifts, and behave in a generally permissive way, very uncommon between men of different generations in societies like these. Although Radcliffe-Brown also noted a similar relationship between the grandson and the grandfather, he maintained the position that these two permissive relationships are different. Actually, they seem to be much the same and, as noted above, Ego even addresses the two types of relations by the same term in some Omaha systems.

Hence, it seems possible that Omaha classification is not only or primarily a reflection of lineage solidarity, but also an index of a set of coalitions that grow out of alliances and oppositions in terms of control of fluid forms of wealth in a situation where lineages are still valuable for exploiting land agriculturally. Figure 5.7 illustrates this. The circle of kin adjacent to Ego are his chief competitors, and the next circle out, his allies.

While Omaha terminology occurs in conjunction with patrilineal descent, not all societies using it have strong patrilineages. The Pokot, for example, have very shallow lineages, and men, as earlier explained, do not even know who their great-grandfathers were. Since the rule of descent governs transmission of property and if the kinship classification governs the way people relate, if some societies with Omaha terms have weak lineages, there is further support for the idea that the terminology relates in various ways to the structure of wealth and how people relate to it. Thus, while Figure 5.7 correlates very nicely with the kind of terminology found among the Soga and the Turu, the Maasai and the Nandi cases appear to introduce a complicating factor represented by the equation of maternal and paternal GF who, on the other hand, are differentiated from MB. This amounts to an intrusion of considerations of generation, the significance of which is not clear.

Compared to Iroquois a characteristic which should be emphasized is the specific lack of cousin marriage. Often it is the case that cousin marriage is not merely lacking but specifically forbidden. Put in other terms, the marriage system is extensive, as compared to the intensiveness of Iroquois. The sensible person is one who avoids marriage with all the relatives he can, because he already has economic ties with them. He reaches out to marry strangers, thereby establishing new links. In societies like Omaha, where there is mobile wealth, it appears to be good strategy to make as many links with strangers as possible, whether through marriage or otherwise.

DESCRIPTIVE

I have chosen to discuss Descriptive terminology next because it seems to follow naturally out of a discussion of Omaha. Like East African Omaha, it is associated with cattle and camel raising, but unlike Omaha, which occurs across states and stateless societies, it seems to be a terminology that goes with statelessness. I hasten to add, however, that this does not mean that statelessness causes it. Both are derived from the nature of the economies that exist in this area. These are highly capital intensive; that is, they depend more on cattle than on labor in the production of wealth. Furthermore, Descriptive terminology accompanies a decline in the value of fixed assets, as compared to Omaha.

Murdock's sample for the world shows that Descriptive terminology, in which all of the parents' siblings and their offspring are indentified uniquely, such as by the designation "mother's brother's son" or "father's brother's daughter," is typically not associated with unilineal descent. In Africa this does not seem to be the case, but to judge by such people as the Turkana, it is certainly true that unilineal relations decline in importance in favor of more individualistic relations. Even the apparently strongly patrilineally oriented Nuer, supposed paragons of strong lineage, show signs of bilaterality (Evans-Pritchard 1940, 193):

Agnatic (patrilineal) kinship between lineages is called *buth*. *Buth* is always an agnatic relationship between groups of persons, and only between persons in virtue of their membership of groups. *Buth* agnation is to be distinguished from kinship in the sense of relationship between persons, e.g., between a man and his father's brother and mother's brother. Cognation in this sense the Nuer call *mar*. Any person to whom a man can trace any genealogical link, whether through males or females, is *mar* to him. A man's *mar* are consequently all his father's kin and all his mother's kin, and we call this cognatic category kindred.

Further emphasizing his point, Evans-Pritchard points out that a man is not allowed to marry any woman who is a member of his mar.

We might summarize Evans-Pritchard's argument as follows: Among the Nuer, relations of property are agnatically, or patrilineally, determined. However, relations among kin crosscut these patrilineal lines such that persons who are bilaterally related form some sort of cooperative group which is so strong that it has even become exogamous. Thus, in a sense, Murdock's conclusion about the relationship between Descriptive terms and nonunilineality is borne out both by the Nuer and by the Turkana. Furthermore, as we saw in the case of Eskimo (that is, American), the decline of unilineality is associated with the rise of individuality.

HAWAIIAN

Hawaiian terms are not as popular in Africa as they are in the rest of the world, taken as a whole, but they are still second in frequency. They well outdistance their closest rival, Descriptive, even though they are far behind Iroquois (25 percent compared to 35 percent). In Africa, Hawaiian seems generally to be associated with patrilineal descent, even though there is a bilateral dimension to it. As Bascom explains of the Yoruba (Bascom 1969, 42):

> Yoruba kinship is bilateral in theory, with incest taboos and kinship terminology extended to known relatives through both male and female relatives, but in practice it is strongly patrilineal. The importance of bilateral relationships is restricted because they depend upon the ability to trace them through all the connecting relatives, and few Yoruba can remember their genealogies for more than four generations back. In contrast, patrilineal descent, in which only male ancestors are counted, is insitutionalized in the clan and does not depend upon individual memory.

Hawaiian terminology makes no distinction between one's own siblings and any cousins, cross or parallel. In addition, it groups together F and all his

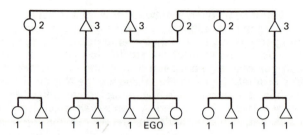

FIGURE 5.8   Hawaiian terminology
(note: numbers indicate persons called by the same term)

brothers and all of MB's. Similarly, all women of M's generation on M's and F's side are called the same, hence its seeming bilaterality. But, to reemphasize a point made earlier, the reckoning of descent occurs independently of kinship classification. That a cross cousin in your mother's lineage is called "my sibling" is not a hindrance to understanding that such a person is of a different matrilineage or patrilineage.

Despite its tendency to occur in connection with patrilineal descent in Africa, Hawaiian fits with matrilineal emphasis also and, in fact, is most appropriate for ambilineal descent, which I spoke of in the last chapter in connection with ramages, ambilineal counterparts of lineages. Nadel (1942, 32) speaks of how the system works among the Nupe of Nigeria:

> Generally speaking, matrilineal descent in Nupe, including here both descent from the mother as an individual and from her family, has essentially the significance of an ultimate safeguard in case the patrilineal arrangement proves insufficient. In Bida society (one of the Nupe), with its great inequality of wealth and status, rich or powerful maternal relations may be as valuable as paternal relations; political connexions, especially, through the mother's family will often be utilized profitably. We realize that these "matrilineal" rights do not follow rigid rules of descent and succession; rather they represent a "second line of defense" on which individuals can fall back in case the "first line of defense"—claims derived through the father—has failed. If we speak of the Nupe extended family as "patrilineal" it will be understood that we refer only to the preponderance and the more rigid formulation of rights and duties transmitted in the father's line. The kinship organization as such, in which the alternative methods of reckoning descent stand in that relation of "first" and "second line of defence," can be most aptly described by a term which was suggested by R. W. Firth as "ambilateral" (i.e., ambilineal).

How Hawaiian terms coordinate with ambilineal tendencies is best seen among the ambilineal Palauans of the Pacific. A man is born into a matrilineal descent group, but if his father can accrue an amount necessary to pay the bridewealth, he may take his son into his own lineage. Thus the fact that the son refers to both his father and mother's brother by the same term accords with a general situation in which the descent status of any person is ambiguous.

As I have already said, ambilineal is not the same as bilateral. It is unilineal descent in which the ancestor through whom lineage is traced may be either the father's or mother's brother depending on circumstances. The resulting ramage is still a discrete descent group, like a unilineal descent group, but unlike a kindred because descent is still traced through only one parent, not through both as in the bilateral case.

Hawaiian terminology seems to be similar to Iroquois in that it fits with either matrilineal or patrilineal descent, but in Iroquois the line which is utilized seems more stable. In Hawaiian the two lines are not kept well separated with the result that prohibition of cross-cousin marriage in Hawaiian makes sense because such a person might become one's lineage mate as in the case where mother's brother is able to keep control of his own sons and those of his sister at the same time.

The "bilaterality" characteristic of Hawaiian should be distinguished from that which we detected in Descriptive. In Descriptive systems, this bilaterality seems based more on a decline in the importance of descent and a tendency for affines to form cooperating business enterprises. In the Hawaiian case, lineages continue to be strong, but there is ambivalence about which of the parents' lineages to associate with.

The economic basis for this ambilineal shifting is not altogether clear. Hawaiian terms predominate in the eastern part of West Africa, which has been one of the economically most volatile regions. As Nadel says of the Bida, there are great variations in wealth and status. It seems clear that for any individual, access to wealth is uncertain enough to lay the basis for ambilineality. However, there is inequality of access to wealth in Iroquois systems too. The fact that in Iroquois, the pattern of descent is firmer, therefore, suggests that while in both systems there is inequality in access to wealth, the possibility of obtaining it is surer in Hawaiian systems than in Iroquois. It is precisely such subtle differences as this, dependent on finer measures of the operation of economies than have been usual in anthropology, which might provide us with the elusive answer to apparently inexplicable differences in terminological systems.

CROW

Crow terminology is the strangest of all. As we know, it is very uncommon. This suggests that what produces it is a very special set of circumstances. In

MATRILINEAGES

	WIFE-TAKING LINEAGES	EGO'S MATRILINEAGE	WIFE-GIVING LINEAGES
1	F 3	MB 1	
2	FZS 3	EGO	MBS 4
3		ZS 2	S 4

GENERATIONS

FIGURE 5.9 Crow terminology
(note: numbers indicate persons called by the same term by Ego)

Crow something happens which is like a reverse of Omaha. This is illustrated in Figure 5.9. If the figure represents a society with matrilineages, Ego's matrilineage is that of his mother's brother. Terminologically he lumps generations in his affinal lineage together, just as Omaha does, identifying his biological father with FZS, who is of Ego's father's lineage, just as Ego is a member of his MB's lineage. On the other side, MBS is identified with Ego's son. These would not be of the same lineage, but they are of lineages from which Ego's has taken wives, and they are of different generations, a characteristic Omaha-Crow trait. In the Crow system, then, it is the wifetakers (father's lineage) who are raised up because FZS is equated with F, and the wifegivers who are lowered, because MBS is equated with one's own son.

The reason for Crow terminology is very unclear, due in part to its rarity over the world (unlike Eskimo, which is only rare in Africa). It occurs only sporadically, except in the Mongo cluster of societies in the center of Zaire, people about whom we do not have a great deal of information (Vansina c1965). However, evidence from the Wambugwe and the Mongo gives some suggestions about its causes. Interestingly, it turns out to relate in some ways to Hawaiian, rather than to Omaha.

Although it has been commonly thought that Crow fits with matrilineal

138

descent as Omaha does with patrilineal, in Africa it is related to both forms of descent in curious ways. For example, in both the Wambugwe and the Mongo cases, marriage is patrilocal and descent, essentially patrilineal, sons inheriting primarily from their fathers. The key element in Crow seems to be a certain ambiguity about descent, however. This is best illustrated by the so-called *nkita* system of the Mongo (Murdock 1959, 287–288; Vansina c1965, 86). In this system, residence is ordinarily patrilocal and patrilineal. The father of a young man is expected to provide brideprice for his son. However, if he cannot do so, the son can invoke the "right" of his mother, dependent on the fact that her marriage payment provided the brideprice for his marriage. The son can require her brother to give to her son a brideprice, a right which takes precedence over the claims of his own sons. In other words, if a father cannot provide for his son, the social structure reverts to matrilineal, and the sister's son becomes a member of MB's lineage, acquiring rights in MB's estate. Among the Wambugwe, similarly, despite the existence of matriclans, residence is patrilocal, and sons inherit from their fathers. However, they also inherit the brideprice cattle paid for their mother from MB.

The curious thing about this arrangement is the special claim ZS has on MB, much greater than normal. However, interpretation of the rest of the terminology system is a problem. Certainly there is no clear pattern corresponding to the one we found for Omaha.

Economically speaking, the Crow people are not poor. The Mongo are banana and cassava raisers, and the Wambugwe, like their Iraqw neighbors, who are also Crow, are rich in cattle, as are the Crow Sukuma of the south side of Lake Victoria. The nkita system and the customs of Wambugwe with respect to inheritance suggests some kind of maldistribution of access to wealth, but how this is to be differentiated from the situation among Hawaiian users is not clear.

SUMMARY

Even though the causes of various classifications of kin are thus not altogether clear, some tentative conclusions are possible. Most particularly, we have seen that there is an economic dimension to kinship which seems to add considerably to older attempts to explain kinship purely in sociological terms (for example, Omaha results from extreme emphasis on patrilineality, as if the choice of patrilineality were arbitrary.) Actually these economic causes are not altogether different from older causal statements. The economics is merely more explicit.

Table 5.2 summarizes certain points I made in the foregoing. It is not

TABLE 5.2 Variable Features of Kinship Classification

	IROQUOIS	DESCRIPTIVE	OMAHA	HAWAIIAN	CROW
COUSIN MARRIAGE	Cross Cousin	Some Parallel	None (extensive marriage)	None	None
ACCESS TO MOBILE WEALTH	Low	High	High	Variable	Variable
EMPHASIS ON UNILINEALITY	High	Low	High	Low	High (but ambi-lineal)
TYPE OF DESCENT	Patrilineal or Matrilineal	Patrilineal	Patrilineal	Patrilineal	Patrilineal and Matrilineal

meant to be an exhaustive summation of differences in these systems of terminology. It does show how small differences in combinations of elements relate to apparently large differences in terminological structures through a multivariate approach. Also it supports the point I have stressed so heavily in this account of the Africans, that it seems important to learn more about the rates of access to wealth and production of wealth in order better to understand these systems.

POWER
AND AUTHORITY

Among the topics usually treated by an ethnological approach to Africa is government, as in Mair's book *Primitive Government* (about East Africa), or the chapter on "Government" in Murdock's *Africa*. However, this word connotes rulers, leaders, administrations, and authority and therefore does not do justice to an appreciable number of African societies, especially in East Africa, where there is no government in this sense. Nevertheless, processes of power aggrandizement, sometimes leading to the establishment of authority, are also present in these societies and are really what the subject of government is about. So we will be investigating processes of achieving power and authority in this chapter, not government as such.

While the relationship of economics to power and authority has in fact been more often recognized than has been the case with descent and kinship or even marriage, there is still a surprising tendency to see processes of power and authority as cultural constructions, rather than as products of exchange, notably in the appearance of states. Yet, as we shall see, the relationship between economics and power and authority is more apparent than in aspects of descent and kinship.

There are still chiefs and kings in some places in Africa, just as there are still societies without authority, headless, acephalous, or stateless societies. While they may operate in ways similar to precolonial and preindependence forms, in most cases the traditional organization has been heavily affected by the power of modern national governments. In the cases of states, where the strength of leaders was in the past mainly dependent on their economic resources, they have lost control of the resources. In more recent times, where such rulers have been allowed to survive, as in Kenya or Botswana, their greatly diminished power often depends on services they perform for the leaders of the new states. Surprisingly, in the cases of headless societies, many have continued to operate according to old patterns up to very recent times, or are still doing so. Often because they exist in remote areas and because they lack chiefs, new central authorities have had difficulty asserting power over them. The Maasai or the Turkana illustrate this point. The reader must therefore remember that the forms of overall organization I am about to discuss may be long gone or may exist in a much modified form.

In this chapter, as implied, I will be concerned with two types of overall systems of organization of power and authority, states and acephalous, or headless, societies. I will examine their forms and their economic bases. Acephalous societies should be differentiated from the simple hunting and gathering societies like the !Kung or the Hadza, in which independent families or groups of families are the largest organizations. True acephalous societies, like the Maasai, are far more complex.

THE ECONOMICS OF POWER

Power in traditional African society came with control of wealth, just as in any other society, and the search for power was universal and persistent. Power can be obtained in two ways. First, it can come from gaining control of or access to some critical resource which is in short or monopolizable supply. Clients give support to its possessor, who translates this support into authority and chiefship. The majority of African societies were shaped by this process although they varied greatly in the degree of complexity to which stateship evolved, varying from petty chiefships based on petty wealth, to great kingdoms based on great resources. Also power could be obtained by force, and we shall see that military means were used in Africa. However, it is useful to think of military activities as an offshoot of the control of resources.

The second way to gain power is by capitalistic manipulations where wealth is in long supply and elusive of control so that it cannot be monopolized. As a result, large numbers of people compete to outdo each other. In such societies chiefs do not emerge, only big men. Such headless societies, therefore, are merely a variant to states based on differences in the nature and conditions of the production and control of wealth.

STATES

The Great Kingdoms and Chiefdoms

The glamor of the great kingdoms and empires of Africa has excited most students of African people and formed the basis of instant prestige for many new countries. For instance, such old empires and kingdoms as Mali, Ghana, and Benin have been exploited through the use of their names by modern governments in West Africa. These large-scale African states had rulers or kings who were designated by a word for king, as European powers have done when they called the king of Germany, the Kaiser or the ruler of Russia, the Czar. The head of the Ashanti state was the *asantahene,* that of the nearby Fon-speaking people was *akwamuhene,* and the head of one famous Yoruba kingdom was the *alafin* of Oyo while that of another was the *oni* of Ife.

Many of the best known of these great kingdoms appeared in clusters (see Map 6.1), as if the forces that created one were responsible also in some way for the others. For example, the so-called Interlacustrine (interlake) States, including Buganda, with its king, the *kabaka,* Bunyoro with its *mukama,* Bunyankole with its *mugabe,* or Rwanda with its *mwami,* all in East Africa, are linked together by certain similar rites and customs, associated with a postulated prehistoric invasion of the area by cattle people from the north who left their mark on the whole area, much as the Romans left their mark on the individual states of Europe (including, often, the title Caesar, of which Kaiser and Czar are variants).

Another cluster is in southern Africa with the states of the Zulu and the Sotho (pronounced sutu), among others. The Zulu king was called *inkosi* and the king of the Swazi, *ingwenyama.* In the southern part of Zaire, the Lunda empire created another cluster, including the *mwaant yaav* of the Lunda, the *ngola* of Kimbundu, the *nyimi* of the Kuba, and the *litunga* of Lozi. Moreover, there is the cluster of what may be called the Fipa kingdoms in southern Tanzania and northeast Zambia, all of whose rulers were called *mweene.* In addition to the cluster of kingdoms in the eastern coastal area of West Africa there were also clusters in the western part of the West Sudan. However, these various clusters do not exhaust the list of African kingdoms as Map 6–1 shows.

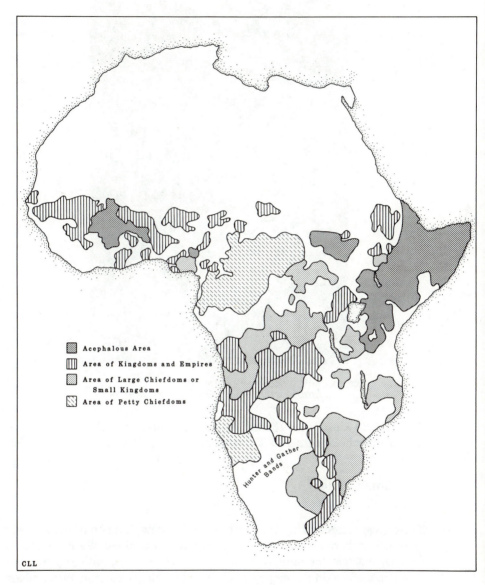

MAP 6.1   Partial Display of Overall Organization

Acephalous Area

Area of Kingdoms and Empires

Area of Large Chiefdoms or
Small Kingdoms

Area of Petty Chiefdoms

Hunter and Gather Bands

CLL

The King of the Bakuba
(photo courtesy of Barbara W. Merriam)

The Amhara kingdom in the Ethiopian Highlands or the Shambaa kingdom near the northeast corner of Tanzania are just two illustrations of the point.

Small States

These great states or kingdoms tend to overshadow those on a smaller scale in which authority was not so elaborate and centralized. So it should be remembered that for most Africans who lived in states, authority was not vested in a great king or emperor but more humble, more anonymous rulers. Probably most ethnic groups had no central king; some had only regional chiefs, as appears to have been the case, for instance, with the Kimbu and the Nyamwezi of western Tanzania. The Shona and the Tswana are further examples. In some places, notably in what is now Cameroon and the northeast part of Zaire, as well as in many places in Tanzania, authority was petty, a single village or a small group of villages had a ruler who was independent of all others. The famous nineteenth-century explorer of Africa, H. M. Stanley, illustrates what these petty chiefs were like in a passage from his book *In Darkest Africa* (1891, 442) where he describes some chiefs he encountered to the southeast of Lake Victoria in the Sukuma ethnic area:

> As we marched from one petty district to another, each independent from the other, governed by its own chief and council of elders, exclusive from its own peculiar customs, habits, or passion, varying differently from the other according to the age, intelligence, and disposition of the chief, our duties and rule of conduct varied. We moved through petty spheres, wherein our duties varied according to the demands made upon us. Here was the small district of Sinyanga with a population not exceeding 2000. The chief and his headmen were as proud of their little state as any monarch and his senate might be of an empire. The chief was conscious of weakness, and that imprudent aggressiveness would prove speedy ruin; but he exacted his dues all the same. We paid them freely and with kindly words. The chief reciprocated the kindness, returned a gift to mark his pleasure, then his people flocked to the camp to exchange their grain and produce for cloth and beads, during which many a friendship and brotherly act was formed between the natives and our men.

Courts

In the great kingdoms, encounters with the leading authority were much more impressive. Mair (1977b) has attempted to detail the complexity of such an establishment, that of the Kabaka of Buganda as Speke, the first European to encounter the Kabaka's court, might have seen it. In the first place, the Kabaka had a clearly recognizable court, a place where people dependent on the king gathered. Since the state of Buganda was so large and rich, the court became enormously complicated. At the bottom were servants doing the things necessary to maintain the splendor, formality, and hospitality of the court. Then the court had officials who directed the humble workers. These included such people as custodians of the royal graves, custodians of the royal drums, caretakers, a "putter-on" of the royal crown, custodians of spear, stool, and other regalia, and those keeping a watchful eye on cooks, bath attendants, herdsmen, potters, barkcloth makers, musicians and so forth. In short, the day-to-day operation of the court was involved and a major administrative task for the ruler. In the smaller kingdoms the prime minister, the man who ran the daily affairs of the kingdom for the king, might also take as his responsibility the running of the court, but in the case of Buganda, the *katikiro* or prime minister's duties appear not to have included housekeeping. Then there were officials in charge of royal rituals of whom in Buganda the most important seems to have been the *kimbugwe,* who kept a shrine beside the entrance to the palace. It contained such things as the sacred fire and also the king's umbilical cord encased in cowry shells.

In addition to all this, the visitor to the royal court of the Kabaka would have encountered not only the king, whose formality and social distance from the visitor would have reflected his wealth, but also the powerful prime minister, the "mother" and "sister" of the king (who might or might not be his actual mother or sister), other powerful and impressive people, including ministers and district rulers, subject to the king's command. Stanley was able to patronize the petty chiefs of Shinyanga (as we now spell it), but Speke and those who followed him kept a healthy respect for the Kabaka and other such kings who, like the modern Idi Amin, were despots, used to taking lives.

Variability

African kingdoms were not fixed or static. A map of systems of overall organization such as Map 6.1 can only suggest what the general situation might have been like at the beginning of colonialism. Kingdoms rose and fell (Buganda was a fragment of a larger previous kingdom, Kitara), and petty chieftainships were aggregated from time to time and then dissolved again. The Kimbu of western Tanzania had only district chiefs until Arab trade for ivory and slaves penetrated that area, beginning in the early part of the nineteenth century. Fighting among themselves for control of this trade and using the profits from it, chiefs became bigger and bigger until finally, just before colonial rule entered, a king of the Kimbu emerged, Nyungu-ya-Mawe (Shorter 1972). Similarly, the Zulu kingdom seems to have arisen for the first time just after 1800 and was responsible, through the violent impact it had on southern African people, for spawning kingdoms as far away as among the Ndebele of Zimbabwe and the Ngoni of Malawi. Kingdoms, in other words, are not cultural inventions established and perpetuated by custom. They are an important result of political-economic processes which determine how small or large they may be and the extent to which they will fluctuate in size. A state like that of the Kimbu, built on ivory trade, will suffer decline when the ivory is all gone. On the other hand, there is reason to suspect that the great Interlacustrine States grew because of a decline in cattle holding due to tsetse fly infestation of the interlacustrine grasslands.

Common Features of States

While African states may therefore differ greatly in size, from a widespread empire like the Lunda, through so-called segmentary states, like that of the Alur of western Uganda (Southall c1954), where the king and district chiefs competed for power, to petty chieftainships like those Stanley saw in Shi-nyanga, an interesting fact about them all is their structural similarity. This has been the subject of some attention by scholars (Murdock 1959; Mair 1977).

Murdock's characterization is the most comprehensive. To begin, these monarchs and chiefs, he said, all enjoyed absolute power, at least in theory. For example, they typically were said to be owners of all the land, so that any individual landholder possessed his title through the sufferance of the ruler. While the king of the Galla monarchy of Jimma Abba Jifar in Ethiopia does not exemplify this (H. S. Lewis 1965) exactly, he serves to make the point while also demonstrating that this characterization is not unqualifiedly true. The king of Jimma did not own all the land. Individuals did hold land in their own right. However, he was the largest single landholder, and all unused, open lands and all forests also belonged to him. Thus the kingdom was filled with tenants beholden to the king for the land they used. Perhaps it is not too much to guess that the extent to which a king controlled all the land reflected the extent of his power, and in Jimma we have a relatively new kingdom. However, I do not mean to suggest that the process of centralization is inexorable. A king, like the Alur king, might fail to gain total control. But, insofar as he did, he would probably end up owning all the land by divine sanction.

Another trait of African kings mentioned by Murdock was their divinity. In fact, not all were divine. The Jimma kings were not. Nevertheless, it is a very common aspect of kingship. The *oba* of Benin, near the Niger Delta in Nigeria, illustrates (Mair 1977a, 163) this. He was accorded a status on the level of the highest gods of the pantheon of gods headed by Edo, the Creator. As king of the dry land he was linked with Olorun, the king of the waters, the god of the sea from which all life is believed to have sprung. He was thought of as giver of life and might be addressed as "Child of the Sky whom we pray not to fall and cover us, Child of the Earth whom we implore not to swallow us up." It was believed that he was immune from ordinary physical needs, that he neither ate, nor slept, nor washed, and that he could never die. To maintain this fiction, he led a life of seclusion. This ritual isolation, while by no means universal, was another common feature of African kingship. It seems logical to assume that it is but an extreme form of a normal distance between a powerful ruler and his subjects, even though in the petty chieftainships, this distance might be minimal.

Insignia of office also seem to have been a universal trait. Chiefs in West Africa often wore beaded crowns and used umbrellas to indicate rank. In western Tanzania, chiefs frequently wore conch shells, and the kings of the Interlacustrine States commonly used drums as royal insignia so that in Rwanda it was said "He is king who has the drums." In Buganda a huge special drum, placed at the main gate to the palace, was beaten only when the king was present. In southern Africa, the chief often appropriated to himself the power of rain making and all its paraphernalia. In the Kuba kingdom of southern Zaire, the most important chiefs had the right to wear eagle feathers.

FIGURE 6.1 The Zulu capital—early nineteenth century

Rulers usually had capital towns distinct from other types of settlement, which were often simply overgrown homesteads isolated from those of other people. Often these capitals were mobile, for the king moved from place to place within his kingdom. However, we must not exaggerate this last trait. Such kingdoms as Benin or Dahomey had permanent capitals consonant with the fact that the people were settled agriculturalists. No doubt in areas where swidden production was intensive, or pastoralism important, as in Central and East Africa, the capital complex would move more often. More consistent was the elaborateness of the capital, a feature correlating with the size and wealth of the kingdom. An early trader who visited the capital of Shaka, the Zulu king, tells of how 80,000 warriors were drawn up inside the capital corral. Figure 6.1, which is a nineteenth-century engraving of the capital of Dingane, successor to Shaka, illustrates the kind of capital that would be more characteristic of a mobile, cattle-oriented people than, say, that of the Oba of Benin.

Special royal protocol and officials who had charge of affairs of the court and of the kingdom have already been mentioned. Territorial bureaucracy, in which subchiefs (often kin of the king) acted as agents of the king were characteristic of the larger kingdoms. While in some of these bureaucratic systems, the structure of the kingdom reflected the segmentary lineage structure described earlier. Subchiefs might also be appointed. One of the most interesting features of many African monarchies was the role sometimes played by women, as in the Buganda kingdom. Often there were king's "sisters" and "mothers" with considerable power. For contrast, the kings' wives seldom had important roles (Mair 1977a, 50). Thus in Bunyoro the king had an official sister whose power was equal to that of senior chiefs. In other places women often played important roles in the central administration, even if not that of official mother or sister. In the northern Nigerian Hausa kingdom of Maradi, a royal lady was appointed to handle women's affairs in the court. Women as supreme rulers, equivalent to Queen Elizabeth I of England, were almost unknown; however, there was one important exception, the so-called Rain Queen of the Lovedu of South Africa (Krige and Krige 1943).

Law

Another characteristic of states is the kind of law they have. Most of us think of a complex system of law as necessary to society. We are like the functionalists who think the state is necessary to keep order. However, it has been observed (Black 1976) that the amount of law that a people have rises with the increase in complexity of stratification. This means that even a petty village state has more law than an acephalous society, but that it has less law than a kingdom. Furthermore, it has been said (Middleton and Tait 1958) that states have criminal laws, or their equivalents, where headless societies do not. What all this seems to mean is simply that a counterpart of the rise of authority in society is the rise of rules to govern interactions between people to protect the power of the ruler, who is represented as society, and to protect the rights of clients relative to the ruler. Law orders the transactions between ruler and ruled. Treason, a crime against the state, can only occur in a state.

Examination of states and stateless societies shows that both have law, but between the two, it is different. In the state there are more laws, the number increasing with the complexity; there are criminal laws, covering challenges to the authority of the state, and there is regular force backing up the law. I might even add that physical punishment is more characteristic of some laws in states than in stateless societies. By contrast, in the stateless societies, relating to the difference in economic base, the prominence of "civil" law is merely recognition of the common practice of adjudicating by negotiation and exchange of property. As I. M. Lewis (1961) says of Somalis, if the elders decide that a decision running against their client is just, they will see that it is paid. However, they do not accept it without question.

Similarly, Gulliver, speaking of the stateless Arush Maasai on Mt. Meru in northern Tanzania explains how settlement of disputes is accomplished in the absence of central authority (Gulliver 1963, 232):

> The Arusha answer to questions of this kind ... "We discuss and discuss the matter ... and then we agree. When we agree, that is the end. What else is there to do?" In other words ... the process of

establishing a settlement consists of discussion and negotiation, argument and counterargument, offer and counteroffer, between the disputants' parties in an endeavour to find an area of mutual agreement. Being mutually acceptable, the question of enforcement does not arise, or at least only marginally.

Why do Africans, like ourselves, generate laws, rules governing relations? The answer at the simplest level seems to be that contractual relations between human beings (*homo reciprocus,* as Howard Becker called us) are normal. Law makes explicit the rules of interaction, of exchange. Where there are states a most important element of exchange is social exchange. It is not too much to say that to an important degree, criminal law is the rules governing social exchange between subject and lord, the political authorities and the weak. Civil law covers material exchange and since it predominates in stateless societies, this is why they have no criminal law. Force does not take the form of police but of self-help, as individuals are required, to a certain extent, to protect themselves and to use force to protect their rights.

Having said only this much I will leave the subject of law without further comment. Anthropologists have not in fact studied law in African societies with enough consistency to generalize very deeply about it, and illustration of how settlement of disputes is accomplished would take up far too much space. Suffice it to mention some of the best works which characterize what little has been done: P. Bohannan, *Justice and Judgment among the Tiv* (1957); P. Gulliver, *Social Control in an African Society* (1963—about Arusha); M. Gluckman, *The Judicial Process among the Barotse of Northern Rhodesia* (1955); W. Goldschmidt, *Sebei Law* (1967); E. A. Hoebel, "Three Studies in African Law" (1961); and I. Schapera, *Handbook of Tswana Law and Custom* (1938).

Kimbu Chiefs

In order to obtain a more integrated view of the structure of an African state, I propose here to describe briefly one of the less pretentious systems, the chiefdoms of the Akimbu people of western Tanzania (Shorter 1972). Before the centralization of Ukimbu by Nyungu-ya-Mawe, the people of Ukimbu had a multitude of more or less independent chiefs. The people of the chiefdoms were linked through certain ethnic ties, such as rituals and a common language, but each chief had political independence in his zone. At the onset of colonialism, there were more than thirty-eight chiefdoms in an area of about 20,000 square miles and a population something less than 50,000 people. Each chiefdom, in fact, was little more than a single village or cluster of villages. However, there were economic links between these independent rulers based on kinship such that a chief might have certain obligations to his father, chief of another area. In fact, these chiefdoms were typically just households carried in some cases to a very high level of development, based on economic differences. Apparently the chief's mother and sisters had no special political roles, but it is easy to guess that they did, in fact, have more power than ordinary mothers or sisters simply because Kimbu chiefs would certainly honor their mothers and value their sisters as any African man would do. As a matter of fact, in the nearby Nyamwezi chiefdoms, which were similar to the Kimbu, marriage among chiefs, as we saw earlier, was matrilineal but patrilineal among ordinary people, obviously because a chief's sister was too valuable and costly for ordinary marriage, and probably because the chief used his sister politically to tie valuable sons-in-law to his household.

The Kimbu chiefs, who ceased to rule effectively when colonial power was established, were called *umwaami* So and So and addressed as *umweene,* much as an Englishman would say King So and So and "your majesty." The chiefdom was clearly delimited by certain landmarks, like hills and ridges, and although most of it was forest, all of it was thought of as the domain of the chief, who was literally called "the earth" and whose kinsmen were called sons of the earth. A physical symbol of the position was the side-blown horn *(imbutu),* four or five feet long, used only on certain rare occasions and only in honor of chiefs, living and dead. These horns usually had carved on them the Kimbu symbol for the sun, *ilyuva,* who was associated with Matunda, the Creator of the earth of which the chief was a holder of a segment. The chief wore a large conch shell on his forehead which was pure white, a color and shape again associated with ilyuva.

The chief ruled with the advice of a council of elders *(ivanyaampala)* who were patrilineal relatives of the king, thus members of the royal lineage. They controlled the regalia for installation of a chief and therefore, could at any time, put someone else through the installment ritual, a fact which caused the chiefs a good deal of discomfort. The chief's sons ruled over divisions of the chiefdom known as *itumbi,* which were fortified villages, often with outrider villages around them. The king's difficulty in controlling his sons is a common theme in the Kimbu accounts of chieftainship. After conferring a subdivision of his chiefdom on his sons, they would often rebel and assert their autonomy from him.

Reasons for Structural Similarity of States

Why did African states tend to have structural features in common? Murdock (1959) said that Africans acted as if they had a little plan for the state built into their heads so that whenever the possibility of forming a state appeared, the same structure emerged everywhere. In a sense, this is true. The African state tends to certain features that are basic to all African life or are logical developments from it. For example, the peripatetic capital, where it occurs, is a larger manifestation of the fact that in most places, Africans move their homesteads about to one degree or another. However, since the chief or king may be above local kinship ties, he moves his capital across kinship boundaries and over longer distances. Because African men honor their mothers and value their sisters for reasons explained earlier, it is not surprising to find that when they gain great power, their mothers and sisters also benefit.

However, when trying to understand the reasons for the state in Africa, it is probably a mistake to emphasize these structural similarities too much, at the expense of political and economic forces. To do so seems to suggest that the cause of states is cultural, diffused from a common source; rather it is the result of dynamic processes which generate a state in one place but a headless society in another. As in modern society, we sometimes forget that democracy is not simply a tradition which can be chosen or not as the basis for government, but a political system that demands certain economic conditions (a large rate of capital growth, for one thing). To describe democracy simply as a result of a common tradition in the West would therefore be a mistake.

Competing Theories of the Causes of States

We must therefore turn our attention to the explanation for African states insofar as it is dependent on more than tradition. Why do Africans have states? Before we can even attempt an answer to this question, we must first be clear about what is meant by state. Some people make a distinction between kingdoms and chiefdoms, which can therefore be placed alongside headless societies to form an exhaustive classification of types of overall organization. However, the economic differences between headless societies on the one side and chiefdoms-kingdoms on the other are far more profound than the differences between chiefdoms and kingdoms. These latter systems vary only in degree, for example, in the fact that kingdoms have administrations but small chiefdoms do not need them and cannot afford them. An administration is merely the result of a chiefdom's becoming too large for the chief to run it out of his hat, so to speak. Nevertheless, both are states, having in common the essential features differentiating them from headless societies, people (ordinarily men) with authority, who occupy a position or office and work within a framework of law, possessing regalia and symbols of authority, including myths, often associated with divine right. In the headless societies, perhaps excluding the small hunting and gathering societies, there are people who are wealthy and respected and who lead, but they do not govern. Because there is so little doubt in the minds of ethnographers about when we are dealing with states as opposed to acephalous societies, people like Vansina (c1965, 17) are able to say that in much of Zaire, the role of chief is clearly defined. Similarly, there is little doubt among East Africanists which societies are headless and which are states.

The various competing theories of the rise of states parallel the general theories of African behavior reviewed in the first chapter. One, favored by a few even today, is that the state is a natural development, a progressive movement in time from a more primitive to a more advanced condition. A respected contemporary theorist (Sahlins 1962) once referred to headless societies in Melanesia as "underdeveloped." Another student of states (Kottack 1979, 159) says:

> It could be reasonably argued that the state ranks alongside exogamy, symbolic communication, and tool making as a major achievement of human evolution.

A diffusionist view still prevails in some places, as suggested previously, according to which the similarity of structure among African kingdoms is due to the fact that they all derive by a process of diffusion from the same source. The functionalists explain the rise of states as a result of the fact that through the rule of law and the use of coercive force, the state maintains order where otherwise Hobbesian anarchy would prevail.

The marxist explanation, related to the progressive view, is well represented, particularly in the writings of Maquet (1972). He sees the reason for the large number of kingdoms in the matrilineal belt as a function of a combination of habitat and technology which made possible the production of a surplus of grain. Powerful people took possession of the grain, used it to aggregate others to them, and on the basis of this clientship extorted even more grain from the people.

I have already said something about the deficiencies of these various theories, but it would be worthwhile to summarize them here before offering my approach to the rise of states, which is more in line with accepted current views. A progressive theory simply begs the question. It is obvious that states do not automatically arise everywhere and, further, such a theory is clearly prejudicial to the acephalous societies. The diffusionist approach places too much emphasis on structural features, which could be explained as fundamental and indigenous to African societies. It does not place enough emphasis on the dynamics of states, the economic and political reasons for their being. The functionalist view, like the progressive approach, is prejudiced against the headless societies. It places too great a value on the rule of law and does not focus sufficiently on the more fluid economic processes which form the basis of order in society. Finally, the marxists seem inherently prejudiced toward the stateless societies, to which their theories falsely ascribe a poverty of production. Ironically, the states of the matrilineal belt, which Maquet sees as so productive, actually encounter some of the highest labor costs for the lowest production of any African societies.

Population and States

While on the subject of the cause of states it will be useful to take note of an interesting point made by Stevenson. He notes there is a correlation between states and population such that states are more populous than headless systems. He even claims that large population causes the state (Stevenson 1968, 232). My feeling is that such a claim does not take sufficient cognizance of the relationship between economic modes and population and so closes the door to the distinct possibility that in conditions of production which value labor over capital, forces that work toward increased population are stimulated. Actually, it seems, the state is produced by conditions augmenting clientage, forces which themselves also favor increased population. On the other hand, in northeast Africa, where cattle are a chief form of wealth, labor is not in such demand, and increased population not only is not desired, but actually has a negative impact on the economy by reducing grazing land and availability of capital for investment. Hence pastoral people seem to limit their populations in some way.

Control of Resources

Researchers on the subject of the rise of African states are today moving in the direction pointed out some years ago by Lucy Mair, in the first edition of *Primitive Government* in 1962. Mair said that states arise wherever someone is able to collect around him a group of followers and to keep them tied to him. The followers inevitably promote the leader to a position of legally supported authority, thereby making him into a chief or king. More recently Lemarchand (1977, 8) put it this way:

> Monarchial *legitimacy* stems from the nature of exchange relationships between the monarch on the one hand, and his "publics" or "sectors" on the other. Mutually beneficial transactions between them enhances the regime's legitimacy.

Carol Smith (1976, 311) has also recently stated in general terms how this can happen:

Agrarian societies are societies economically divided between food producers and nonfood producers in which the bulk of the population is engaged in food production. The basis for stratification in all such societies—that which divides the elite from the peasantry and which defines other economic classes—is, without exception, control over some critical resource by select members of that society. The critical resource may be a means of production, such as land, or a means of destruction, such as fire power. But it may also be a simple means of subsistence, such as salt, that cannot be locally produced or procured. In any case, if a stable system of inequality is to be sustained, the stratification system is institutionalized by a system of exchanges in which the elite control the critical nodes or *means of exchange* (my emphasis).

In other words, stable stratification is the result of more or less permanent differential access to or control over the means of exchange, and variation in stratification systems is related to variation in types of exchange between producers and nonproducers. Relative to Africa, the only qualification to this quotation which I would make is that stratification does not occur only in agrarian societies but can occur also in pastoral societies where the means of production and exchange can be monopolized, as has happened in southern Africa among the Zulu, Sotho, Tswana and others.

Smith may seem to be saying the same thing as Maquet, but there is an important difference between them. Maquet believes that wherever a surplus of grain is produced, there is an opportunity for someone to get control of it and make himself into a ruler. Implicit in Smith's theory is the idea that permanent control of this resource must be obtained—it is not a foregone conclusion that it will be controlled. Otherwise all African societies with grain surpluses would be chiefdoms, but not all are (for example, the Turu, Kipsigis, Teso or Nandi are not).

It is common among writers to assert that the scarce or critical resource on which authorities based their power is land. Lloyd (1965, 73) explains that land is of critical importance in subsistence societies and is therefore the prime economic constraint. Goody (1973), comparing the production systems of Africa and Asia, questions this and makes the point now familiar to the reader that it was labor, not land, that was in short supply in Africa. Plows and other capital did not exist although if they had, these probably would have been the chief constraint, thrusting labor into the background, as in India where instead of bridewealth, a dowry is paid to a husband to take a daughter off her father's hands. Allowing for this, we must not jump to the erroneous conclusion that land was of no importance. It took second place to labor only where it was available and, as in the Kimbu case about to be discussed, chiefs could base their power on its control. Furthermore, in the stratified pastoral societies, control of capital (cattle) laid the basis for authority, and, as Smith suggests, states may also be built on control of the means of exchange (the trade system) and on control of force. In fact, the largest of them used both.

Smith's point can be illustrated by reference to the intense commercial system that grew up in the Niger Delta in earlier days. Alagoa (1970) gives an indication of how control of trade fostered states in that area when he examines the question of whether it is true that the European slave trade was the cause of the rise of states in the Niger Delta. He shows that, in fact, trade for other goods than slaves preceded the arrival of Europeans. He points out that the saltwater swamp environment of the eastern Delta was not suitable for agriculture so the people had to trade for vegetables from Ijo and the north. This trade was accomplished with dugout canoes which made the swamp easily passable. If anyone could make a canoe one might expect that this trade would generate egalitarian relations as every man could be an entrepreneur by choice. However, it turns out that the right trees for the canoes came from a limited area, such as Apoi in the central Delta, and although Alagoa does not say so, it seems possible that control of the supply of canoes in Apoi, or control of the source of supply by some local importer, could and did lay the basis for kingship.

The Economics of Kimbu Chiefdoms

States built on control of land and of exchange may be illustrated by the chiefdoms of Ukimbu (Shorter 1972). The Kimbu, before Arabs appeared in the nineteenth century creating a demand for ivory and slaves, had petty chiefdoms based on control of land, poor as it was. There appears to have been great competition for land among people of this area. They had to resort to extremes of shifting cultivation because of the poor soil and their utter dependence on it since they could raise no cattle in this tsetse fly area. Shorter says that a chief was a man who could utilize his sons effectively to capture and hold bush land and who could obtain followers from those to whom he allowed access. The size and complexity of a state depends on the level of production of wealth which it can achieve, regardless of what it produces. That is to say, reiterating an earlier point, the production regions of Africa, displayed in Map 3.4, do not correlate with state or nonstate systems, seen in Map 6.1, because one livestock- or grain-producing economy may generate great production and high levels of economic activity whereas another will not. In the case of the Kimbu, the level of production and of the economy appears to have been low so the highest level of chieftainship it could attain was one in which a chief loosely held a small area of a few outlying villages and controlled similarly small areas through his sons who, as was noted, were likely to rebel, probably because the resources of the chief were insufficient to hold them in check. One of the puzzling things about chieftainship is why anyone would consent to subserve a chief, despite the fact that there is some kind of inequality in the relationship. The answer may be that where one does rebel against the chief's legal authority, in most cases the usurper finds himself in exactly the same position as the deposed chief, subject to rebellion himself. There is no point in rebelling unless a new exchange relationship can be established that will satisfy the subordinates. Conversely, when the economics of the situation change, it is a wise chief who adjusts the equation of exchange to fit the new reality. A good case in point is the rebellion of the district chiefs in the kingdom of Shambaa in the latter part of the last century (Feierman 1974). When attacks on them by powerful gun-bearing Zigula from the south could not be repulsed because the king of Shambaa refused to trade with Arabs and so prevented the acquisition of guns, the outlying chiefs saw it in their interest to obtain guns. In so doing, they made themselves more powerful than the king, whom they then abandoned.

The level of complexity of the Kimbu chiefdoms began to rise with the slave and ivory trade so the basis of the kingdom shifted from control of land to control of exchange. The Kimbu chiefs were able to defend their claim to part of the ivory felled by the hunters, the tusk that touched the ground, and to use the ivory to obtain guns from the Arabs. In turn, the guns were used to capture slaves, who were also sold, and the proceeds were used to obtain more followers. In the end, as we saw, one of the most powerful chiefs grew bigger than all the others, Nyungu-ya-Mawe, and made himself king of the Kimbu just before the Germans took over.

The Kimbu example suggests an interesting hypothesis. Small states are more likely to be based on control of land than larger ones, since in the African context, land cannot generate enough wealth to support a large state, which requires trade.

Economics of States: Military and Slavery

While trade of some valued item or items may supersede control of land as the basis of state formation and may produce states of greater complexity, another process which frequently underlies the rise of kingdoms is the development of military power. In fact, the prevalence of warfare in state formation once led scholars to think that conquest was the principal means of state formation. The states of the western sudan utilized military means, including cavalry, in varying degrees to further their ends (Goody 1971). The great Zulu state, as well as some of its offshoots, like the Ndebele and the Ngoni, utilized conquest to lay claim to strange lands. In East Africa, the great state of Buganda used warfare as a production device as did the other states in this area where plantains were the staple. In fact, this area of Africa was noted for the degree to which militarism underlay state formation leading to their being called "predatory states." Because plantains give such a high return relative to labor costs, they support a large population and free men almost entirely from subsistence activities. The men can be used by leaders to create a military machine to extort wealth, such as women and cattle, from their neighbors. The most interesting thing about such states (Little N.D.) is that the large ones were more offensive in operations than the small ones, because the continuity of the state depended on acquiring spoils to pay off the clients of the leaders. Where the leader could no longer do this, the state dissolved into small village units which were purely defensive. In the Interlacustrine area, then, rulers sought to obtain valuable resources by utilizing surplus labor which, however, had to be paid off. When the state failed to produce enough to do this, the state fell.

Central African Militarism

Paradoxically, in Central Africa, military organization was sometimes the result of a shortage of labor, not, as in East Africa, because of a surplus. Ordinarily in African societies in which labor is the chief constraint on production, the supply of labor necessary to meet the demand for products can be obtained by the usual processes of marriage and lineage cooperation. Sometimes, however, the demand for labor severely outstrips this supply mechanism and leads, as we saw earlier, to various kinds of practices, including slavery. Particularly in the large states of West Africa (Hopkins 1973, 23), it acted as an alternative to a free labor market, presumably because under those conditions, the production and use of slaves was cheaper than free labor. The reason labor was in such demand in these complex societies was because it was the basis on which they grew, and the bigger they got, the richer they became. The Chokwe were one of the large states in Central Africa about whom we have information on the dynamics of state formation (Miller 1970). Before slavery and warfare were suppressed, the state's military power depended on its ability to mass men to capture women to support the production system of the state. With the abolition of slavery, the state fell apart.

It has been observed that there is a high correlation in Central Africa between matrilineality and the states, and in the last chapter we saw that there is an association of Iroquois kinship terminology with societies in this area. The apparent reason for this is again the problem that these societies depended heavily for the production of wealth on labor but had insufficient mobile wealth to finance movement of labor. As we have seen, matrilineality is but an expression of the inability to obtain control of women through material exchanges. Iroquois terminology is an index to the presence of the need by men to make alliances with more powerful men in order to get wives and of powerful men to obtain political subordinates and labor in the absence of means to mutiply material wealth. Regionally, Central Africa, as the presence of slavery, matrilineality, and Iroquois terminology shows, had unusually severe production problems.

Symbolic and Ritual Aspects of Chieftainship

There is one other aspect of the causality of states which requires attention before we leave the subject. Many scholars seem to feel that the symbolic and ritual aspects of chieftainship have power to cause the state to persist, despite the failure of economic support. The argument for this is simply that if the symbols and rituals are powerless to maintain monarchy, why do they exist? The answer to this question anticipates the next chapter on African philosophy and religion but can be dealt with briefly here.

Later in this chapter we will be looking at stateless societies where men of power arise from time to time but are unable to institutionalize this power as chieftainship or kingship. As political scientists like Lemarchand would say, they cannot attain legitimacy as rulers. In contrast, we saw how petty Kimbu chiefs had authority, wore conch shells, symbolizing the sun, and used side-blown horns to represent their right to rule. The Lozi king's superior status, like many in Africa, is symbolized by drums. Furthermore, many kings, like the king of Shambaa, are supported by myths, in this case the myth of Mbegha, which explains why the king is and must be. In this myth, a mysterious hunter enters the country of Shambaa and proves skillful at settling disputes so he is asked to remain and be king. The descendants of Mbegha then employ the myth to support their power.

Despite the existence of the symbols of chieftainship, which seem to insist that a particular chief or king was divinely appointed and should therefore be honored in all circumstances, chieftainships fall, kingdoms disappear or are overthrown by their subjects. The answer to this enigma seems to be that the symbols of chieftainship are not a mandate to rule but a way of expressing or modeling a complex socioeconomic situation in such a way as to convey the notion that under prevailing circumstances, the monarchy is necessary and inevitable. For example, the Lozi king is said to be the Great-One-of-the-Earth, the land. This accords with the essential part played by the Zambezi flood plains in the economy and with the fact that in order for that economy to work, there must be a clear right to the land. The king establishes his prior right to all of it, a right, which if challenged, would endanger the rights to it of all his subjects. Suppose, however, that conditions were to change, that an economy not dependent so much on land were to arise, as in England during the Industrial Revolution. Then despite the myth, drums, conch shells or whatever, the power of the monarchy would decline or disappear, having become obsolete. The economic reality would not now accord with the "theory of society" embodied in the royal symbols and myths. Theory, as we all know, has to a certain extent a life of its own, and economic reality and political reality might grow out of phase from time to time. Nevertheless, in the end, an accomodation must be made.

Balandier (1970), speaking of the Mossi people of Upper Volta, expresses the idea in this way. The sovereign of the Mossi, the Mogho Naba, symoblizes the universe of the Mossi people. Associated with this is the concept of *nam* referring to a force received from God that enables a man to dominate others.

> Its dual origin, divine and historical, makes it a sacred power that confers on the group that holds it supremacy (a "noble status") and the ability to govern. Although the *nam* is the condition of all power and authority, it is never acquired permanently. Its possession is the object of political struggle: failure brings its loss, as well as the abandonment of power and prestige. This notion primarily concerns legitimate domination and the struggle for the positions from which it can be exercised.

The Lozi Kingdom

During the period in which the most intensive study of African societies was being carried on, it was not customary to pay much attention to economics as I have defined it, and ethnographers were generally naive about it. A trustworthy economic analysis of statehood is therefore difficult. Nevertheless, some accounts, like that of the great ethnographer of the Lozi people of western Zambia, Max Gluckman, make possible a plausible estimate of what may have been going on. Reanalyzing some of Gluckman's data will illustrate the economics of large statehood in one area of Africa, and the treatment of symbolic aspects of kingship will anticipate the following chapters on philosophy and religion.

The Lozi are one of the most famous kingdoms in Africa, mainly because of the writings on Gluckman. When he went to study them first in 1940, he found a kingdom, Bulozi, about 120 miles long and 25 miles wide, at its widest, stretched along the upper Zambezi River on a north-south axis (Map XIV), with a population in excess of 150,000. The kingdom was divided into two major sections, the north, headed by a king, Litunga, or "earth," also known as "Great-One-of-the-Earth," and a southern section headed by a Princess Chief, Mulena Mukwae, known as "Earth-of-the-South" and also Litunga. In practice the Princess Chief was entirely subordinate to the male Litunga of the north so that the reason for the existence of this dual division is not altogether

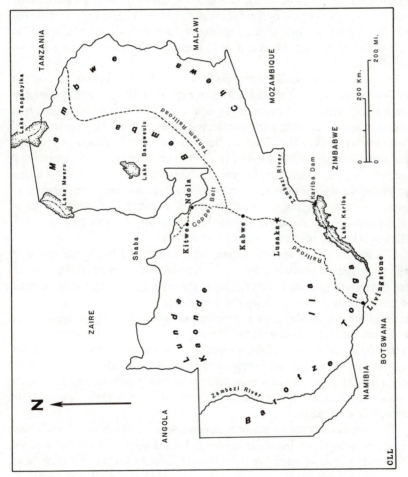

MAP 6.2 Zambia

clear. Anticipating my later discussion of African modes of thought, I would suggest that it is largely a symbolic statement of the particular history and conditions of tension in the Lozi kingdom, manifested in terms of a binary system of classification. The Great One is associated with maleness, north, peace, security, and probably the right hand, whereas the Princess is associated with femaleness, south, insecurity, and probably the left hand. The insecurity represented here is a result of the fact that the Lozi kingdom was conquered in 1838 by Kololo, a south African Bantu leader who had fled to this area as a result of the Zulu wars. He was able to penetrate the south because of civil war in that area.

For practical purposes, then, this is a centralized kingdom, run by the Great-One-of-the-Earth from the northern capital while the southern capital is a major administrative subcenter. In addition, the kingdom is divided into a large number of sections, each containing villages, including central royal villages, scattered over the Zambezi flood plain. These villages, which are further administrative subdivisions, are all built on mounds which are isolated by water during the floods from December to March, after the harvest. During the period of floods, the people migrate to the margins to carry on agriculture by inferior means, ranging from cultivation of swampy areas on the edge of the plain through decreasingly favorable conditions to swidden in the dry woodlands. Harvest in these areas occurs in April.

In addition to the village system, which is the basis of production of goods and of administration, there is a crosscutting *makolo* system which groups men other than by locality. This is the basis for organizing large-scale labor projects (like canal building) and warfare.

The Lozi are divided into a complicated system of statuses which have both vertical and lateral dimensions. Taking the latter first, the occupants of the fertile flood plains think of themselves as *malozi toto* or True Malozi, while other, presumably conquered, people on the periphery are also Malozi, but not True Malozi. The True Malozi have distinctive tatoos, brands, ear lobe holes, and other marks that distinguish them and which are their "passport to Nyambe," God, after death.

The vertical system of statuses is composed of the Royal Family and descendants from kings, based on bilateral descent (the Lozi are unusual for the bilaterality and, significantly, their use of Hawaiian kinship terminology because both are rare in this part of Africa). These royal people are differentiated as Linabi, or Lozi, on the one hand, and Bana Bamulena, descendants of the conquering Kololo, on the other hand. They are the people who occupy the two capitals and the various royal villages. Next in order of importance are husbands of princesses, *boishee,* and commoner relatives of the Royal Family, *likwanabi.* Then there are the freemen or commoners, including immigrants who were brought into Loziland as free men. Formerly there would also have been a final low rank, the serfs or slaves, although this status has been abolished since the British established colonial rule.

Gluckman tells us that the Lozi raised cattle on the flood plains where they grazed from May to December, apparently in between the cultivated fields and otherwise in the woodlands. They also caught fish in the rivers, streams, some dammed areas, and special areas, which were especially productive. They also grew sorghum, maize, and "root crops." In the woodlands they grew tobacco, cassava, millet, groundnuts, collected honey, and manufactured dugout canoes, mats, baskets, fishnets, bark rope, beeswax, and other products of forest materials. Problems for an economic analysis of Lozi production are apparent in the list. For example, we know that root crops differ in labor costs, as between cassava and yams, but Gluckman does not tell us what these root crops are. There must also be variation among the crops of the plain, for example, in return relative to cost of production, but he says nothing of this, and we learn nothing of differences in emphasis on sorghum and maize, at least in the account used here (Gluckman 1951). In fact, Gluckman had a primitive notion of the role of labor cost, but he thought all modes of production were equally labor costly, including the herding of cattle. This might have been true, but there are no facts to determine the matter, and it seems unlikely.

Even more curious is his idea that these products of Lozi labor are all "consumables," having no economic importance because they are perishable. Cattle, of course, are stores of wealth, but fish can be dried for storage, and sorghum and maize can also be stored. Cassava can be made into storable flour. Moreover, dugout canoes, baskets, and the like are durable. Furthermore, the Lozi system was elaborately built on tribute paid to the king through his regional officers who in their turn dispersed goods to clients.

What seems to have puzzled Gluckman was why, if Lozi production was so high, as it undoubtedly was with fields in the fertile, alluvial flood plain, no large-scale trade developed. He considered it to be due to the fact that goods were not durable.

My own suspicion is that the matter was complex in the following way. In the first place, the Lozi had no good means of storing wealth in repositories like cattle. The ratio of cattle to people was certainly below one to one. Hence the individual farmer was forced into agriculture as the main means of creating wealth, and, as we have seen, this produces hierarchy through the fact that the land is scarce and owned by a few (like the Great One).

Although the Lozi were then condemned to hierarchy, so to speak, they were somewhat redeemed by the unusual productivity of the flood plain. It is reasonable to suspect that in a manner parallel to Buganda, the superior production capability reduced labor costs and allowed for the emergence of the Makolo system. Under this system, on the one hand, the king could achieve economies of scale in projects that further increased productivity and which, on the other hand, allowed formation of a military machine which conquered surrounding people, confiscating their wealth, exacting tribute (like Ila cattle), and producing slaves to bring back to the plains and woodlands to further relieve True Malozi of production activities.

Thus, by supporting their king, the Lozi enabled him to increase their standard of living, even though they could not escape hierarchy through the exploitation of a set of circumstances that made the use of the military as a means of production.

In the Lozi cosmology the king, as we have seen, is identified with the earth. Bulozi is "the soil of the king." "The king is the land and the land is the king." This expresses the True Malozi recognition that the affluence they enjoy is due to the richness of the soil *and* the central organization which is able to exploit this benefit and convert it into greater wealth through the Makolo system. The Lozi have a straightforward understanding of their relation with the king, Gluckman says. "The king exists in his subjects and the subjects are nothing without the king." The kingship is seen as having been created by men. The relations of king and subject are based on exchange. The individual owes to the king the obligation to fight for him, work for him, and give him tribute. The king must provide protection, adjudicate disputes, and dispense land and goods from his own stock.

The imbalance in this relationship, which is made possible by the enormous power of the king, seems to have given rise to an ombudsman type institution called *ngambela*. Every level of administation had a Ngambela. At the top the king's Ngambela was a kind of "deputy," but his authority was independent of the king. The king was identified with the land; the Ngambela, with the people. The Ngambela was said to protect the nation against the king. The Ngambela could upbraid the king in private. He had to be a commoner who could not succeed to the throne. Yet the Ngambela was clearly subordinate to the king.

In short, then, the Lozi kingdom probably grew to a critical mass, as I. M. Lewis (1976) puts it, on the basis of the resources and opportunities open to it. It was a kingdom because of the nature of its method of producing wealth, and it was a large kingdom because of the good production possibilities it faced. However, since colonial times, production and elaboration have fallen because of the abolition of slavery, and the conquered people have shown increased desires for equality before the government. This reflects the Lozi's inability to utilize military means to exploit others. Furthermore, the penetration of the area by capitalist operations must further reduce the power of the king, making him more a figurehead than in the past, and it has caused people increasingly to move out of the plain to the margin. On the other hand, the dominance of the Zambian nation by Bemba to the east may have strengthened the monarchy, which serves, in manner parallel to the past, to unify Malozi and to protect them from exploitation by Bemba and others in seats of national power.

ACEPHALOUS SYSTEMS

My account to this point might have driven the reader to the conclusion that the conditions for the creation of states are so prevalent that any other type of overall organization is impossible. But, in fact there were acephalous societies, most notably in East Africa but also in parts of West Africa and elsewhere. Information on the exact political condition of all African societies is not available, but a good deal is known, as Murdock's *Ethnographic Atlas* (1967) attests. From this it is possible to estimate that 67 percent of African societies had hierarchical forms of one sort or another, the largest group consisting of petty chiefdoms; 32 percent were headless. As I explained earlier, it has been conventional to ignore such societies on the grounds that they are undeveloped and not worthy of much attention. It may be true that some of these societies, as in parts of Zaire, are simply very poor, unable even to generate petty chiefs. I also suggested that people who live in states, particularly those with some power, would have personal reasons for feeling negative toward types of societies in which it is not possible to obtain chiefly power. In fact, acephalous societies are not necessarily inferior but simply different, based on different economic processes.

This point is best illustrated in East Africa (Schneider 1979), the area whose headless societies are best known. East Africa can be divided into two major zones, the Agricultural Zone and the Pastoral Zone. The former is for the most part infested with the tsetse fly which prevents the raising of cattle in any significant numbers while the latter zone is free of the fly. Nearly without exception, the societies of the fly-free zone are headless, including some of the most famous in Africa: the Maasai, the Turkana, the Kikuyu, the Somali, the Borana Galla, and the Samburu. In all these societies, the ratio of cattle to people is one to one or better, a fact which I underscored in an earlier chapter. Thus cattle (and sometimes camels), in sufficiently high ratios, and under certain circumstances, such as open grazing or easy access to grazing, constitute a type of property from which states apparently cannot be developed whereas in the fly area states do arise. Before discussing in more detail the reason for this, we shall take some time to have a look at the general structure of relations among people in such societies.

Two aspects of these headless societies are especially prominent, the tendency to lineage localization in the form of segmentary lineage systems among some of them, and the importance of age grading in others.

Lineages and Agriculture

Those societies, such as the Turu, the Lugbara, and the Nuer, which employed the lineage principal in spatial organization and otherwise, seemed to do so because land and agricultural production continued to be important even though the ratio of cattle to people was high enough to turn them into acephalous societies. In Chapter 4, it will be remembered, it was pointed out that the segmentary principle of lineage construction was valuable for control and exploitation of land and that mobility, as among the high ratio acephalous societies in East Africa, works against it for the most part (the Somalis may be an exception). It was also pointed out that while lineage as an organizing principle is not incompatible with chieftainship, the presence of chiefs waters it down. For one thing, as we have seen, chiefs typically take control of the land and by allocating it according to considerations of clientship, must attack the unity of the lineage itself. Furthermore, a lineage is in a sense a system of rules for control and succession of land. Since a chief typically institutes laws or new rules, they must work counter to lineage to some degree. The fact is that the segmentary lineage system, as such, is an acephalous organization which begins to change shape and in some cases declines almost to invisibility when it competes with hierarchical processes. The segmentary lineage systems I discussed in Chapter 4 are all acephalous.

While agriculture continues to be important among these headless East African societies whose ratio of cattle to people is less than five to one,

An East African herdsman

segmentary lineage as an important organizing principle seems to be common only at the lowest levels, less than two to one. In such societies the number of cattle possessed is sufficient to create headlessness, but agricultural production is still economically very important.

Age Organization

Many of these headless societies depend heavily upon age grading in preference to lineage to organize relations. Probably all societies organize people according to age to one degree or another, but in some of these East African societies, age organization is vastly more developed into what are called age-set and generation-set systems. While not the most complex of the age systems, that of the Pokot will illustrate this point.

The Pokot have what is called a cyclical system, in contrast to the linear systems that are possessed by other East Africans, such as the Maasai. There are a series of age sets, in this case seven, which cycle through time. Figure 6.2 illustrates this system. At the time I lived with the Pokot in the early 1950s, membership in the *first* set was being filled whereas the second was completed as were all the sets ahead of it except for six and seven. They were empty because all previous members had died and new recruitment still had not begun. This meant, of course, that there were very few members of set five around since most had died, and the remainder were mostly very old.

While it is still recruiting, each set takes on new members each year over a period of about fourteen years through the rite of circumcision. If, in a certain year, a young man succeeds in persuading his father to let him go

FIGURE 6.2   Pokot cyclical age set system

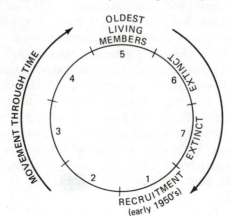

through the arduous rite, at its completion, he joins the set currently recruiting and can participate in its joint activities. These include the *kerket* feast in which an ox is ceremonially consumed; the feast can only be attended by circumcised men. Henceforth, wherever he may be at the time of kerket, he may participate even if all the other men participating are strangers, so long as he takes his proper place in the ceremonial setting with members of his own set.

These East African age-grading systems are further complicated by the existence, side-by-side, of two principles, age sets and generation sets, which may or may not coincide. The age-set principle groups men (women do not have sets) according to age. While literal age is seldom reckoned, boys of about the same age are put in the same sets, with the result that members of a junior set are young and those of a senior set are old men. Generation sets go by genealogical relations so that, for example, all men who are of the same generation, calculated from an apical ancestor, are in the same set and are therefore in a different set from men who are classified as their fathers. If we remember that one's first cousin, who is of one's own generation, may be much older than oneself, it will be immediately apparent that members of the same generation set can vary in age, sometimes enormously while, on the other hand, members of one's age set may include people who are classified as one's fathers or sons.

The Pokot system, like most in East Africa, in effect combines these principles by keeping men of about the same age in the same set but making sure that literal fathers and sons are in different sets. However, the Borana Galla do not. Their so-called *gada* system, which is probably the most complex in East Africa, has two different types of age groups that crosscut each other, generation-set groups and age-set groups. A man belongs to one of each of these groups simultaneously, a generation set composed of his generation equals, and an age set composed of his age equals.

In the most recent book on age organization in East Africa, Baxter and Almagor (1978) raise the question which always confronts students of age organization, why do they exist. These authors believe that they have existed and continue to do so where they have been the vehicles of rituals which the actors have continued to regard as important, that is, rituals which are "beneficial" to them. Goldschmidt (1976), with whom these authors dispute, voices the more generally accepted explanation, which is that they are a device that is highly adapted to the function of governance, the maintenance of order, and the protection of property in predominantly pastoral societies.

It seems to me that in a certain sense both of these explanations are true. However, we can get a better idea of the causes generating them and therefore an explanation for them, by examining more closely the economic basis of pastoral societies.

Kinsnip

Earlier I remarked that in southern and central Africa, Iroquois kinship terminology is typically associated with state systems, apparently because it is compatible with promoting clientship through marriage. In East Africa the distribution of types of kinship terminology between the Agricultural and Pastoral Zones also has implications for the relationship of economy and politics. In the poorer states, as in western Tanzania, Iroquois again is dominant. However, in the larger states of the Interlacustrine area and in the southwestern part of the Pastoral Zone, where cattle wealth is typically lower than in the more arid northeast, Omaha terminology dominates. Descriptive terminology is most common in the more nomadic part of the Pastoral Zone. In the last chapter, I spoke of how Omaha terminology is compatible with competition for mobile property. Also it is compatible with the continued importance of lineage and land. Hence, the explanation for the fact that Omaha terms crosscut the larger states and lower-ratio pastoral societies seems to be the presence in both of important amounts of mobile property (usually cattle in both the larger states and pastoral systems), even though the ratios in the states are low, connected with the importance of land and agriculture. In the more nomadic systems, where lineage has declined in importance and where cattle and camel wealth is very high, Descriptive terminology has emerged as compatible with systems almost entirely devoted to manipulation of capital and in which ad hoc business arrangements have superceded kinship as the basis for cooperation.

Egalitarian societies in East Africa, which is what these headless societies are, manage to provide certain basic organizing structures, whether lineage or age grade, which get certain organizational chores done, without resorting to chiefs and kings. They are not anarchies. However, they are also not so strictly ordered as chief-controlled societies. They are famous for the fact that their members are highly individualistic, even truculent, and for the fact that they scorn men who try to set themselves up as authorities. As observed earlier, they have less law or, to put it another way, they have only civil law. A man can be charged with violating the rules of exchange of livestock or for destroying or stealing another's property. In that case, a judgment may be rendered by respected men which may have the effect of forcing the guilty party to make restitution by paying a fine in livestock. However, enforcement depends very much on reaching a consensus, as in the Arusha illustration, and upon moral suasion from respected elders and age mates. Killing another person, to take the extreme case, is not seen as a crime against society but as an attack on property for which compensation must be paid. Hence blood money will be extracted from such a person; he will not be executed. (However, friends of the deceased may institute a feud and, in turn, kill him, but then they will have to pay a fine, too.) Order in these societies is based far more than in chief-controlled societies on the dynamic give-and-take of material self-interest. Powerful persons, big men as they are called in other parts of the world, exist, but they are big because they are successful operators for whom others have respect, not because they have authority.

The lineage-organized pastoral societies are less committed to age grading, although it may exist among them in simple forms. In these societies, the reciprocal obligations of kinship create the basis for order although as in the age-organized societies, it is an order based on negotation rather than rigid law, where each localized lineage is always prepared to fight others. In the more nomadic Pastoral Zone, age organization emerges, apparently as a functional substitute, crosscutting society, since each age set has members everywhere. It imposes upon members certain rights and obligations, resting on bonds of reciprocity, that make possible the pursuit of cattle wealth even among strangers. This is what Goldschmidt meant by his explanation for age sets. But, as Baxter and Almagor also claim, the age system lays the groundwork among its members for the creation of wealth, the emergence of stock associateship.

Pastoralists as Capitalists

Increasingly students of these egalitarian societies have tended to describe them as capitalists. The word capitalist has many interpretations and is emotionally loaded, but there is no better term so it will have to serve. When it is used in this context, the intended meaning is that these people are decision makers, free-wheeling entrepreneurs who are continuously involved in the manipulation of cattle, camels, women, and other forms of capital in order to increase their wealth. This is in contrast to the agriculturally oriented people who supposedly lead simpler lives. They have only to decide to apply their labor to the land each year and once having done so are committed to an inexorable process of planting, weeding, and harvesting, with little opportunity to respond to quickly changing conditions in order to profit. The pastoralist is seen as continuously involved in taking chances and is forced to do so, even if he does not want to do so. The agriculturalist (that is, the nonpastoralist agriculturalist) has little opportunity to do anything that will markedly increase his wealth. That is why he ends up committed to a chief; he finds his future in subordinating himself to a man of power, rather than in investing for a profit.

This meaning of pastoral capitalism is useful, since it contains a grain of truth. Economic historians have recognized that even in the growth of Western economies, land is the enemy of man, so to speak, for it is in short supply and is only capable of yielding returns through the sweat of the laborer's brow. Capitalist industrial economies often provide opportunity for profit and power because, unlike the land, opportunity for economic growth is less limited.

Although it is more difficult to understand, I propose a definition of capitalism which may be applied to these pastoralists and which takes more account of basic economic processes. A *capitalist* is one whose production activities involve, more importantly than labor, the manipulation of capital as the main means of increasing wealth. That these pastoral societies are capital- rather than labor-oriented has profound implications. The main one is simply that where labor is the primary constraint, possibilities for growth in wealth are limited to the few people who control the land, whereas where capital is the primary constraint, and where there is wide access to it, growth is more generally open. Certain conditions must prevail for this to be true. In East Africa in the past, the main ones were the unlimited number of cattle a man could own and the high rate of growth of the herds (Dahl and Hjort 1976), conditions which worked to make access to wealth widely available. However, since droughts appeared at regular intervals thereby reducing herd populations and offsetting growth, there was a check on the ecological effects of herd growth combined with a continual redistribution of cattle and camels due to the sale of cattle for grain. Nevertheless, this apparently did not impede incentives because individuals were always lucky enough, on occasion, to escape the effects of drought or cattle raids. In any case capitalist operators by their nature seem to be oriented toward short-term incentives. Ordinarily, a successful pastoralist could in a year expect to exceed in the growth of his wealth, the best that most farmers could do.

Pastoral Finance

To understand pastoral capitalism requires a grasp of the financial implications of high-growth, capital-oriented economics. These days we are used to ideas about inflation and deflation. Probably any reasonably educated person knows that inflation represents an increase in the supply of money (or means of buying things) over the supply of goods. With more and more money competing for the same amount of goods, or the amount of goods increasing more slowly than the money supply, the price of goods goes up. The educated person also understands the more difficult notion that for growth in production of goods to be stimulated, there must be some inflation. Producers will not put themselves out to produce goods, indeed cannot do so, unless there is enough money around to be had and to use for further production, to make it worthwhile. If the supply of money gets too low relative to the supply of goods, they will not produce goods for fear they cannot be sold. Thus governments have monetary policies designed to regulate the supply of money in order to keep production up. The Federal Reserve is responsible for this in the United States. In 1979 its head pronounced that an annual increase in the money supply of 3.4 percent was about right to maintain production without producing runaway inflation (a kind of violently self-destructive growth of money supply).

Elemental monetary principles are applicable to these African economies, too (Einzig 1966). Two things act to hold down the growth of the money supply in the Agricultural Zone and thus keep production down, while promoting hierarchy. The first is simply that the techniques of production and the kind of wealth made possible by the culture and environmental conditions are such that producing new money (cloth, crops, salt, or whatever) cannot keep up with the natural tendency for the currency supply to shrink, unless it is constantly replenished. Cloth wears out; salt deteriorates, even if not consumed; and shells are lost. It is costly in terms of labor inputs or in other terms to produce new money. Secondly, it is in the interest of chiefs to maintain what amounts to a monetary policy which keeps the supply of money down because if subordinates have too much wealth, they do not need the chief, a fact which chiefs clearly recognize at times. This can be done in many ways. Monopolizing the production of salt or increasing the amount of tribute demanded are two ways. A good illustration of how this works comes from MacGaffey's (1970) account of the Kongo kingdoms where he explains that at the death of a chief, it often happened that a large number of slaves were killed to accompany him. One suspects that the total supply of slaves was not so great that, whether the dead chief's successors realized it or not, this act had some impact on the money supply, since slaves were important media of exchange.

Cattle and camels are radically different from wealth produced in agricultural societies because they depend only on grass. Furthermore, they reproduce themselves with a minimum of human care, far less than is necessary to produce equivalent wealth in agricultural societies, and they are difficult for a small group to monopolize if grazing is common or easily accessible. Thus pastoral societies are basically inflationary and egalitarian whereas agricultural societies are basically deflationary and hierarchical.

Cattle as Repositories of Value

But my point cannot be fully comprehended unless we consider one other aspect of these economies stressed in Chapter 3. Most students of pastoralists are not economists and do not understand the economics of raising livestock for their own sake as repositories of value. Thus they conclude inappropriately that the reason for raising them is to provide subsistence. That they do provide various amounts of food—milk, meat, blood—cannot be disputed. However, recent studies of this subject (Dahl and Hjort 1976; Meyn 1970) also demonstrate conclusively what has been apparent to some outside observers for years (Herskovits 1926) and what is proclaimed by the people themselves, that they do not produce enough to feed the people. Agricultural products, particularly grains, are essential to all the pastoralists. Most would grow some grain if they could do so without interfering with the production of livestock. Thus trade between specialists in livestock production and agricultural production was universal.

This simple fact lays the basis for financial manipulation of livestock in the Pastoral Zone. The demand for these animals by agriculturalists and other pastoralists, not the value of the animals as food for the pastoralists, determines how the animals are handled. If the animals are husbanded to produce the maximum amount of milk or meat, they will be treated one way; if simply to produce the maximum number of animals, another. Also, as in Gresham's Law, where bad money drives out good, small, skinny animals come to be preferred over large, fat animals.

Stock Associateship

Where cattle are in great demand as repositories of value, where manipulation of herd structure is necessary to make the most of breeding potential, and where cattle are used to obtain wives as a valuable labor source, a special structural pattern is created. These conditions were not altogether lacking in the Agricultural Zone where there are some cattle, but they were pronounced and became the basis for egalitarianism in the Pastoral Zone. This is what Gulliver has called stock associateship, the intricate spread of crosscutting ties of joint ownership of cattle. It was mentioned in Chapter 3 in connection with the Pokot tilia system, Turu uriha, and Rwandese ubuhake. Each man during his lifetime makes contracts with other men for the exchange of values including cattle, especially female cattle. The use of the cow over a period of time is balanced by some value paid to the owner of the cow. This associateship could take many forms. In marriage, as we have seen, an equation was balanced in such a way that the cattle given for a bride balanced off the value of the bride, and the balance was continually reevaluated during the marriage and readjusted from time to time. Similarly, a man might give a heifer for a steer to slaughter but continue as part owner of the cow due to the fact that the cow is more valuable than the steer. His continuing ownership of the cow is manifest in the fact that he shares the future offspring of the cow with its new holder. Alternatively, a man might give a cow to another to hold for him because he has insufficient pasture or because his new associate has a reputation as an expert husbandman. In exchange, the associate gets some calves or the use of the cow's milk and manure. To name just one more example from innumerable possibilities, a man might borrow a heifer from another in return for a steer and continuing rights in some of the calves of the heifer so that the borrower can restructure his herd to more efficiently exploit its production potential.

We have seen that in agricultural societies, because of the scarcity of mobile wealth and the lack of inflation of wealth, people are forced into patron-client relationships. In the Pastoral Zone, the prevalence of livestock leads instead to the appearance of widespread ties of associateship, each man becoming the focal point of a network of relations spreading out from his community to his whole ethnic group or beyond. People are interlocked directly and indirectly and this provides the basis for countering monopolistic forces. The richer the man, the wider his network. For the poorer people the advantage lies in the fact that the rich need them to maintain their positions, even if only to lend animals to them in order take the pressure off their own grazing resources. In the low-ratio cattle areas, stock associateship is an important alternative to kinship ties while in the high-ratio areas, associateship becomes almost the entire basis for interaction. Affines even become business associateships in societies like the Turkana.

Thus there developed in East Africa an economic world no less esoteric than ours in the West, where gold is the key, and where production of goods for use or to get gold or its equivalent, is the driving force behind the economy.

Equalitarianism in association with pastoralism is a phenomenon that has been recognized in other parts of the world, such as among the Middle East Bedouins or even among Plains Indians where it occurs in conjunction with horse raising. It also occurs in other circumstances than production of livestock. One of the most famous areas of big-men systems is Melanesia in the South Pacific. In Africa, East Africa is the area where it occurs most prominently. Its rarity elsewhere suggests the difficulty associated with establishing an economy that can produce it. It seems to be generally true that Africans, like ourselves, prefer egalitarian systems if they can have them (excepting, of course, the royalty and aristocrats who have control of the agricultural systems).

Nonpastoral Acephalous Societies

Outside of East Africa, a prominent site of headless societies is one which cuts West Africa into two parts and which is located in northern Ghana. Otherwise, acephalous societies are scattered and their economics poorly understood, compared to East Africa. A prominent example of an isolated headless system is that of the Tiv of Nigeria, along the banks of the Benue River. Numbering nearly a million people, they are not a small group. Tiv society was character- ized by very dynamic competition among big men whose power and influence was markedly associated with dynamic markets (P. Bohannan and L. Bohan- nan 1968, 189). One may speculate that for some reason, land was not in short supply in Tiv country, and that it was also highly productive of rice, cassava, bulrush millet, and other products. In fact, the Tiv were famous in the last century for the production of cotton and, from that, of cloth money. Thus the Tiv economy seems to have provided the basis for large profits for individual entrepreneurs who traded with others, including foreigners, and laid the basis for an egalitarian system. Why the big men were unable to gain control of the marketplaces and land and so convert their positions into chieftainships is not clear. The Ibo people parallel the Tiv in many ways. The special entre- preneurial, capitalistic character of the Ibo produced big men also.

The two other areas of Africa best noted for cattle are southern Africa and the Western Sudan. That cattle don't always promote headless societies, even where there are high ratios of cattle to people, is well illustrated in the southern African case, although they seem to have accomplished this with the Ila of Zambia (Fielder 1973). However, there is no reason, under the right conditions, why cattle, like other goods, cannot be monopolized by a few and so serve as the basis for authority, as in the case where grasslands come under individual control. The reason for this development in South Africa is still not understood and is the basis for speculation among students of that area.

In the Western Sudan, headless societies also are not common, despite the presence of cattle in the savannah region. For some reason, the ratios of cattle to people seem too small to accomplish statelessness. The exception is the pastoral Fulani, as Stenning (1959) calls them. Fulani are often thought of as predominantly pastoralists, the pastoral conquerors of the Hausa and other Western Sudanic societies among whom they are scattered. Only a few continue to be real pastoralists in the sense in which I have defined the term. Small populations exist in the Senegal-Gambia region, in Chad, and the north- ern reaches of the Sahel in general, in the Jos Plateau and the Adamawa Highlands of Nigeria. These pastoral Fulani appear to manifest many of the features of East African pastoralists. Leaders are selected by acclamation, and individual households are highly independent. They are antiauthoritarian, dealing with each other through "economic reciprocity."

Recent evidence suggests that the Kru people of Liberia and the Ivory Coast (Massing 1977) are stateless, in part, because they were heavily engaged in seamanship. This outlet for entrepreneurial activity generated the opportu- nity to accumulate wealth that countered chieftainship. It is a common feature of so-called "developing" areas of West Africa today, as we saw in Bledsoe's account of independence among modern women traders in West Africa, that as opportunities to obtain mobile wealth appear, so does decline of authority.

CONCLUSION

Despite the fact that we in America have no kings or chiefs, our history is full of them and so, apparently, we have always been better able to visualize African kingdoms than acephalous societies. We think we understand societies in which it makes sense to say "take me to your leader." Stateless societies are another story. Students of such a society have a difficult time getting on the inside (literally as well as analytically). In a chiefdom, they simply go to the leader and if he gets on with them, they get the sanction to study the society and a well-defined system of organization.

Ethnographers going into a headless society find only a maze. No one is in charge, and anyone they stop to talk to is suspicious of their reasons for doing so. They see people going about their business in a reasonably orderly way (although all the men seem to be armed with some kind of weapon), but they see no one directing activity. They wander through the community looking for authorities, but all the houses are the same. They are driven to conclude, as was Evans-Pritchard of the Nuer, that what they are witnessing is ordered anarchy. I hope that in this chapter, I have been able to convey to the reader my belief that this apparent formlessness is the manifestation of a kind of economic process (in fact similar to our own) in which high economic growth works against political centralization.

RELIGION AND PHILOSOPHY: THE GREAT TRADITIONS AND MODELING

THERE WAS A TIME not too long ago when ethnographers felt that Africans had no systematized beliefs about the nature of the world so there was no point in looking for such beliefs. This seemingly patronizing view had a certain logic to it. When we consider the amount of specialization which goes into complex modes of thought in our Western society—great universities devoted specifically to the subject—it seems reasonable to think that people like our Africans, with much simpler production and economic systems, would have less resources to devote to such pursuits, even if they should desire or need to indulge them.

COMPLEXITY OF AFRICAN BELIEFS

We now know that this presumption is false. While there may be great variations in the degree of elaboration, such as the variable cosmologies developed by the priests of the Fon cults of Dahomey, even the seemingly least complex African people sometimes have surprisingly sophisticated notions about a lot of things. Often their ideas are not codified the way we codify them in books, but that they exist is implied in actions and concepts. For example, until Placide Tempels wrote his book *Bantu Philosophy* (1959) many people thought that African notions of witchcraft were disorganized superstitions (that is to say, irrational). Temples' achievement was to show the systematic thought behind such views, derived from Bantu concepts of reality.

Why then have the existence of African belief systems been denied or ignored by ethnographers? American and British ethnographers have been most interested in social processes. They have paid a lot of attention to such things as structure of the family, kinship terminology, lineage structure, and much less attention to thought processes. There are important exceptions to this generalization. For example Evans-Pritchard's classic study of Azande sorcery and witchcraft (Evans-Pritchard 1950) was concerned with the logic of these beliefs, and Turner's famous studies of Ndembu systems of classification (Turner 1961, 1967, 1968, 1969) did not follow the trend. However, the fact remains that these men, important and famous as their work was, did not represent the main trend.

Furthermore, many ethnographers were affected by the views of Marx and certain other social philosophers who established the idea in the minds of researchers that the chief causal element in society is production and economics. As Marx's scheme was interpreted, for example, the means of production (the methods of production and the property relations) determined the social superstructure which in turn determined thought. What you are economically and socially determines what you think. This being the case, it would be natural to concentrate first on means of production and leave religion and philosophy to the last, or ignore it.

A further reason for neglect of philosophy is the especially intimate knowledge of a people which is necessary to acquire in this subject. While most anthropologists learn the language of the people they study with some degree of competence, understanding religion and philosophy requires the greatest control of language and very extended fieldwork. When failure to acquire deep linguistic competence is combined with lack of central interest in philosophy the subject is likely to be relatively neglected.

What I have said applies more to the British and Americans than to the other great group of ethnographers, the French. The British approach to the study of African thought has been empirical, focusing on facts while resisting attempts, like Temples', to leap to very systematic conclusions. On the other hand the French, like Levi-Strauss, whose structuralist technique finds human beings very systematic in their use of classifications, formalize, some British would say overformalize (Richards 1967). Probably the most famous example of this is the book by Marcel Griaule, in its English translation called *Conversations with Ogotemmeli* (1965). This "introduction" to Dogon religious ideas is 223 pages long with 33 chapters, each developing some new aspect of Dogon thought. The ideas were conveyed to Griaule by Ogotemmeli, a blind man of great renown in his country who chose to give Griaule a full account of Dogon cosmology. This is remarkable enough, but Griaule points out when he has completed his account that what Ogotemmeli was in fact doing was explaining the rationale of the signs of the zodiac. His explanation apparently predates the historical appearance of the zodiac in the West and hence constitutes a more ancient explanation than the one developed in the West which relates it to the motions of the planets. The British seem to find such explanations too good to be true. Do the French oversystematize while the British undersystematize? The answer is probably yes. On balance, however, I tend to side with the French and feel that the British and Americans have generally understated the orderliness and complexity of African philosophy.

CULTURAL AND NATURAL ELEMENTS

Before we turn to look at African systems of thought, there is a matter which was adumbrated in the first chapter which it would be well to underscore here. In preceding chapters it was sufficient to maintain that observed behavior could be explained for the most part by resort to the concept of society or the concept of culture. Behavior was either explained as a kind of exchange interaction between people or as an accident, invention, or transmission. When we get into the subject of modes of thought, a seeming paradox arises. That aspect of human behavior which seems most human, philosophy and religion, is in important respects most obviously a reflex of our nature as animals. For example, apparently all Africans, just like ourselves, create binary classifications of opposites, like man-woman or sun-moon. That Americans associate the right hand with goodness in some way and the left with evil makes us identical with Africans, who do the same. Such similarities, I noted, are difficult to explain in terms of culture alone and, as in some current sociobiological theories, seem to a degree to represent a natural manifestation of behavior. As Levi-Strauss (1962) has claimed, all human beings seem to have the ability to classify and model reality (that is, build a theoretical picture of it) although different people show great variability in certain aspects of this process, such as their beliefs about how creation was accomplished or what things belong on the right hand or on the left.

THE GREAT TRADITIONS

In African thought, as in that of other historic people we know, cultural variability in religion and philosophy seems most apparent in what Marriott (1955, 171) has called great traditions. Whole groups of societies follow to one degree or another a great tradition of Christianity, and others, Islam, Hinduism, or Buddhism. Interestingly, there is a strong tendency for these great traditions to follow along the lines of linguistic divisions. Christians are Indo-European speakers (and within that group, the Romance speakers are generally Catholics, and the Germanic speakers, generally Protestants). Islam is nearly universal among the Arabs, and Hinduism, among East Indians. However religious traditions do not follow language lines exactly: Poles, who are slavs, are Catholics; Indonesians are often Islamic; and Buddhism extends outside India to other southeast Asian people.

In Africa also there appear to be great traditions: the Bantu Tradition and the Nilotic Tradition, in addition to the Coptic Christian Tradition of the Amhara of Ethiopia and the Islamic Tradition of the Somalis. Not nearly as much is known about the Bantu and Nilotic Traditions as about the other great traditions but it can no longer be doubted that they exist. As in Europe and Asia, these traditions follow closely, but not exactly, along language lines. For example, while the Abyssinian Amhara and the Tigre of highland Ethiopia are Coptic Christians, the type of Christianity once practiced by all Egyptians before the rise of Islam, these Ethiopians speak a Semitic language, related to Hebrew. Of course, it might be argued that this is not a contradiction since before Islam, it could be said of Arabic and perhaps non-Jewish Semitic speakers that as Christians, they still were a special type, Coptic.

Another, perhaps better, example, is found in western Kenya where it appears that the Bantu Abaluyia have taken important ideas from the Nilotic tradition, as I will demonstrate. In the Western Sudan, as a result of strong Arab incursions over the last thousand years, Islam is the religion of many West Africans who presumably at one time had beliefs more like those still held by the West Africans in the tropical rain forest, nearer the coast.

The Coptic and Islamic Traditions

For our introduction to African thought, let us begin then with a look at some elements in these great traditions. We will start with the better-known ones,

Coptic Christianity and Islam. These will be followed by the traditions of Congo-Kordofanian speakers and finally the Nilotic traditions. In certain respects, Islam and Coptic Christianity can be treated together because both are variants of Middle Eastern religions, just as the language of Abyssinia, the seat of the Coptic faith, is Semitic while the languages of surrounding people and those to the north are Cushitic, both varieties of Afro-Asiatic. In fact, this evokes an interesting point relative to the previously posed question of what an African is. I explained that there is no exact dividing point between Africa north and south of the Sahara, but as one gets into the area of Ethiopia, certainly the Oromo (Galla) and Somali regions, few would dispute that we are dealing with Africans, people who in some sense are different from Mediterranean people. What makes them different, in good part, as we have seen, is the economics and production of these areas. Africans do not use plows (at least they did not in the past), and they have the "cattle complex," just to name two important elements. Also we have seen that many of these Africans speak

A Model of a Coptic Church, Ethiopia

Afro-Asiatic languages, the language of the whole southern Mediterranean coast and of all the Middle East.

The fact is that below about the latitude of Khartoum people, Africans whether they speak one of the great African languages or Afro-Asiatic, shift the form of their economies and with it, to a great extent, their social structures although their great religious traditions may be Mediterranean and Middle Eastern. Thus, for example, the Somalis are Moslems as are many of the people of the Western Sudan. The Ethiopians, or to be more specific, the Abyssinians, are apparently an exception. The Coptic Christianity they espouse derives from Old Egypt (Davis 1973) and in fact is continuous with the pre-Islamic Egyptian church. In the seventh century, Islam conquered Egypt and excluded Coptics from the main centers of society. This led eventually, for all practical purposes, to the demise of the Coptic Church in Egypt and left the Abyssinian Coptics isolated. Unlike the Somalis, however, the economy and social structure of Abyssinia is more like that of the Mediterranean, for example in the use of the plow. The Abyssinians are essentially Mediterranean people while the Somalis and Galla are Africans, despite their Islamic faith (not all Gallas are Moslems, however).

Even to a specialist in Christian theology and liturgy, the Coptic Church is not very different from the kind of Christianity practiced in the Catholic and Orthodox churches of the West. The Copts are monophysites, holding to a view of the nature of Jesus different from the one that emerged victorious in the Latin and Byzantine churches, but they possess essentially the same sacraments or basic ceremonials and rites of passage. The structure of the church is a complex hierarchy with an archbishop of the Ethiopian branch under the Patriarch of Cairo (a kind of Pope). Under the archbishop are chief priests, the most senior of whom (like Orthodox priests) do not marry, in contrast to the Roman Church where none are allowed to marry. In addition, there are other lesser officials under these priests to perform less and less critical functions.

In a certain sense it may be said of Christianity, at least the Mediterranean and Coptic branches, that they are forms of religion suited to very hierarchical societies. In contrast, Islam is much more egalitarian. There are no priests, bishops, and the like, and people have a direct relationship with Allah. This fact, however, poses a peculiar paradox. Strong central leadership is not foreign to Islam. Caliphs, sultans, and emirs abound in many parts of Islamic Africa as well as in the Mediterranean. In a sense the egalitarianism of Islam may be attributed to the long preservation in that religion of certain principles which always characterize new, revitalized faiths, of which egalitarianism is one. Why should it have been preserved in Islam while it disappeared from Christianity (except where it reemerged during the Reformation in Europe with the rise of Protestantism)?

Perhaps the answer resides in the fact that, much more than in Christianity, the people over whom Islam flowed, at least in the Mediterranean and Middle East, and including the Somalis, very often had livestock-oriented economics (camels more than cattle) and were egalitarian. To such people, Islam would be a more satisfying creed than hierarchical Christianity of either the Roman, Orthodox, or Coptic variety.

A word should also be said about pre-Islamic creeds which existed in Africa among Cushitic-speaking people. In fact these are not all gone. The religion of many Oromo is neither Islamic nor Coptic. However, as one might expect, it contains elements which are similar to these creeds, just as Christianity itself has similarities to Judaism and pre-Christian creeds in Europe.

West African Traditions

The great traditions of the Bantu and Nilotes have many important differences, greater in fact, it would seem, than the differences between Christianity and Islam. Both are clearly removed from the latter, except for the fact that there may have been some borrowing of elements of a general kind of Middle Eastern set of beliefs, such as washing sins in the blood of sheep, which caused some early scholars to designate the Eastern Nilotes as Half-Hamites or, as we might say today, semi-Afro-Asiatics. Within these great African traditions, it seems necessary to distinguish the Western Sudanic and tropical West Africans from the Bantu, despite their common membership in the Congo-Kordofanian language groups, for example, because of such things as the special emphasis the West Africans place on fate in their beliefs. Turner feels this may be due to the fact that West Africans are more sedentary than are Central Africans. The West Africans may have had the opportunity to sit and speculate about cosmology and develop more complex systems of belief while the Central Africans, due to their dependence on chitemene agriculture in a rather hostile environment, have had to move around much more, composing and decomposing social groups. Perhaps, also, the difference reflects differing degrees of stratification; the West African system is affected more by the growing complexity of hierarchical societies.

Many scholars have remarked that there is an isomorphism in the beliefs of certain West Africans, like the Yoruba, the Dogon, far off to the northwest in Upper Volta, and the Mediterranean people. For instance, like the classic Greeks, the Dogon believe that the essential parts of matter are earth, air, fire, and water. Moreover, the Yoruba have a high God, Oloran, under whom is a pantheon composed of innumerable subdeities, of which one prominent one is Shango, the god of thunder. Among these subdeities is Elegba, the so-called trickster, or messenger god, like Mercury in the Greek pantheon, who delivers to people the fates decreed for them by God.

Elegba (or Eshu as others know him) brings us back to the element of fate. Yoruba beliefs about deities and about the nature of evil and goodness have been described by Bascom (1969) and are far too complex to detail here. Nevertheless, it is useful to take notice of their view of fate, or destiny, as it relates to beliefs in deities to get some feeling for the complexity and nature of their cosmology. Ifa is the god of divination, who translates the wishes of Oloran and the other deities like Shango, to man, through Eshu. He is the "scholar" god, closest to Oloran. What he has in store for humans can be divined through the complicated system of Ifa divination by which specialists, casting palm kernels, can discern one of 256 possible sets of verses which, when recited, give the client the needed clues, as in a horoscope. Technically each individual's fate is foreordained but by praying to Eshu, which all Yoruba do whatever other deities they may follow, people attempt to get him to alter fate and thus preserve them from a bad fate. Thus, oversimplifying, Yoruba express through their set of beliefs and the actions based on them, their perception of the existence of good and evil in the world, a world in which they would like only good for themselves. They strive to do what is right, but through the complexities of the nature of the cosmos, bad fates may occur. Contrasting the Yoruba with the Bantu, when a wall falls on you, it may simply be Eshu who is responsible, acting unpredictably. To the Bantu, the action must be due to evil intent by another human being, a witch, controlling supernatural forces. To anticipate, for the Bantu, the forces of the universe as they relate to good and evil are much more embedded in ideas about human malintention than they are for the Yoruba. The Yoruba also believe in witches and they also ascribe some evil at least to distant, somewhat impersonal forces, perhaps because the Yoruba are much more subject in social life to highly bureaucratized, urbanized impersonal political forces.

Notions of fate do not depend only on this, any more than they do in Western thought where we relegate them to the category of accident. Fate is also important to the belief system of the Tallensi of northern Ghana, who perceive it as a manifestation of complex and impersonal forces working within kinship groups. Meyer Fortes (1960) compares Tallensi notions of fate to Oedipus in Greek mythology and contrasts them to their ideas about predictable order, which he compares to the relationship of Job and God in the Old Testament. Oedipus is a man who, despite all attempts to avoid such behavior, finds himself inexorably led to kill his father and marry his mother, both unspeakable acts. In other words, there are forces which lead us in unpredictable, unavoidable, sometimes immoral directions, despite our wishes to avoid them. Job is a saintly man, pictured as sitting among the ruins of his prosperity, railing against God because he has been so unjustly rewarded. That is to say, the Jobian view of life is one in which the future can be controlled by making exchanges with God. In Tallensi life, relations among patrilineal kin are Jobian, and this order is expressed in the ancestor cult, in which the relations among members of the family, which are ordered and predictable, at least most of the time, are transposed to the religious plane. However, relations between brothers and between fathers and sons have inevitable elements of friction, and it is this, the Oedipal element in life, which works contrary to the predictable. In the ancestral cult, it is symbolized by the fact that each man has his own specific set of ancestors who are his guardians and who are responsible for his particular life cycle (Fortes 1960, 32).

> One lives according to one's mundane lights, guided by the jural and moral sanctions of society, knowing that the ancestors dispense justice by their own standards and that one cannot please all of them at the same time.

However, like the Yoruba, a man is not condemned by his fate, for by honoring his ancestors, he can counter this unpredictable element and restore order and goodness to life. Thus the Tallensi, like so many other people faced with disorder in the world, bring it under control through religion.

West African thought has much more to it than notions of fate and pantheons of deities. Earlier I mentioned Ogotemmeli and his view of the zodiac. Turner (1973) has tried to summarize the system of beliefs that Ogotemmeli expounded. Quoting extensively from what he says, we may obtain a rare example of a view of a West African cosmological system:

> Among the Dogon ... a symbol becomes a fixed point of linkage between animal, vegetable, and mineral kingdoms, which are themselves regarded as parts of (a gigantic human organism). The doctrine of correspondence reigns—everything is a symbol of everything else, whether in a ritual context or not. Thus Dogon establish a correspondence between the different categories of minerals and the organs of the body. The various soils in the area are conceived of as the organs of the "interior of the stomach," rocks are regarded as the bones of the skeleton, and various hues of red clay are likened to the blood. Sometimes these correspondences are remarkably precise: one rock resting on another represents the chest; little white river pebbles stand for the toes of the feet. The same ... principles hold true for the relationship between man and the vegetable kingdom. Man is not only the grain of the universe, but each distinct part of a single grain represents part of the human body ... The Dogon further conceive of a subtle and finely wrought interplay between speech and the components of personality. The body constitutes a magnet or focus for man's spiritual principles, which nevertheless are capable of sustaining an independent existence. The Dogon contrast visible and invisible ("spiritual") components of the human personality. The body is made up of four elements: water (the body and bodily fluids), earth (the skeleton), air (breath), and fire (animal warmth). There is a continuous interchange between these internal expressions of the elements and their external aspects. The body has 22 parts: feet, shins, thighs, lumbar region, stomach, chest, arms, neck, and head make up nine parts

(it would seem that Dogon reckon double parts, as they do twins, as a unit); the fingers (each counting as a unit), make up ten parts; and the male genitals make up three parts. Further numerical symbolism is involved: there are believed to be eight symbolic grains—representing the principal cereal crops of the region—lodged in the collarbones of each Dogon. These grains represent the mystical bond between man and his crops. The *body* of speech itself is, like the human body, composed of four elements: water is saliva, without which speech is dry; air gives rise to sound vibrations; earth gives speech its weight and significance; and fire gives speech its warmth. There is not only homology between personality and speech, but also a sort of functional interdependence, for words are selected by the brain, stir up the liver, and rise as steam from the lungs to the clavicles, which decide ultimately whether the speech is to emerge from the mouth. To the 22 parts of the personality must be added the 48 types of speech, which are divided into two sets of 24. Each set is under the sign of a supernatural being, one of the androgynous twins Nommo and Yourougou ... The twins are the creations of Amma. Yourougou rebelled against Amma and had sexual relations with his mother—he was punished by being changed into a pale fox. Nommo saved the world by an act of self-sacrifice, brought humans, animals, and plants to the earth, and became the lord of speech. Nommo's speech is human and can be heard; the fox's is silent, a sign language made by his paw marks, and only diviners can interpret it. These myths provide a classification and taxonomy of cosmos and society; explain many details of ritual, including the forms and color symbolism of elaborate masks; and, indeed, determine where and how houses are constructed.

The Dogon are here modeling the world, a practice which we all indulge in, and about which I will speak further shortly. The existence of such a complex representation of the beliefs of one African people gives strong support to the point made earlier, that African modeling may not all be subconscious. It is true that in a sense this representation of Dogon beliefs derives from Ogotemmeli, a specialist, and would not be possible for all Dogon, although all would understand the truth of what he says, allowing for the fact that Ogotemmeli has probably put his personal mark on the exposition.

Bantu Tradition

In Bantu thought (Tempels 1959, Beck 1974) God, unlike the Creator in Nilotic religion, in Christianity, or in Islam, who created all things, is generally removed from men. There are no cults of God or his subdeities, only cults of the ancestors. Nevertheless, God is not indifferent to the human condition. He is benevolent, having arranged the universe so that good and justice are dominant, although He also allows evil to play itself out. God is not responsible for evil; man is. However, he passes no moral judgment on the acts of men because although men may act evil, in the end good will triumph. The effect of all this is to allow to men the maximum influence in planning their lives.

The elements of the universe are arranged in a hierarchy with the Creator at the top, followed by the founders of the clans (or the founder of a tribe whose sons are the founders of the clans), below whom are the specific ancestors of a clan. These are followed by living human beings, after which come animals (who may be arranged in degrees of power), and finally, the inanimate and animate mineral and vegetable parts of the universe. This hierarchy reflects varying degrees of power, or what Tempels calls "vital force" which is available to the entities. A man has greater vital force than an animal. For a man, the central motivation in life is to maintain and increase his vital force or, on the other hand, to prevent it from being diminished. The greatest evil, in human eyes, is for someone to attempt to reduce the vital force of another, an act which if attempted by another living being is witchcraft. If attempted by a dead ancestor, it is not evil, but punishment. Ancestors reduce the vital force of their descendants to punish them for inattention; another living being has no such rights.

In contrast to West Africans, then, when misfortune afflicts a man it is never due to fate but always to the machinations of another person who attempts to increase his vital force at the expense of the victim. However, as suggested above, the world of beings who are interacting this way consists not only of the living, but also of the dead, proximate ancestors. In Turu belief, for instance, the tendency for an ancestor to interfere in the lives of his descendants declines with distance. This means that when a man or woman is afflicted, they look either to a proximal ancestor—father, mother, grandparents, or great-grandparents—or to a living person. Which of these is the cause is determined by visiting a diviner who, at least in the Turu case, gets applicants to project their suspicions of who is the perpetrator. This determines the subsequent course of action: to accuse someone of witchcraft or to sacrifice to an ancestor.

A man can increase his vital force in several ways. The most direct method is working to increase his wealth and standing in society and drawing upon the vital force of his ancestors by seeking their help. As can be imagined, this latter is a metaphor for seeking a coalition with living people, symbolized in joint honoring of the ancestor through the ancestor cult. The most common way that a man's force is decreased is by not honoring the ancestors and by being challenged by another person, the challenge being manifested in accusations of witchcraft. To a Bantu, nothing happens by accident. Even if a man seemingly injures himself, as by falling out of a tree, he immediately suspects either an ancestor or another person as being the ultimate cause. The logic he uses, as Gluckman once pointed out, is this: he knows that gravity is the agent of his injury if he falls out of a tree, but not everyone falls out of a tree so he asks why this happened to him and not to someone else. Science can determine cause and effect relations (and all men employ logic to explain cause and effect), but science cannot say why an effect should happen to any particular person. In Bantu thought, even death would not occur except through the negative utilization of vital force.

Thus, when West Africans sometimes explain the existence of uncontrolled, antistructured forces as manifestations of disorder in the universe (fate) and counteract it through the use of the ancestor cult and the cult of the trickster deity, the Bantu, according to Tempels, live in a universe of free will in which the manifestation of disorder is explained through evil manipulation of vital force.

Nilotic Tradition

In Nilotic philosophy we see yet another configuration. Divinity is less anthropomorphic than in Bantu religion (where, in a sense, it is identified with the ancestors) and less substantive. Whether the Dinka *nhialic,* the Nuer *kwoth,* or the Pokot *tororut,* it is a formless wind or spirit. Associated with it are subforces represented in natural phenomena, such as the sun of the Ingassana or the rain of the Pokot. Evans-Pritchard says of the Nuer Kwoth (1960, 69):

> God is everywhere; he is permanent and changeless in his relations to the constant elements in the natural and moral orders; he is one, and he is all-powerful, just, and compassionate. The spirits of the air are in particular persons and places, and even when their prophets are politically important persons, they have a limited spread of influence; they have fallen from the clouds in recent times and their renown depends on the personal prestige of their prophets and on political circumstances, both of which are unstable factors and may be ephemeral . . .

The Nilotic God takes a direct interest in human affairs, and people pray directly to him, as Nuer do when, associating Kwoth with the sky, they look up to the sky while praying, or as Pokot do in the Kerket when they call upon Tororut to help them. Where in Bantu sacrifice, the prayers are addressed to a proximal ancestor, the Nilotes sacrifice an animal directly to God; they offer it as a substitute for human beings who would otherwise be the victims.

It also seems to be a part of the Nilotic tradition to expand enormously concepts of cleanliness and uncleanliness as an explanation for evil, in contrast to Bantu ideas of fiddling with vital forces. The best study of this is to be found in the writings of Gunter Wagner (1954) on the Abaluyia Bantu of eastern Kenya. They seem to have been affected in their beliefs by association with the surrounding Nilotes. They hold that God not only created the world and man but also established things in a way proper and essential to the survival of man. He provided men with women so they might multiply, air to breathe, the sun for warmth, the moon to light up the night, water to drink, plants and animals to eat, and so forth. He did not create the evil things of the world, the disruptive forces that interfere with man's happiness. However, God can alter such disruptive forces so people pray directly to him to do so. All actions or occurrences which deviate from this normal order are evil (*luswa* for humans and *kiragi* for animals). Such abnormalities cover a wide range of things. For instance, an infant who cuts its upper teeth first is luswa, as is a small child who cries excessively without reason, a circumcised person who rides an ox or cow (that is to say, an adult who acts like a child), a woman who climbs on the roof of a house (men are roofers and so the roof is their exclusive territory), incest, a man viewing a widow or his mother-in-law without clothes, indecent behavior by a person in the presence of another of the opposite sex, a beard on a woman's chin, homosexuality, a cow twisting its tail around the trunk of a tree, a bull attempting to mount a human being, or the birth of twins. In addition to these, there are certain occurrences which, while normal in one sense of the word, are viewed as fraught with danger. They are in some sense contrary to proper order and therefore ritually dangerous and unclean, such as a woman who has given birth, a warrior who has killed an enemy, or a widow, conditions associated with death or with a fundamental transitional period of life. Similarly, witches are unclean because they perform acts which are unclean, killing or harming others.

The Pokot, whose ideas on this subject are very close to the Abaluyia, even conceive of a superclean person, one who is supernormal in his or her behavior, principally in having avoided association with evil (or nearly so, since no one can avoid it altogether). One example might be a woman none of whose children have ever died. Such people have a special status in rituals.

In contrast with Bantu philosophy, animal sacrifices are not undertaken to placate ancestors but to promote cleanliness and pure ritual status, to cure uncleanliness or to maintain cleanliness. While such sacrifices are symbolically complex, an important component is the use of animal blood to cleanse, sometimes by sprinkling it on the victim. In one such rite which I witnessed among the Pokot, a young man and a woman accused of adultery were seated under a tree. From a branch hung a sheep whose throat was cut to allow the blood to flow over them, thus washing them in the blood of the lamb, so to speak. This idea is also familiar in the Middle East and in Christian theology, from which, perhaps, some of these Nilotic ideas came (or vice versa). Symbols which occur in many of these rites include the color white, associated with the Creator, the right hand of anything (for example, a strip of the hide of the sacred animal sacrificed is tied to the right wrist), honey, the early morning, virginity, flowing water, and certain wild plants, all symbolizing purity and cleanliness.

Even this superficial survey of elements of Nilotic philosophy shows how divergent it is from the Bantu in such things as the conception of the relation of God to man (close rather than distant) and the relation of men to their ancestors (distant rather than close). While this survey is only suggestive, since we cannot yet be very sure about the composition of the various great traditions, it helps support the hypothesis that such great traditions exist in Africa as well as in the other areas of the world.

ENCOUNTER WITH A RAINMAKER

The various great traditions which we have been inspecting may be said to represent a human need to understand the nature of the forces which rule the universe. Each group of people seem to generate somewhat different, historically determined, ways of doing this. But, even so, to some degree at least, the cosmology is also related to society. While not all Moslems are pastoralists, many are, and their conception of the nature of the world and of God leans toward egalitarianism. Bantu people tend overwhelmingly to depend on the principle of lineage as the basis of social organization, and so their God is closely related to ancestors, He *is* an ancestor in a sense.

On the other hand, there is a degree to which the great tradition serves its purpose by not being too closely related to any specific type of social system otherwise the tradition would come under attack every time a radical reformation occurred in social structure. Thus, when we look for beliefs that are not so constrained, which are amenable to close conjunction with social structure and specific environmental and economic problems, we turn to the seemingly more naturally founded sets of beliefs, particularly binary classifications, associated with rituals and symbol systems, witchcraft, and sacrifice.

But before doing this, we shall inspect some current views among those who have written about African religion as the modeling of or theorizing about the universe which provide the basis for action. As an introduction, it will be useful to review a famous meeting between the explorer David Livingstone and a Tswana rainmaker (Livingstone 1857):

> Livingstone: Hail, friend! How very many medicines you have about you this morning! Why, you have every medicine in the country here.
>
> Rainmaker: Very true, my friend; and I ought; for the whole country needs the rain which I am making.
>
> L.: So you really believe that you can command the clouds? I think that can be done by God alone.

A coat of arms of the modern state of Botswana, featuring the moto *Pula,* meaning "rain"

R.: We both believe the very same thing. It is God that makes the rain, but I pray to him by means of these medicines, and the rain coming, of course it is then mine. It was I who made it for the Bakwains for many years, when they were at Shokuane; through my wisdom, too, their women became fat and shining. Ask them; they will tell you the same as I do.

L.: But we are distinctly told in the parting words of our Saviour that we can pray to God acceptably in His name alone, and not by means of medicines.

R.: Truly! but God told *us* differently. He made black men first, and did not love us, as he did the white men. He made you beautiful, and gave you clothing, and guns, and gunpowder, and horses, and wagons, and many other things about which we know nothing. But towards us he had no heart. He gave us nothing, except the assegai (spear), and cattle, and rainmaking; and he did not give us hearts like yours. We never love each other. Other tribes place medicines about our country to prevent the rain, so that we may be dispersed by hunger, and go to them, and augment their power. We must dissolve their charms by our medicines. God has given us one little thing, which you know nothing of. He has given us the knowledge of certain medicines by which we can make rain. *We* do not despise those things which you possess, though we are ignorant of them. We don't understand your book, but we don't despise it. *You* ought not to despise our little knowledge, though you are ignorant of it.

L.: I don't despise what I am ignorant of; I only think you are mistaken in saying that you have medicines which can influence the rain at all.

R.: That's just the way people speak when they talk on a subject of which they have no knowledge. When we first opened our eyes, we found our forefathers making rain, and we follow in their footsteps. You, who send to Kuruman for corn, and irrigate your garden, may do without rain; *we* cannot manage in that way. If we had no rain, the cattle would have no pasture, the cows give no milk, our children become lean and die, our wives run away to other tribes who do make rain, and have corn, and the whole tribe become dispersed and lost; our fire would go out.

L.: I quite agree with you as to the value of rain; but you cannot charm the clouds by medicines. You wait till you see the clouds come, then you use your medicines, and take the credit which belongs to God only.

R.: I use my medicines, and you employ yours; we are both doctors, and doctors are not deceivers. You give a patient medicine. Sometimes God is pleased to heal him by means of your medicine; sometimes not—he dies. When he is cured, you take the credit of what God does. I do the same. Sometimes God grants us rain, sometimes not. When he does we take the credit of the charm. When a patient dies, you don't give up trust in your medicine, neither do I when rain fails. If you wish me to leave off my medicine, why continue your own?

L.: I give medicine to living creatures within my reach, and can see the effects though no cure follows; you pretend to charm the clouds, which are so far above us that your medicines never reach them. The clouds usually lie in one direction, and your smoke goes in another. God alone can command the clouds. Only try and wait patiently; God will give us rain without your medicines.

R.: Mahala-ma-kapa-a-a! Well, I always thought white men were wise till this morning. Who ever thought of making a virtue of starvation! Is death pleasant then?

L.: Could you make it rain on one spot and not on another?

R.: I wouldn't think of trying. I like to see the whole country green, and all the people glad; the women clapping their hands and giving me their ornaments for thankfulness, and lullilooing for joy.

L.: I think you deceive both them and yourself.

R.: Well, then, there is a pair of us.

What we observe here is two people, one a nineteenth-century Victorian Englishman, representative of the European nation which was a leader of scientific thought and of the industrial revolution in the West at the time, and a Tswana specialist in making rain. Each is engaged in an activity thought useful and necessary in his time. England in the nineteenth century was ablaze with fervor to convert the heathen nations, some say because it served British economic ambitions; others, that it served to verify Victorian notions of the Industrial Revolution as the highest attainment of progress. (That is, missionary work was a by-product of English models of history which generated various courses of action, this being one.)

The Tswana live in a place in Africa where there are lush grasslands which support huge herds of cattle, making these people wealthy in African terms where, as we have seen, cattle are currency, repositories of value, financial items. However Tswana, like many South African ethnic groups, including the Zulu—to judge by the fact that the great Zulu emperor took to himself exclusive right to make rain—are apparently threatened continuously by the possibility of failure of rain which would lead to huge losses of cattle and crops. While rain is a chancy thing in all the savannah areas of Africa, not all Africans have rainmakers or stress rainmaking so much. The Kipsigis, for example, do not, but the people in the northern part of the Eastern Nilotic area do, as one would expect in this drier area. In Botswana today, the national coat of arms has as its moto *pula,* meaning rain, and the currency is called pula.

In the preceding dialogue, the Rainmaker's concern is not simply with rain. Apparently, the group to which the Rainmaker belonged was constantly threatened by surrounding people seeking to absorb them. In other words, the Rainmaker's science was intimately connected with a social condition. This provided a bridge between the seemingly mechanical process of rainmaking and the theory of evil we saw operating in witchcraft in the Bantu area. It provides an answer to the question of why some one person should have suffered the consequences of some destructive act like falling out of a tree, and not another. The Rainmaker's reasoning apparently followed the line that although God made the rain, the reason it fell on one place rather than another was because of the actions of the Rainmaker, actions which not only made the rain but also countered the evil intentions of other tribes.

The Tswana theory of causality is not necessarily different from our own. At one level scientific theory may, in some circumstances, make possibly false hypotheses about the nature of causality which promote the interests of scientists insofar as their audience believes them. Both rainmaker and missionary doctor were powerful figures at the time Livingstone wrote this and both benefited from people's belief in their powers. Since the two were in competition for leadership of the Tswana, one would expect Livingstone to challenge the Rainmaker's theories, even if they were true, the way the Catholic Church challenged Galileo's theories of cosmology in the Middle Ages, even though they were in some sense true. When human beings theorize about nature, they never do so as perfectly objective observers, but as social beings.

Put another way, Livingstone was working with a statistical theory of causality, basic to the scientific method, which associated the efficacy of his cures with the statistical frequency of success. The Rainmaker, on the other hand, thought of *any* successful occurrence as proof of causality. To judge by the success of the scientific method throughout the world in winning the minds of men, we may judge that in the end Livingstone's theory of causality won over the Rainmaker's. However, like many false theories, the Rainmaker's was plausible and held its own as long as people believed in it and as long as it helped satisfy their need for a defense against their enemies. Similarly, there are still plenty of false theories in Western science whose success is dependent on the same social process which supported the Rainmaker's theory.

My point can be further underscored by reference to social anthropology itself. In his essay on "Objectivity in Anthropology" which I alluded to in the introduction, Maquet claimed that structural-functional theory, which presents African societies as static, served the class interests of anthropologists, who as academicians were of the higher classes in Britain. These interests were supported by colonialism, which in turn benefited from scientific support for the idea that African societies are naturally static therefore requiring no investment of resources in helping them change. Thus, the surplus could go into the coffers of the colonial government and return in one way or another to Britain to support the class system. Despite whatever truth there is in Maquet's accusation, as I also pointed out earlier, static models of social systems do have some scientific validity. Human beings model reality; their theories may be right or wrong or half right. Furthermore, theories are always placed in some social context which they serve as much as they serve the search for truth.

MODELING

One of the most prominent students of African thought, Robert Horton (1964; Fernandez 1978, 221ff) claims that African systems of belief are attempts to model in the same way that Western scientific theories model (or theorize) about important events. He therefore criticizes some Westerners who speak of African idea systems as having no intellectual content. Horton believes there is an important difference between African and Western models. Westerners are more prone to model the relations of *things,* whereas Africans model the relations of *people.* Note, for example, in the exchange between Livingstone and the Rainmaker how the heart of the Rainmaker's theory is built on conflicts between people, resulting in the failure of rain. On the other hand, Livingstone's is one describing the relations between physical facts. Yet we should not forget that at least on the surface, the Rainmaker claimed to be dealing with the relations of things (medicines and rain clouds), and Livingstone's apparent concern with natural facts hides a concern with human relations, the status of the doctor and missionary relative to other people. However, insofar as Horton is correct, it seems plausible that African emphasis on modeling human relations relates to a mode of life in which production is ordinarily dependent on labor-intensive operations and requires complex social relational systems to accomplish production. Western systems are capital intensive, depending more on machines. Both Africans and Westerners are ultimately concerned with social relations, but the emphasis is different. Perhaps this is why belief in witchcraft has declined in the West since the Industrial Revolution, and why witchcraft seems so much less important among nomadic, pastoral people in Africa than among even pastoral agriculturalists.

The process of modeling can take at least two forms, the scientific one we know, which stresses precise measurement and testable hypotheses, and the other, a form which is more metaphoric or poetic, which says something intellectually satisfying about the nature of the world. The way many Westerners felt about the theory of biological evolution developed by Darwin before they had the paleontologic and genetic knowledge to verify it illustrates the point. This type of modeling is not confined to "primitive" people; it is a human trait. Onwuejeogwu (1975) gives an example. He argues that in the modeling done by Catholic Christians with respect to the concept of the Trinity, there is a syllogism that goes like this: high nature combines mystically with super nature (the supernatural) in the form of low nature and is transformed mystically into super nature and high nature. That is to say, the Virgin Mary combines with the Holy Ghost in the form of the Dove to produce Jesus. Onwuejeogwu believes that this symbolic logic is illogical according to scientific precepts, but it is a legitimate mode of reasoning which occurs among all men. For example, Australian Aborigines, using the same syllogism, believe that woman (high nature) combines with totem (super nature) in the form of fish (low nature) to produce son (super nature, because the son becomes high nature but is from a totem and returns to it when he dies).

What is lacking in Onwuejeogwu's discussion is an explanation of how the symbolic system or theory relates to ritual and what social meaning it has. At the base of the syllogism seems to be an attempt to answer the question: what is the relationship between the natural and the supernatural? Or, how is it possible to obtain a supernatural form (Jesus, totem) from a lower-natured form (Virgin Mary, Aborigine son)? It seems that this is related to the question of how women can at the same time be below men in nature and still produce men. In other words, among other things, such logic is concerned with the question of how women can be both human and subhuman, a question which, we have seen, must concern many Africans who must treat women at the same time as mothers, to whom they are deferent, and as labor, which they exploit. Of course, the syllogism does not refer to this problem alone. Characteristic of such modeling are multiple and complex meanings.

Luc de Heusch (1975), a person who has given a good deal of attention to African religion, particularly in Central Africa, believes that symbol systems are related to ritual in a dialectic which is much more than a simple attempt to validate social order. That is to say, rituals do not just support social structure, and symbolic syllogistic systems do not just defend social order. They interact to address important human questions, like the one about the status of women. This compares with marxist concern over the status of workers in industrial societies.

De Heusch points out that the myth and accompanying rituals of the founding of the Luba state do more than just give support to the divine right of Luba kings to rule. The myth takes up the question of the opposition of culture and nature (civilization and savagery, if you like), and how their seemingly unresolvable natures are brought together. The original Luba king is seen as an uncouth hunter, Nkongolo, whose mouth is open too wide, who laughs too loud, who eats and drinks in public, and is a glutton. His Queen, Lueji, is also pictured as uncontrolled, by having a continuous menstrual flow. Lack of control by both the king and queen is a sign of sterility. Mbidi Kiluwe, a celestial hunter, comes into the picture by marrying a sister of Nkongolo and siring Kalala Tlunga. Kalala Tlunga eventually takes an army from the home of his maternal uncle, with whom he grew up (this is a case of avunculocal residence in a matrilineal society) and slays Nkongolo, thereby reinstituting fertility in the kingdom and the more elevated customs of divine kingship. In other words, this mythic dialogue is a discourse on the relationship between nature and culture, sterility and fertility, orderly state life and disorderly anarchy. By employing the methods of structuralism, (not to be confused with structural-functionalism), which studies the logic of symbols, de Heusch demonstrates that kingship is associated with the rainbow, which in turn is associated with the sun, the earth, and dry season, in opposition to the moon, sky and rains. The rainbow, a symbol for the first king, also represents incest, sterility, and death. It is barbarism. However, it is barbarism brought under control, a control derived from the mating of the first king's sister to a visiting, civilized king whose offspring combines the self-control and refinement of the visiting king with the energy of the first king. Or, put another way, kingship is a civilizing process, but it is also dangerous, drawing on barbaric forces. Some Western political scientists would say the same. Others would say this is simply an engaging theory designed to convince people that they have no other choice than kings!

SUMMARY

It is clear to present day scholars that Africans do have complex philosophical notions which are particularly manifest in their symbolic myths and rituals, notions concerned, like our own, with the relations of men and women, nature and culture, good and evil. While these concepts have clear relation to society, they are not just servants of social structures but transcend them to some degree. They are concerned, at a more general level and among other things, with the nature of the world. In the next chapter we will look at the substance of the binary classification systems used by Africans and, following de Heusch's point that symbolic systems and rituals are related, examine the chief "rituals," or action systems that accompany this binary mode of thought. Finally, we will examine revitalization movements and their relationship to symbols and ritual.

RELIGION AND PHILOSOPHY: BINARY CLASSIFICATION AND RITUAL

THE LAST CHAPTER dealt with the great traditions of African religion and with the concept of African thought as modeling. In this chapter we take up the classificatory structure of this modeling and how it is represented in rituals. Finally, we examine revitalization processes as they occur in life-crisis rituals and social upheavals and as they draw upon this structure of thought.

RIGHT AND LEFT

In Africa as well as in the rest of the world, among ourselves for example, a binary classification is used to arrange the world metaphorically in terms of the bilaterally split body. If we think about it for a minute, we realize that we have a pretty complex classification of this kind of which we are barely aware and which we have difficulty explaining when it is brought to our attention. For instance, why do we shake hands with the right hand? This is sometimes explained as a leftover from the past when people were at war with each other all the time, and the weapons were carried in the right hand. Shaking with the right hand meant removing the weapon from that hand and so was a sign of peace. Such an explanation will not stand close scrutiny. For example, why should so many other people in the world, including Africans, follow the same practice despite having different histories?

The right hand is associated with good in some sense. For instance, saints are thought of as being on the right hand of God. We speak of left-handed compliments, insults disguised as compliments. Moreover, the word sinister means left hand. In politics we speak of the political left, the radical or liberal side, as compared to the right, which is conservative. And, how do we interpret the fact that during the marriage ceremony, the groom stands on the right side facing the minister or priest while the bride is on the left?

In a study of this phenomenon in America, P. and I. Karp (1979) have established some of the following associations:

Left	Right
west	east
death	life
dark	light
night	day
black	white
Church	God
female	male
lack of control	control
feet	head
distaff (weaving)	swordside
animosity	warmth

The place of the right-left system of classification in social processes is much less apparent in our thought than it is in African thought. One of the best accounts of this is Rigby's (1966) for the Gogo of central Tanzania. In their system, the right and left hands or sides of the body are related to various things in their lives, as shown in Table 8.1. This Gogo classification is parallel to one used by the Kaguru (Beidelman 1961) who also equate the left side with the hand used for wiping oneself, weakness, and the side the female lies on during intercourse, while the right is associated with the hand used for eating, strength, and the side the male lies on during intercourse. However, the Kaguru differ remarkably from the Gogo by the addition of certain oppositions evidently distinctive of their society (even though historically the Gogo and Kaguru are closely related). The matrilineal Kaguru (the Gogo are pat-

Young girls wearing sacralized hide of sacrificial steer on their right arms

rilineal), put the matriclan and matrilineage on the left hand and father's matriclan and patrilateral kin on the right. Also, they put bridewealth given by the clan of the bride on the left and bridewealth given to the father of the bride on the right. There are more oppositions of this type, all of them related to the fact that the Kaguru, while possessing a matrilineal form of organization, seem to strain toward patrilineal organization. Among the Gogo, this has been attained, and is replaced by a distinction between the father's line and matrilateral or affinal alliances as well as maternal lines in general. This translates into an opposition between the existing organization (on the right), emphasizing the individuality of the family and patrilineal inheritance, and an alternative possible organization (on the left) composed of matrilineal clans with matrilineal descent.

If we look at the Meru on Mt. Kenya (Needham 1960), we can see the intrusion of special, local considerations into what otherwise contains many universal, suprasocial considerations (like the opposition of night and day) in a society which emphasizes age organization rather than lineages. Here subordinate age divisions are on the left, and dominant age divisions are on the right. Furthermore, the Meru seem to have certain special religious conditions of a revitalization nature which lead them to classify a type of prophet called the *mugwe* on the left, opposite the elders of the society, a prophet whose left hand is also sacred.

TABLE 8.1   Gogo Binary Classification

LEFT	RIGHT
female	male
hand used for wiping anus after defecation	hand used for eating
weakness	strength
stupid	clever
side on which woman lies during sexual intercourse	side on which man lies during sexual intercourse
seed planting	bush clearing
winnowing, grinding	threshing
west	east
north	south
down	up
death, sickness	fertility, health
hot (as in intemperate)	cool (as in calm)
poisonous plants	medicinal plants
red/white	black
young people	old people
junior wives	senior wives
mother and all of her maternal kin	father and all of his paternal kin
economic cooperation	economic competition

If we go over to the Western Sudan, we find that the Fulani (Stenning 1960) have a left-right system also, with many elements similar to the Gogo, such as the opposition of feminine (left) and masculine (right). However, they place genealogical juniors on the left and genealogical seniors on the right, corresponding to the ranking in this society of genealogically related people which is lacking in some other societies, such as the Gogo. When we leave the specifically social elements in the classification, there are some differences. The Gogo place east on the right, but the Fulani place it on the left, although they agree that north is left and south right.

THE MEANING OF RIGHT AND LEFT

Anthropologists have puzzled over the meaning of such schemes. For example, there is a tendency to jump immediately to the conclusion that things on the right are good and those on the left are bad. However, this cannot be true in any absolute sense. The Gogo, whose scheme closely resembles that of the Turu, with which I am familiar, do not consider females to be wholly evil or bad. There is a good deal of tension in Turu society between men and women, and men tend to think of all women as inherently prone to witchcraft. On the other hand, they also associate women with the moon, which is cool, tranquil, and on the right, while men are associated with the sun, which is hot, cauterizing, and on the left. Furthermore, men certainly do not think of their own mothers as evil.

An explanation for such systems of classification, if a full one could be made, would probably plumb the very depths of the world view of a people (something like Moore's [1976] account of the Chagga world view or the summation of the Dogon world view in Griaule's conversations with Ogotemmeli, shown in their system of binary classification [Griaule 1965, 222–223]). Any explanation is therefore bound to be somewhat superficial.

However, I would like to suggest an explanation which will do for now and which will help cast some light on African thought and society. In a scheme like that of the Gogo, the right hand may be thought of as the side associated with order and tranquillity, whereas the left is associated with tension and disorder. If we look again at the Gogo classification, we may speculate, based on comparative evidence from the Turu and other Africans, that the male feels a unity with and placidness about other males, taken as a class compared to females, who as a class are a source of tension and sometimes even fear. The Turu feel that all women are potentially witches because they are less cooperative than men and more prone to scheme and threaten the interests of men. Turu women, as I explained earlier, even have a secret society professing to train women to cooperate with men but which the men see as working to further the interests of the women against men. This does not mean that all men have only placid relations with other men. The division of men and women into different categories is only relevant in terms of the two sexes taken as a group and in terms of the general system of relations between them, just as in our own society we sometimes think of women as a unit and men as a unit, distinct from relations with specific men and women.

The explanation for the next item in the Gogo classification, wiping and eating, is more complex and draws upon the writings of Mary Douglas, who worked with the Lele (Douglas 1966). Africans, like other people, symbolize social relations through the body in other ways than just left and right. The well-being of society is symbolized by eating, taking in food. On the other hand, defecation represents a breaching of the boundaries of society, a lessening of society, and a source of tension. Thus, more specifically witches, who are the most extreme form of antisocial people, use bodily refuse, including feces, to perform magic which threatens life. Parenthetically, during revitalization movements, where inverting symbols is a common and essential practice, as in the case of the Mugwe's sacred left hand, this breach of society is represented as good, and dirt, so to speak, becomes a sacred symbol. It follows, then, that schemes like that of the Gogo are appropriate only to society in its "steady state," not to its revitalistic, or revolutionary, state.

During the steady state, strength and cleverness, as well as fertility and health, are sources of contentment, whereas weakness, stupidity, death, and sickness are not. Young people are threatening to older people because they want to displace them in order to pursue their own lives; junior wives disrupt the household whereas senior wives work with the male head of the house to promote order; the kin of one's mother intrude on the affairs of the family as a source of unpredictable and upsetting claims for more compensation for their women, whereas one's own paternal kin are predictable, orderly and helpful. Interestingly, what Rigby calls "economic competition" may be rephrased as the ability to pursue one's economic ends as opposed to "cooperation," which is interference in one's operations by kin making claims for help.

Some of these items cannot be understood without further study. It is not obvious why east, south, and up are right while west, north, and down are left. As we shall see later, the colors have been explained by Turner. If the Gogo are like the Turu, the east is the direction from which the sun, which is a cleansing agent of evil, comes, and the west is the place the sun goes to deposit all the evil it has burned out of the world. Planting, winnowing, and grinding are probably on the left because they are purely women's occupations whereas men thresh and clear bush.

It is therefore possible that this system of classification is related to the general structure of order and disorder, peace and tension, that characterize a particular society. It is probably obvious to all, even those, like women, who are placed on the left. Some items, such as the opposition of men and women, to judge by the similarity of Gogo and Fulani classifications, are shared by most or all African societies. However, some items are particular to a people, such as a cosmology which finds evil deposited in the west, or the social system which finds the mother and her maternal kin, but not her paternal kin, on the left.

RIGHT-LEFT AND KINGSHIP

The use of binary classification extends to a justification of kingship. In the last chapter we saw Nkongolo, obviously a left type king, conquered by the forces of order, thus giving rise to the divine kingship which maintains order in Luba society. Similar myths are found elsewhere, for example, among the Shambaa where the gist of the mythology of the rise of the first king, Mbegha, is that the founder was a wild, powerful force who was tamed for the good of the people. In this symbolic account, the people are inferior to the king, as indicated by a binary classification built into the myth. Mbegha (the right side) is a provider of meat, a powerful man, protector of territory, king, owner of the country, receiver of women, and a judge. The people of Shambaa, on the other hand, are providers of starchy food, weak women, performers of repetitive work, subjects, inhabitants of the country, providers of women, and litigants (Feierman 1974). This classification, it would seem, is rather self-serving for the king in that it attempts to associate the right side with the monarchy and because it relates the Shambaa people in general to women and weakness. The king is the source of tranquillity; the people without him, in a Hobbesian sense, are pictured as the source of disorder. In order to bolster the association of the king with tranquillity, he is represented in the myth as having moved from the forest, the uncivilized place, and is transformed in his journey from Zigula, a society to the south, to Shambaai, by bringing his power under control and civilizing it. He changes from a hunter in the wilderness to a hunter near homesteads, from a dangerous being to one who brings order, from an eater only of meat to an eater of meat and starch (porridge), from a solitary eater to one who lives by exchange, from a witch to a bringer of solidarity, from a stealer of wives to one who is given wives, and so forth. This transformation is symbolized in a royal sacrifice in which the descendants of Mbegha used to sacrifice and eat the meat of a dog, ordinarily considered to be polluting. The dog, as among the Yoruba so far away, by combining both wild and domestic characteristics, symbolizes the king as one who has the power to harm and therefore the power to rule (Feierman 1974, 62ff).

Mair, discussing rituals and kings (Mair 1977a, 41), makes the point that despite the fact that many rituals of accession establish certain divine characteristics of the king, the one thing they all do is confer power on him. Thus, as in the case of Shambaa, the rituals must establish why, in the face of the fact that kings are not always necessary, one is necessary in this case. The king may be admonished to be aware of his responsibilities toward the people and be reminded of the fact that they ultimately chose him, but it is he who has the power. The problem addressed by royal rituals is the question of why it is necessary to give power to a single person. The way this is treated in the myth of Mbegha suggests that he must have power to maintain order, a theory some Western social philosophers would support. So the Shambaa myth turns out to be a kind of political theory.

THE LUGBARA MODEL OF SOCIETY

These ideas about good and evil associated with the binary system may be found united in a model among the Lugbara whose view of spatial and temporal relations is detailed by Middleton (1965) in Figure 8.1. What this model says is that the Lugbara regard people, both their own ancestors and Europeans who are remote in time, as being somehow "inverted" or radically

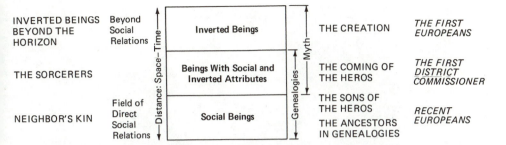

INVERTED BEINGS BEYOND THE HORIZON	Beyond Social Relations	Inverted Beings	THE CREATION	*THE FIRST EUROPEANS*
THE SORCERERS		Beings With Social and Inverted Attributes	THE COMING OF THE HEROS	*THE FIRST DISTRICT COMMISSIONER*
NEIGHBOR'S KIN	Field of Direct Social Relations	Social Beings	THE SONS OF THE HEROS THE ANCESTORS IN GENEALOGIES	*RECENT EUROPEANS*

FIGURE 8.1 Lugbara spatial and temporal views of social relations
(from The Lugbara of Uganda *by John Middleton. Copyright© 1965 by Holt, Rinehart and Winston, Inc. Reprinted by permission of Holt, Rinehart and Winston)*

different in some sense. Similarly people who are remote in space are evil. However, there is a medial category, people who are nearby in time such as dead ancestors, and nearby in space, as on the next ridge, who are not exactly inverted but who are not quite normal either. The normal people are those who are your near kin and neighbors and your recently dead ancestors.

Such a scheme, which would place distant people on the left hand and close people on the right, seems bizarre at first, until we realize that at the heart of it, the Lugbara are saying that those people are normal with whom one has ongoing, regular relations of exchange, while those people with whom one exchanges irregularly and infrequently, are out of one's control and potentially dangerous. Remote people, with whom one has no relations, are unpredictable and very dangerous. Put another way, the degree to which people are threatening (left) or potentially dangerous is proportional to their distance from one in time and place, a perfectly reasonable social law. It is not really different from the way we think. During the last century social science developed in a world where some people thought of the antipodes, the obverse side of the world, like Australia relative to England, as peopled by strange, quasi-human beings, some of whom even walked on their heads. In this climate there developed an evolutionary theory of social development in which the more remote from England or America people were in time and space, the more different (and threatening) they were. If we went back in time, we would find savages (inverted people) who practiced promiscuity, ate each other, and had rudimentary industries (spear throwers, for example), and if we went out spatially, we would find the same people still living in Australia, or Tierra del Fuego, and other remote places, practicing ways of life that offended the sensibilities of Europeans and Americans.

This comparison can be carried even further. Some of the great ideas in Western social thought include the evolution of society from the rule of brute force to the rule of contract (Rousseau), the evolution of the state as a means

Africans as perceived by ancient Europeans

of bringing order to the lives of otherwise unruly men (Hobbes), or the evolution of men from a prehuman to human state, where they have the *natural* propensity to be orderly and respect each others' rights (Locke). Whether a man without government is a brute, or whether prehuman animals are disorderly are legitimate questions for investigation. This is the province of sociology and social anthropology. Such concerns, we see, are also African, symbolized in models of opposition of order and disorder, left and right.

Basically, then, left-right classification deals with evil and good, tension and peace, as it appears in man's world, social and otherwise. Because this way of thinking seems universal among men—some of the categories are even universal—it may be said that structuring thought in this way is as human as our built-in ability (according to Chomsky) to handle speech. Only the categories (words and parts of syntax) vary from language to language, just as in binary classification where the categories are arranged to fit special circumstances.

NDEMBU COLOR CLASSIFICATION

Victor Turner (1966) has most extensively analyzed the use of color to represent good and evil. However he has also demonstrated that through an examination of the use of color, it becomes evident that the Ndembu classification system is more complicated than simply black (left) and white (right), containing also a third category, red, in between. (Incidentally, although Turner tends to think that the association of black and white with left and right is very widespread in human society, as for example in our own, it should be noted that in the Gogo classification, as well as Turu, I believe, black is on the right.) Under white, the Ndembu place goodness, strength and health, purity, good fortune, having power, lack of death in one's kin group, being without tears, chieftainship, honoring the ancestors, life, fertility, huntsmanship, generosity, laughter, eating, openness, maturity (as in becoming an elder), cleanliness, and respectability. As one can see, this is a recipe for the good life. Black, on the other hand, connotes evil, bad luck, suffering, disease, sorcery (in opposition to legitimate power), death, sexual desire (lust), and night, to name some of the categories.

Alongside this binary system they place red, which represents the blood of animals, of parturition, menstrual blood, blood from murder or assault, and the blood of witchcraft. Red things act both for good and evil. Blood is power. Men and animals have blood and can act, speak, sing, and laugh while bloodless things have no such mobility. However, sorcerers can give an inanimate thing blood so that it can thenceforth move and kill people. Semen is white blood, but red (or black) semen is infertile.

De Heusch (1975), commenting on Turner's analysis, adds that apparently red, taken by itself, denotes war and homicide, as opposed to black, which is totally negative in the sense of association with death. War is dangerous and unsettling, but it has good qualities.

Of interest is the way the Ndembu tie these colors in with ritual. The Ndembu circumcision site, where the operation is performed, is called *ifwilu,* "the place of dying" while the place where the novices sit while recovering from the operation is a red gum tree log whose name is derived from the word "to mature." Thus *mukanda,* the circumcision rite, Turner says, might well be called "from death to maturity." Black objects play an important part in circumcision rites, and at the end of the rites, when the boys return to their mothers, they beat sticks with alternating bands of white and black, signifying life and death, over their heads. Similarly, when a girl leaves puberty rites to first sleep with her bridegroom for a night, she signals her guardian the next morning if the encounter has been satisfactory whereupon black mud from the river (which is cool) is sprinkled in a dry powdered form, on thresholds of every hut in the village. Black which has become cold signifies the cooling of tension and the onset of a happy, peaceful marriage. The lust is cooled, and cooperation takes the place of passion.

TYPES OF RITUALS

Turner says that African *rituals,* which are stereotyped sequences of activities involving gestures, words, and objects, performed in places set off for the purpose, are designed to influence supernatural forces or entities on behalf of the actors' goals and interests. There is some dispute about this. Lienhardt (1961), for example, takes the position that Dinka cattle sacrifice is a drama performed, not to gain any direct payoff, but as a sort of general and indirect way of maintaining order, the way a Catholic takes communion. Nevertheless, even this scholar admits that ritual drama has a purpose, albeit remote.

Rituals are of several types; two of the most common are seasonal, occurring in a regular sequence, like the Turu circumcision which comes before the harvest each year, or contingent, held in response to individual or collective crisis, like the special Pokot animal sacrifice called *ime,* designed to curse an unknown thief after the loss of some valuable good. In fact this distinction by Turner is confusing because certain life crisis rituals, like circumcision, are also seasonal, occurring each year at the same time in some societies in response to regularly recurring rises in the tension between generations. Turu ancestral sacrifice, on the other hand, is an example of a crisis ritual which occurs irregularly. A steer is immolated, and the hide is symbolically offered to an ancestor, requesting that he stop causing harm to his descendant. The point I am stressing here is that while a distinction may legitimately be made between rituals which are rather *pro forma,* like going to church on Sunday, and those which respond to emergencies, like funerals, emergencies (crises) may occur rhythmically, too. Ultimately all ritual deals with crisis and attempts to set things right in some way.

Besides these two major types of rituals (seasonal and crisis), Turner finds others, such as divinatory rituals in which the future or some secret is revealed; civil rituals in which leaders or chiefs promote the fertility and wealth of the community; initiations into priesthood; the ceremonies of secret societies; and small daily rituals which offer food to deities and ancestors. Each African society has a specific and finite number of rituals appropriate to its needs and history. The number and type may change over time, but at any time, allowing for some ambiguity where rites are dying or being created, the number is known and can be specified, as any good ethnography will show.

Central to ritual action is a special kind of symbolizing which is different from that occurring outside ritual. There are visual, behavioral, and auditory symbols which have multiple meanings (which is one of the reasons they are so difficult for the uninitiated to understand). The symbols unify apparently disparate things and condense many ideas, relations, actions, and the like into simultaneous representations. They polarize meaning such that at one pole there are grouped indicators referring to the moral and social order and at the other, indicators which stimulate desire and feelings.

An example from Turner's writings is the *mudyi,* or milk tree, of the Ndembu people (Turner 1973) which is the focal symbol of the girls' puberty rites. At the normative pole, the tree symbolizes motherhood, womanhood, and the unity and endurance of Ndembu society. The various aspects of this unity are indicated at various steps in the puberty ritual, all of which is condensed in the symbol of the mudyi tree. At the sensory pole, the same symbol stands for breast milk (the tree exudes a milky latex), mother's breasts, the bodily slenderness and mental pliancy of the novice, and the like. In other words, then, the mudyi tree in Ndembu society, when viewed by a normal adult Ndembu, is as rich in multiple, complex meaning as is Christ and the cross to Christians. The lion is as significant to the Turu and to many other people, among whom it appears in the last sequence of rites in the women's secret society, in conjunction with the birth of twins, as well as in accusations of witchcraft against women, to name just two diverse contexts. In each total system of rituals, there is a nucleus of dominant symbols which are characterized by extreme multiple meaning and a central position in each ritual performance. However, for any given type of ritual, the number of manifestations of any central symbol varies. Deciphering such symbolism is not easy in any society.

SACRIFICE

Probably the most common and one of the most important religious acts in Africa is sacrifice, a crisis ritual designed to seek the aid of supernatural forces for people who are beholden and subordinate to them. It is an exchange between clients and patrons. Often sacrifice is equated with ancestral sacrifice, but this is incorrect. Like witchcraft beliefs, sacrifice is universal, but the structure of sacrifice depends on the great tradition of which it is a part and on the structure of the specific society. Only among those people for whom lineage is a central structural feature can ancestral sacrifice be said to be the usual form. In many Nilotic groups, as we have seen, sacrifice is not to ancestors but to Divinity and associated spirits. However, in all cases, sacrifice is a kind of exchange act in which human beings attempt metaphorically to sort out relations with the powerful forces which rule their lives, an exchange symbolizing or modeling the social forces as they relate to men.

In those places where lineage is dominant, whether in West Africa, Bantu, or Nilotic areas, sacrifice takes on a common form in that the congregation of worshipers comprises either an exclusive kin group composed of members of a unilineal descent group or a group cutting across unilineal descent, depending on the special structure of kinship of the society. Put another way, depending on how the localized kin groups come to be structured, with more or less contact between affines and unilineal kin, the congregation of worshipers will vary. The Turu sacrifice of a steer to an ancestor is attended by the members of the localized, patrilineal descent group—the village group—of the person offering the sacrifice, plus a classificatory maternal uncle of the ancestor. In other places, strangers or even more affines might be included. Ancestral sacrifice is performed by a group of people who have to deal with each other over time, but it is a group whose definition involves descent and ancestors (Fortes 1965).

Ancestor worship is based on a theory about the relations of living men. That is to say, ancestor worship is not a means of insuring a good afterlife. Many, if not most, Africans have rather vague ideas about the afterlife, if it can be called afterlife since the ancestors are believed to be still living, only in a place separate from visible living. The Turu believe that their ancestors live under the ground but in the same coterminous space in which they dwelled during life. They are a separate part of the community and communicate with the living through their vital force. When a sacrifice is made to the ancestor, it is to give him or her something in return for a cessation of a negative use of this force, in the way a son does obeisance to his father in return for peace. However, the evil event which prompts the sacrifice, such as the death of a child or of livestock, is seen as punishment for some social failure, symbolized in the negative act of an ancestor, who stands in some way for the microsociety of the harmed individual. Thus ancestor sacrifice is a symbolic statement of social deficiency by the actor who gives the sacrifice and who attempts to remedy the deficiency by giving a gift to the ancestor. The actual gift, meat, for instance, is to members of his microgroup with whom he attempts to set himself right.

It follows, then, that the symbolizing will model the problem in some specific way and will include members of the group whose relations must be set right. This can be better illustrated by recounting the process involved in seeking the cause of evil. When beset by evils such as the death of a cow, a Turu man may go to a *mughanga,* sometimes translated as doctor, or curer, but who may also be called a diviner, to find out the source of the trouble. There are only two possible sources, a witch (or sorcerer) or an ancestor. The diviner, through a process which might be very complicated, like the Yoruba

Ifa divination system, or as simple as just asking the petitioner who he thinks is the cause, will elicit from the petitioner his sometimes subconscious ideas of the cause. If the petitioner feels no guilt but has enemies, he will end up being told he is being bewitched by his enemy. On the other hand, if he feels guilt about how he has dealt with someone, as for example in having retrieved from a person a cow he loaned that person before the holder could enjoy the milk from its calf, he will be told that an ancestor of that person is bringing the harm to him and that he should sacrifice to that ancestor to stop the harm. (Incidentally, he may not, in fact, make the sacrifice; it depends on how much it costs relative to his suffering.) In such a case, not only will he mollify the offended person and his family with the meat of the sacrifice, but he will make restitution by returning the cow and calf.

Among the Turu, as in witchcraft, no ancestor outside the local lineage is thought to have the power to harm anyone in the lineage. This reflects the fact that important interpersonal contacts, the kind that can produce frictions, are confined within the local lineage. Witchcraft beliefs, then, deal with disorderly conduct within the group, while sacrifice deals with moral failings. It is evil for a witch to kill, but it is morally proper and right for an ancestor to do so because the person sacrificing is the cause of the disorder, whom the righteous ancestor punishes, as a father punishes a son.

Among the Ashanti, only matrilineal forebears become ancestors, receive worship, and stand for the localized matrilineal group. Ashanti also have the *ntoro* cult, membership in which is patrilineally transmitted, but aspects of the personality of an individual, to which it refers, do not survive in the supernatural realm (Fortes 1965, 129). Thus, though sons honor the memories of their fathers in this matrilineal society, it is the mother's brother to whom a stool is dedicated and whose spirit is honored. As Fortes puts it, ancestor worship is a representation or extension of the authority component in the jural relations of successive generations, as between father and son.

The Structure of Sacrifice. All sacrifices, whether ancestral or not, have a threefold structure: (1) sacralization of the time, place, and victims of the sacrifice; (2) communion or sharing of the flesh of the victims; and (3) desacralization and purification (Ray 1976, 79). This can be illustrated by the Ogun sacrifice of the Yoruba (Bascom 1969). The Yoruba, consonant with the general complexity of their social system, have an intricate religious system which includes, as we saw earlier, a massive structure of deities. Ogun, the god of iron, is one of the more heralded of these. Sacrifices to him involve symbols having to do with iron, such as hunting because it uses weapons of iron, but also, nowadays, even bicycles. A family who are Ogun worshippers will assemble during the dry season for this purpose, at the time of good hunting when some game can be obtained for the sacrifice. The ritual is held in the family compound on a date determined by divination. The Ogun priests (Yoruba, unlike most Africans, have specialized cult priests) and officiating family heads prepare themselves by abstaining from cursing, fighting, sexual intercourse, and certain foods. The night before the event, a hunt is made to obtain game, and an all night vigil is held by the shrine of Ogun, a stone column and a tree, which is decorated with palm fronds to symbolize palm wine, one of Ogun's favorite foods. The people themselves drink palm wine and sing to attract Ogun's attention.

All this is part of the process of sacralization, or consecration of the site, which continues the next day with offerings of kola nuts brought by the heads of attending families. As the kolas are offered, the family head asks Ogun for blessings and protection during the year. Then Ogun is presented with his favorite foods: snails, palm oil, pigeons, and dogs. Ogun has an arbitrary and tempestuous temperament so the snails are meant to calm him because they are soft and smooth. Palm oil has the same significance. The dog is appropriate because, as noted earlier, it is wild and dangerous in its undomestic state but friendly and calm when domesticated. The process of consecration is completed by casting portions of the kola nuts before the shrine and, as in Ifa divination, ascertaining from the way they fall whether Ogun wills the sacrifice to continue. If so, the snails are cracked open, and the slime is poured on the altar; the pigeons and dog are beheaded, and their blood is dripped on the altar. (If blood among the Yoruba has the same significance as among the Ndembu, as it probably does, note how appropriate a symbol it is for Ogun.) Thus the transaction is made—the objects are sacrificed for peace and health. Afterwards the participants eat the flesh of the dog and the game.

It is perhaps useful to remind ourselves that the structure of the Ogun sacrifice is basically the same as the Christian eucharist, as is the meaning as well. The Catholic or Anglican participant in communion is presenting to God at Christ's bidding the consecrated real (some say "symbolic") blood and body of Christ in return for salvation. However, in the case of Christianity, there is no actual killing of victims, and the return desired is, at least ostensibly, paradise, although in fact it is plain that the act of communion has important implications for the relations of people in the Christian community.

The Yoruba are a highly urbanized people among whom the simple localized lineage structure appropriate to such people as the Turu is gone. There is a kind of localization of clans, but kinship is effectively bilateral, which means dispersed. Thus their utilization of Ogun worship reflects a move away from ancestral sacrifice to a more generalized kind of sacrifice. In the dispersed pastoral societies of East Africa, where lineage is again much reduced in importance, sacrifice also takes on a form which is not ancestor oriented. The Pokot, for example, sacrifice steers on appropriate occasions, but the participants are whichever people of a miscellaneous lot happen to live in the community at the time. The sacrifice, therefore, is conduced by age sets rather than by kin and is directed to the great spirit Tororut. One of the best descriptions of cattle sacrifice among pastoralists is that of the Dinka by Lienhardt (1961).

On the day of the sacrifice, the animal or animals chosen for sacrifice are killed and left to lie for the time being with their noses pointing to the east (the sacred direction, as among Turu). The women, in single file, dance and luuloo greetings to arriving guests while the men sit in the shade of the huts and trees drinking beer, talking, and laughing. The head of the victim is supported by the bough of a tree, and the body is covered with the foliage of the *dhot* tree, which is placed upon the carcass of a victim as a sign of respect, just as girls' skirts are placed over the haunches of an ox or bull to cover the anus. The Dinka clan and lineage system is more developed than among such people as Pokot so that clan ancestors may be significant, in addition to the divinities, for part of the ritual. Thus the carcass of an animal may be associated with the symbol of clan divinity such as a sausage tree, but it may also be dedicated only to a divinity, such as the free divinity Deng. About noon, the men gather around the carcass with the women on the fringes, and a prophet leads in the singing of various hymns. Eventually, to the rhythm of another hymn, the shrubbery covering the animals is removed and the penis and testicles of the bull are cut off and taken by the women into a house to be eaten by old men of the lineage, to promote fertility. The beast's remainder is then cut up and distributed to the congregation to take home.

Turu man making an offering on the gravestone of his ancester

In Dinka and Nuer sacrifice, the significance of the sacrificed ox is that it is a substitute for humans, who would otherwise be victims. The ox protects mankind. In the Turu case, the ox provides a hide to make a mattress for the ancestor, or an ox and a goat symbolize a cow with calf who provides milk for the ancestor. In both cases, as in the Christian eucharist, no matter how dimly understood by the participants, the sacrifice is a statement about how men must relate to each other in order that life may be good and tranquil. The rather practical and straightforward way Africans often approach such rituals is well illustrated by an incident I once witnessed, in which a guest at the sacrifice knelt down on one knee by the gravestone of the ancestor being approached, turned over the gravestone as if to open the passage to the underworld where the ancestor dwelt, and said to him, "We have come here to provide you with a hide for your bed; now please stop causing distress to your *mwipwa,* Lisu, or we'll dig you up and throw you into the lake!"

WITCHCRAFT

Witchcraft is fundamentally different from sacrifice in the sense that it is action taken by righteous people against immoral, disorderly people who seek to obtain something selfishly and without compensation. Where sacrifice seeks to appease the forces of order, accusations of witchcraft seek to quell the forces of disorder.

The way the process of witchcraft accusation works may be illustrated from the Turu *mbojo* process, which is particular to Turu society, but which contains a general structure common to Africans. The Turu display in their beliefs all the essentials of Bantu philosophy outlined in Tempels' *Bantu Philosophy.* For example, they believe that the animals of the forest, the wild animals, are inferior in force to human beings and can therefore be controlled by human beings. Man-eating lions are endemic in the area during certain times as they migrate through it in a great cycle. During the period of their presence in Unyaturu, they typically kill some people. For example, during a period of fifteen months in 1946–47, they killed over 130 people, an unusually large number.

The Turu do not believe that lions kill people of their own volition. Human beings can control lions, and therefore the lions that kill are controlled by someone. That these lions are not lions motivated by their own interests is demonstrated in Turu thought by the claim that the *mbojo* is a real person dressed in a lion skin, with iron claws, or it is a human being who has been temporarily turned into a lion for the purpose of murder, or it is simply a lion under the direction of the assasin.

As to the question of who would want to use lions this way, the general answer is women. A man may be accused of complicity in an mbojo murder, but a woman is always behind him. Women, Turu feel, are all *watemea,* which may be translated as witches. At heart, they are all opposed to the interests of men and are a disorderly force.

The way a woman goes about committing a mbojo killing is recited easily by any Turu. She goes to a remote part of the subethnic group of Unyanganyi (if the persons questioned live in Wahi) where there is a man who rents out mbojo. She pays him and leads the lion to her home by a rope tied around its neck. She then takes the lion to a woman friend in a neighboring village who keeps it in her dark back room until the time for the murder. The lion is put upon the victim and when the killing is done, the lion is returned to its owner. Important to the logic of this system of explanation is the fact that the mbojo is believed to need to kill so that if the intended victim cannot be reached, it must kill someone, anyone, to satisfy itself.

Subsequent to a killing by a lion, the men of adjacent villages meet out in an open space near the villages, signifying separation from civilization, and decide which woman procured the lion and which woman held it for her. (If they can't identify a perpetrator, they explain the death as simply due to the lion's need to kill someone, anyone; this explanation absolves any women who are neighbors to the victim while retaining the belief that any women are capable at any time of employing mbojo.) The murderer, when identified, is subject to stress, sometimes physical but often only mental, until she confesses. Some confessors do so simply to satisfy the men, but others are under such stress that they make themselves believe they are guilty. The stories told by the women are in close agreement, partly because they confess to a pattern of action like that described above which everybody knows, and partly in response to leading questions, as would be the case with respect to the amount paid to hire the animal.

To the modern Western mind (but perhaps not the medieval Western mind), all this seems ridiculous. Just like Livingstone, we feel it is easy to show that the lion could not be controlled this way and that the confessions are fake. Moreover, like Livingstone, we would make the mistake of ignoring the double meaning of the mbojo process, which is a kind of ritual activity, resembling criminal prosecution. To the Turu, the lion is the symbol of men, but it is also an uncivilized force par excellence. The multivocality of symbols of which Turner speaks is never more evident than here. The mbojo process is an attempt by the Turu to cope mentally with the disorder fundamental to Turu life in the dependence for production and wealth on the importation into a cohesive village of cooperating men of a passel of strange women with interests fundamentally opposed to those of the men. The women are seen as controlling and as using the lions the way they generally control and use men through their secret societies. They cooperate across village lines, the way men do not. Witchcraft, as one man said, is their spear given them by God to protect themselves.

Why do the Turu use the mbojo ritual whereas few others do? The answer is in part because their habitat has provided them with the man-killing lions which may be incorporated into the system of thought. Man-eating lions are not universal. Also, it may be true that the degree of friction between men and women in Turu society is higher than in some other societies, and this leads them to take up a system of explanation which they otherwise might not have, even if the lions were there. For instance, like the Tswana, they could have blamed the lion killings on people of an adjacent society. Through a complex modeling process drawing upon fundamental notions in Bantu philosophy and utilizing the raw materials of their habitat, they have constructed a theory and a mode of action following from it which gives some sort of explanation of the conflict of men and women and of man and nature, an explanation of evil, and a course of action to bring it under control. The upshot of an mbojo process is to make women far more wary in their relations with men, more cautious and less disobedient, and it makes people in general feel they understand the world.

Systems of witchcraft belief, like any good theory, are amenable to a good deal of flexibility. For example, it has been claimed that a distinction can be made between witchcraft and sorcery in African thought (Evans-Pritchard 1937; Middleton and Winter 1963), and that this distinction can be related to subtle differences in social structure. Witchcraft refers to a characteristic of some persons which is inherent in them. A witch's internal organs are different from those of other people, and witches inherit this difference. Such people affect harm to others through mystical means. A sorcerer is more like a mechanic. Such a person is not inherently evil or deformed, but merely a manipulator of objects which can cause harm. With reference to the social structure, a witch would be somebody connected to another person through vital force, a kinsman of that person, able to manipulate the vital force to cause harm to him. A sorcerer, on the other hand, is not a member of one's descent group. In a sense then, a sorcerer is not an evil person as such, but just a stranger using a special method of attack. However, a witch is truly evil, a person who uses methods inherent in his physical form, based on the operation of vital force, to harm his own kin.

In Turu society, as earlier noted, the effective descent group is the village, composed of a single segmentary lineage of the second level. Turu generally believe that no one outside a village can harm a resident through witchcraft (which is why a woman accused of complicity in mbojo must be of the village of the woman or man she kills). However, it is possible to harm people of another village by going to special bewitching shrines in the rocks in the west country, where a specialist will cast the spell. In another place, where intervillage communication is higher, people may believe that bewitching can occur between villages or even different ethnic groups. Pokot society, with its great mobility has generated the belief that any Pokot may potentially bewitch any other.

The subtlety with which the theory of witchcraft may be manipulated is shown in the fact that women may be accused of being witches, combinations of witches and sorcerers, or just sorcerers, depending on the degree to which they are integrated into the families of their husbands (Middleton and Winter 1963). In fact this claim has been disputed, but there is no doubt that there is a substantial amount of truth in it. For example, the fact that Turu women are accused of controlling lions is an accusation of sorcery and reflects, no doubt, the fact that women are only partially under the control of their husbands. Some control still resides in the hands of their brothers and fathers. The term *watemea,* by which their bewitching activities are described, means "cutters," referring to the fact that their primary method for harming men is by lacerating the vagina of a victim's cow, thereby preventing it from having calves.

Witchcraft beliefs derive from the nature of evil in African life, which is defined in terms of personal relations, and which derives importantly from the dependence of men on women for cooperation in production. The beliefs ponder the nature of this evil, why it should be, and how to control it. This point was brought home early in the study of witchcraft by social anthropologists, in fact in the most famous study of it, Evans-Pritchard's *Witchcraft, Oracles and Magic among the Azande* (1937). Here, as earlier explained, the author points out the similarity between notions of witchcraft and our ideas about luck. The African reasons that if you die of some disease, there is no reason not to believe that the agent of your death was a microbe, or whatever. However, this does not answer the question of why it was you, and not someone else, the microbe killed. The ultimate cause of your death was someone who hates you and who directed the microbe to you.

It is an important fact that the extent to which authority or patronship exists, whereby people are forced into close proximity over time as opposed to having only short-term relationships, determines the extent to which witchcraft accusations are made (P. T. W. Baxter 1972). People in the latter societies believe in witchcraft, but they find less occasion to make accusations. Put another way, in societies, such as pastoral societies of the Turu type, where localized lineages are juxtaposed with extensive intervillage cattle exchanges, witchcraft accusations are confined within the village and do not extend to stock associates. Witchcraft accusations appear where people are forced to remain associated. Frictions are sure to develop in such situations, and these frictions become patterned, appearing in relations of certain types of persons, like husband and wife, or father and son, depending on the particular structure of the society. In more open, mobile pastoral societies, the ability to move away or the fluidity of associateship, works against conflicts of interest developing into permanent irritations. Among pastoralists evil is more likely to be attributed to one's own failings, and appeals are more likely to be made to the supernatural to help set oneself right. In such societies, also, curses are more likely to be used to control miscreants. A curse, in a sense, is the opposite of witchcraft, done by a righteous man against an immoral man. Baxter (1972) makes the interesting suggestion that witchcraft accusations are more likely in societies where people have zero-sum relations, where any gain made by one is equally a loss to others. I would rephrase this to say that they are more likely to appear in economies which are stagnant, as opposed to inflationary, growth economies.

Witchcraft beliefs may be more generally described in terms defined by Douglas (1966, 135), as a problem of pollution. In this sense, we share the same problem with Africans and cope with it in approximately the same way. Douglas notes that current debate in America about pollution parallels African thought. Pollution in one sense is dirt in the system, so to speak. What constitutes dirt is relative. Where there is dirt, there is system. That is to say, what constitutes dirt depends on how we define our system. A system may be defined as an ordered set of interactions among people within a certain habitat. No one cared about raw sewage in the rivers of America until this interefered with some aspect of someone's part of the system (sportsmen, campers, the city downriver?). Moreover, there is a double level to this, just as in Africa. Where the actions of one person or class of persons, such as industrialists, are seen as impinging on the actions and freedom of others, the industrialists' physical actions come to be defined as pollution, and the effluents from their factories put into streams become defined as pollution because they are polluted people (witches) and they are polluted because of their products. Such a syllogism exists in precisely the same form in Africa.

The phenomenon of witchcraft beliefs, in some form, is therefore probably universal, but explanations of witchcraft draw for their content upon the great traditions possessed by a society. Bantu philosophy depicts a witch as one who manipulates vital force to harm another person. The Mandari of southern Sudan (Buxton 1963) may display a form of the Nilotic great tradition in their theory of witchcraft. The witch among them is simply another type of God's creation, like lions or other preying animals, born to harm people. They are thought of as working God's will in bringing death to people, but, on the other hand, they are also thought of as hated by God. Thus bad luck and failure are attributed to witches, never to spiritual beings. Here, the witch, as in Bantu thought, is still a disorderly person, one associated with dirt, filth, and unnatural acts.

In West Africa we would expect to find some similarity with Bantu beliefs because of the apparent historical connection between these two areas. However, the separation of the two traditions is apparently old enough to generate at least differences in emphasis, the notion of fate, for one thing, being important. The Tiv (Mead 1955, 96ff) possess two concepts, *tsav* and *akombo,* which together provide the basis for accounting for evil. Tsav is a force, a personal potency like the Bantu vital force, which can be increased by taking actions of various kinds. Akombo are supernatural agents which interfere with the natural functioning of things. In this case, the idea of fate, contained in akombo, is allied with the notion of tsav to explain the sources of evil, akombo explaining bad fate and tsav other evils that can happen to a person as a result of superior tsav being used against him.

The form that notions of witchcraft take in any given society is thus compounded by the interplay of two variables, the particular great tradition used to identify the nature of evil persons and the structure of society with its peculiar points of interpersonal friction which reveal themselves through the forms that witchcraft accusations take. Witchcraft does not deal merely with conflicts between men and women. In the case of the Tiv, witchcraft notions are tied to conflicts between seniors and juniors, big men and little men, in a continuing struggle for power. Senior men and big men have more tsav than others and use it against the younger to keep them in line. That is to say, in this society when a young man suffers misfortune, he attributes it either to a bad akombo or to some senior trying by witchcraft, or the use of superior tsav, to keep him down.

Among the Mandari, those persons born evil, the tools of God, are often strangers incorporated into the ethnic group who are envious of their protectors and resent their patronage. Among the Nilotic Lugbara (Middleton 1963), night witches, the most feared kind, are always old men, who use their power of evil to put down the young men who challenge their authority. One wonders whether in Central Africa slave societies, slaves were not commonly accused of witchcraft.

The place of witchcraft beliefs in African thought can best be summarized by looking at their views of death. It is common to believe that death is caused by witches. (On the other hand, death is necessary; therefore, old, senile persons who are no longer able to adequately care for themselves may be helped to their deaths to solve the problem. It is reasoned that if a person reaches senility without being killed, no one will bother to kill him now because he is no threat to anyone.) That is to say, Africans, of whatever tradition, conceive of an ideal, good world whose aspects are displayed in the qualities of the right hand, of which life would be one while death would be on the left hand. They ask themselves, just as we do, why there is evil in the world. Their answer, condensed into beliefs in witchcraft, bad fate, and malevolent ancestors is that there are imperfections in the natural order—witches, who are something like genetically defective beings, ambitious, greedy and mean persons. Having identified the source of evil, they are also in a position to take action against it, just as we do when we remove impurities from the environment to protect the good life. In the case of witchcraft, this amounts to identifying those members of the community whose selfishness works against others. Africans do not condemn individuality or status variability, but rather they fault manifestations of individuality which are harmful to the rights or opportunities of others and which ignore obligations. A rich man who uses his wealth in an honest way to establish patronage is not necessarily condemned, nor is a woman who attempts to enrich her house. However, the rich man who is mean, and uses his wealth to destroy others, or a woman who in her greed to enhance her house dishonorably interferes with the efforts of her cowives or neighbors is seen as disorderly.

REVITALIZATION

Sacrificial rites occur in response to moral confrontation between men and their divine superiors. Witchcraft "rites," insofar as they are rituals of accusation, like mbojo or Azande seances, take place in the confrontation of moral and immoral persons. Birth and death rites occur in the confrontation of men with the creation and elimination of life. However, in Africa, the life-crisis situation which generates the largest responses, determined by the magnitude of the rite and the number of people involved, is ordinarily the ritual of accession to manhood. Women's puberty rites and ties of accession to motherhood may also be of large magnitude but not as predictably as male rites. Therefore, I have chosen to discuss these rites as a special case because what we know of them helps understand the life-crisis phenomena and the social upheavals that seek change.

In order to accomplish this end, it will be useful to look first at circumcision life-crises ceremonies as they occur among the Turu. In this society men usually go through the circumcision ceremonies at about the age of fifteen, sometimes at the same time as girls, who, however, enter it at an earlier age. Beginning in the period preceding the harvest but, after the final cultivation, the male initiates gather from neighboring or even regional villages at the home of a man who has decided to hold the event for his son or daughter, or both. On the assigned day, each boy is anointed on the head while he sits with his mother on her bed; he is then sent to the circumcision site—a place cleared of stover in the field next to the host's homestead. There, surrounded by the men and removed from the women, who are not allowed to watch, each boy, having in effect been torn away from his mother, unceremoniously has his foreskin cut off while his father and other adult men jeer at him. "I won't ever herd your sheep for you again!" the boy may cry out, and the father replies, "Who cares! You were never any good at it anyway!" Some of the boys cry and curse. Others proudly remain as stoical as they can. For the rest of the day, the bloody, naked, and miserable initiates are kept in a temporary stover hut in the field, where they are alternatively victimized by the men, who force

Young circumcised boys in liminal state, bodies covered with ash

them to stand and sing while doing the *usungu* dance, or they are left to languish while classificatory husbands and wives, as if to mock the boys, gleefully engage in the *ujumya ngoi,* a dance overtly and abandonly mimicking the act of coitus. The mothers who attempt to join the boys to comfort them are driven off by the fathers or are sent away by the boys themselves, who consider that they are men enough to endure the ordeal alone.

The climax of the day occurs when the women, doing the *kilimbida* marching dance, parade to the village water hole in the marsh and return to the homestead with water to cook *nxomba,* a thick porridge made for sick people. It is purposely dirtied and defiled by the women, who throw soiled skirts and other impurities into it. Dancing another kilimbida while holding aloft stirring spoons covered with the repulsive mixture, the women present the food to the boys who are told they must eat it, accompanied by further jeers from the men. Having done so (or refused to do so), the miserable fellows are successfully expelled from the homestead. The following morning, they are fed the liver of a sheep, which has heretofore been forbidden food for them. This is meant to induce fertility. They are then turned loose to go to their individual homesteads, there to construct a temporary windbreak and shade near the entrance to be used during the daylight hours for the next six months or so. (They are allowed to sleep in the house at night because of the danger from wild animals.) During this time, they are refused entrance to their home until

Pastoral Pokot sacrificing a steer

after dark and are forced to seek rest in the hut. From this shelter they wander about like strange beings, their bodies covered with soot, mud, and odd designs, forbidden or disinclined to wash, seemingly driven to hunt strange wild animals, and fed by anyone of whom they request food. They molest women, whom they force to give them white beads and whom they threaten with oddly shaped *igolyo* paddles.

At the end of the six months, when the rains begin, the boys wash. Their temporary shelter is destroyed by the men as if a great war had been fought and the initiates had been conquered, and the boys are received back into their homes by their fathers, whom they accuse of having deserted them and from whom they therefore demand a cow for reconciliation. This is the cow by whose name father and son subsequently address each other. After paying a bracelet made of the white beads he has collected, each young man reportedly succeeds in having coitus with an adult woman (one who is clitoridectomized), and transition to adulthood is complete.

Because circumcision rites like these occur every year and because they are so formalized, it is easy to fall into the error of thinking they are simply *pro forma* rather than crisis rituals, having little real personal significance. To some degree that may be true, but it is never entirely true. Besides the fact that the young men who undergo this ordeal are truly involved in a life crisis, the movement from childhood to manhood, they cannot hide from themselves the fact that such movements always involve conflict with the adult world. Most apparent is conflict with the father, whose role as director of the family's affairs is challenged by the son moving out from under his control. The son threatens the father's financial position by demanding the resources of his mother's house, most particularly the wherewithal to get married, in order to establish his own position. Thus becoming a man through the circumcision rite is not just a formality; it occurs along with real interpersonal conflicts. MacGaffey (1970) shows especially clearly how the *kinkamba* puberty rites of Kongo were related to political instability and messianism.

Turner (1969) shows that life-crisis rituals symbolically represent a dialectic in human life between structure and antistructure. Structure is the aspect of life which corresponds to all that has been described earlier in this chapter as on the right. It is what we think of as normal, the steady or conservative state of society in which logic reigns along with common sense, where people are practical, clever (if they can be), and orderly. Antistructure looks like anarchy or radicalism. It is a kind of behavior, occurring usually over a short time, during which structure seems to be stood on its head and in which crazies are on the loose.

People who are frustrated by structured events, whose attempts to achieve some kind of reasonable place in the structured order are blocked, are *liminal* or borderline and shift into a state of *communitas,* a kind of antistructure society. In this state the members of the communitas, or commune, individually or together, tend to manifest behavioral characteristics which are just the opposite or radically different from those which are respected in the structured state. Turner lists these traits (1969), some of which are

Antistructure	Structure
equality	inequality
absence of property	property
absence of status	status
nakedness	clothing
sexual continence	sexuality
minimization of sex distinctions	maximization of sex distinctions
humility	pride
no distinctions of wealth	distinctions of wealth
unselfishness	selfishness
total obedience	limited obedience
sacredness	secularity
silence	speech
foolishness	sagacity
suspension of kinship rights and obligations	kinship rights and obligations
simplicity	complexity
acceptance of pain	rejection of pain

During the period of communitas, the liminal person is seen as abnormal from the structured perspective. He (or she) is partial to equality, silence, humility, stupidity, and unselfishness and is prone to seek out and accept pain (as in the circumcision act itself). Such persons are black (in Ndembu color classification) or "dead." In fact, there are other things that could be added to this list of characteristics, one of which is hairiness, for which liminal people show great partiality.

Turner recognized a resemblance between these liminal traits, occurring among circumcision initiates, and those manifested by, for example, Hippies during the campus movements of the 1960s in the United States or members of segregated religious orders and cults. We need not stop there. In many important respects, true believers in any revolutionary movement or revitalization movement show many of the same traits. This is why I have said that circumcision, most particularly of African life-crisis rituals, is a human, rather than simply a cultural, manifestation in African behavior. The Turu boy who moves into the circumcision process is a liminal person, in confrontation with his father and the ruling generation. He seeks catharsis for his frustration in a resort to the communitas of the circumcision rites, which send him off into the wilderness (so to speak) for six months, to avoid water, to clean himself with mud (pollution), to paint his body with strange, "nonstructured" types of designs, to hunt strange animals, to manifest a totally communistic form of life in which he does nothing to support himself but depends on handouts from people he meets. At the end of six months, he is reborn into structured society, given a cow by his father (as a sign of reconciliation and reentry into the structured economy), and granted a new name, expressing this conciliation and his rebirth. In Turu society and elsewhere, women may also have their special rituals of life crisis. In some places they actually have a type which parallels circumcision, in which the clitoris is excised. However, often the crisis in a woman's life is much more severe than that of the man because she not only must advance to an adult role at an earlier age, but she must do so in a strange village, among strange men and women, to which she goes when married. Hence the crisis rites for women in Turu society are much more complex, running over many years, through four stages and end in the symbolic capturing of a lion (that is, possibly conquest of the men).

Revitalization can occur as a response to oppositions between other categories than those already mentioned, and the oppositions can also occur on a larger scale, involving whole villages, regions, or societies. For instance, such movements as the Mau Mau, the opposition of Kikuyu of one portion of society to a set of conditions caused indirectly by colonial rule, or TANU, the Tanzanian political movement opposing British rule, which involved many different ethnic groups.

Speaking of the apparently endemic tendency to revitalization movements in Zaire, De Craemer, Vansina, and Fox (1976), three specialists in the ethnography of the area, insist that these movements were not stimulated just by colonial rule, but were a regular part of the life of this area. This point of view offers a healthy counterweight to the idea that African societies were, in their precolonial phase, stagnant or static, although it is at fault in implying that such movements were only characteristic of this area. The best that can be said is that the Zaire Basin was particularly prone to generating such movements, perhaps because of deficiencies of production possibilities which created low-level chiefdoms and caused a great deal of breakdown and recombination of local groups in the areas where these movements took place. These authors discount the economic or situational determination of such movements, but I would insist on their importance. Any African society (and probably all) is likely to find itself at one time or another in a condition so untenable as to generate a religious revitalization movement, but in some areas, problems may have been so severe as to make them more common, as has also been the case with the people of Melanesia, who are prone to generate so-called cargo cults.

Wallace (1956) has said that any religion contains within its structure the remnants of a revitalization phase. For example, Christianity fosters the Ten Commandments, rules which apply well to the liminal person but which do not fit the reestablished steady state of society where, for example, killing and envy, or status and authority, are unavoidable. As these authors note of the Africans of Zaire, the movements are innovative. A leader always arises who may invent new myths which become established dogma. To accomplish this, he draws upon old myths and symbols which are recombined and sometimes augmented with others borrowed from the outside, the way some use the robes and the paraphernalia of Catholic bishops as part of their accouterments.

All these Central African movements aim to prevent misfortune and maximize good fortune. Furthermore, they focus on three major constellations of goods to be obtained by the new society which will grow out of the communitas: (1) fecundity, including birth of children, success in hunting, and abundant harvests (success in hunting would more likely be a desired goal in Zaire than in pastoral societies); (2) invulnerability and impunity, eliminating the risk that the role of chance lays on human affairs; and (3) improvement of status and wealth.

In these movements the goals, summarized in the rituals and symbols, are usually brought together and symbolized in a charm which, when accomplished, is placed in a shrine to keep it undefiled and strong. The rituals use prayer, invocation, and communion to establish and communicate with the invisible world and to indicate purity of intensions. In addition, a binary classification is established to show the nature of the new society, except that where authority emerges, as is usually the case in Zaire, the binary system is compounded with classifications like those spoken of by de Heusch for the Luba or Feierman for Shambaa, in which it is represented as a controlled, wild force. Thus, for example, the rooster is the civilized bird in opposition to the wild guinea fowl, both of which are eaten, but the wild eagle is superior to the rooster and in some sense to all birds, because it is the king, so the eagle feather is the symbol of the king.

Thus, the revitalization movement, responding to unsatisfactory conditions, generates a revolutionary society of communitas headed by a prophet, and if successful, it breaks the bonds of the old and generates, by a process of borrowing and recombination, a new symbolic-mythologic order and social structure to cope with the desire to better achieve the goals of reproduction, security, and wealth. Sometimes the new order may last for a very long time (as is generally the case in America where the present order derives from the period of the Civil War or in Africa where some societies, like the Yoruba, seem to have been very stable for a period going back into prehistory). But, sometimes the new order is short lived. De Craemer and others speak of some of these societies in Zaire as having a life of no more than a few years. While we are most aware of these movements as responses to colonial and modern national rule, we should not fail to be aware that they could have and probably did occur in all times. The African societies we see in the precolonial phase have been shaped to one degree or another by them, the way America was shaped by the Revolution of 1776, giving us a republican government, or France was shaped by the great French Revolution. After it is over, much remains the same, but the often subtle changes may have profound implications.

CONCLUSION

To summarize the last two chapters, African philosophy and religion may be viewed as containing two main dimensions, great traditions, comparable to Christianity and Islam in the West, and elements which are specific to individual societies, which are to some extent simply a product of our nature as animals. The former include such ideas as that God is close to man (Christianity, Islam, Nilotic philosophy) or that God is distant, a disinterested Being (Bantu). The latter, based on a metaphoric association of parts of the body and bodily functions with social processes, pictures the universe as composed of good and evil parts, the right representing the placid part of social life and the left, areas of tension and disorder. In this respect, African religion and philosophy, despite its special African features, is fundamentally like religion and philosophy in the West in its concern with the question of the presence of evil in life and the path to good fortune.

CONTEMPORARY
AFRICA

AFRICA TODAY is not what it was when the colonial powers first took control in the last quarter of the nineteenth century. For example, there are few visible chiefs or kings left; the king of Swaziland, Sobhuza II, is a notable exception. Furthermore, it is not what it was since the new national governments began rising in the late 1950s. For instance, there have been massive changes in production as these nations attempt to find a footing in the new international economy by exporting goods such as cotton, tea, coffee, or cocoa for currencies which can be used to purchase goods from overseas.

Then Africa at the end of the last century was not the Africa that existed 100, 500 or 1000 years before, either. As Johnston explained, over the last 400 years, the Zaire Basin shifted the production of crops from labor-expensive yams and African cereals to cheaper maize, subsequent to the discovery of

America, and finally to cassava, also from America. Cassava is the cheapest labor-demanding crop in Africa except for bananas. This steady move toward reduction of labor costs has surely had social and philosophical effects although in general, we don't know as much about them as we do about areas like Uganda, which saw the rise of banana military states accompanying the appearance of low labor cost plantains.

Africa, like the rest of the world, has been subject to change on all fronts at all times so this chapter does not intend to demonstrate that Africa has changed but rather to show what *kinds* of changes have accompanied large-scale contact with European and Southeast Asian societies. This will further enhance our understanding of African societies. It will give us greater insight into the modern problems of economic development and allow us to better grasp why it may be asserted that Africa, for all its modern changes, will continue for a long time to be recognizably Africa.

LONG-DISTANCE TRADE AND CHANGE

There was a time when it was believed that the massive trade that began between non-Africans and African societies after 1500, centering on the slave trade, had little impact on African societies away from the coast. Since the trade was coastal, it was assumed that interior societies continued statically to maintain their forms. Such views misunderstand the political economics of trade, the indirect impact on societies which may result from economic contact in areas remote from them. Shorter's study of Kimbu chieftainship which was discussed in Chapter 6, illustrates this point. Throughout much of western Tanzania, the indigenous economies were poor, having no cattle because of the tsetse fly and forced, due to low rainfall and poor soil, to depend on labor costly African cereals for the production of wealth. The political economies were labor-intensive, forcing people into patron-client relationships of petty chieftainships in order to gain control of enough land to produce any wealth at all. Into this situation a new element was injected by the appearance of coastal Arab traders who did not, at first, even venture inland but whose activities had profound remote effects. They were willing to pay beads, copper, cloth, guns, and powder, all items in great demand in the interior, for ivory and slaves. Up to that time, Africans had little interest in ivory and while labor was central in importance to their production process, demand for it was for some reason not extreme enough to generate domestic slavery. In Central Africa, we have seen, the pressure for labor was greater, both because the cost of production was high and because there was the possibility of using slaves to augment clans and provide military power to exploit neighboring states. In Tanzania, as Arab-African trade developed, the demand for slaves grew, not only because the Arabs desired them for export, but because the Arabs created a steady and high demand for such food products as maize to supply the needs of caravans and trading stations. It is for this reason, for example, that on Kerebe Island in Lake Victoria, slavery appeared among the indigenous people who used its products for sale to the Arabs, and slavery grew up in Unyamwezi as people used it to produce food. Meanwhile the Nyamwezi concentrated their production activities on securing ivory.

Thus the introduction of Arab trade created new wealth in a way that was not, however, open to exploitation by all. The elephants were thought of as a part of the resources of the land, and the landowner could claim half the ivory produced on his land by the hunter. Similarly, apparently, methods for securing slaves did not present possibilities for the rise of extensive economy. Thus trade with the Arabs did not move societies toward egalitarianism but simply intensified the already present hierarchical system. Chiefs became more and more powerful, giving rise eventually in both Kimbu and Nyamwezi societies to kings.

This last illustration allows clarification of one problem in the interpretation of African history raised by Alagoa with respect to the Niger Delta. Alagoa disputes with other historians the question of the rise of states in that area. He says that there is no doubt that the trans-Atlantic slave trade stimulated the rise of large-scale states. However, those historians who think that this was the sole cause of states underestimate the amount of long-distance trade based on local production that already existed in the area, which also could have led to the creation of states. Alagoa's point is well taken. I have suggested that African societies were never totally isolated from each other and that trade in varying degrees of intensity occurred between societies everywhere. However, Alagoa's argument seems to imply that trade is the only cause of hierarchy. It must be remembered that hierarchy arises wherever production of wealth can be monopolized, or where the exchange of wealth (as in the control of market places) can be monopolized. The Kimbu chiefdoms were built, not so much on trade, as on monopolization of land. This seems to be the case with most of Africa's petty hierarchical systems; intersocietal trade merely amplified the hierarchical tendencies. Therefore, we can be certain that states of one size or another have existed in the Niger Delta for a very long time, merely increasing in size and wealth with the introduction of slave trade.

This tendency can be seen in many parts of Africa. MacGaffey remarks (1970, 244) that the areas of lower Zaire closest in contact with long-distance trade (Portuguese in this case) had the most powerful, most centralized, and most stable regimes, in which concentration of power was marked by rituals and insignia of chieftainship. That West Africa was economically far more dynamic in the production of commodities of all types, including slaves for the European and American market, is well documented (Hopkins 1973). Therefore, it may be said, with a good deal of assurance, that Alagoa's thesis about the Niger Delta can be extended to most of West Africa, where the prevalence of states, especially large-scale states, is understandable. Central Africa, outside the lower Zaire Basin, seems also to have been affected by this process. The European demand for slaves led the area at the mouth of the Zaire River to become the second most important source of slaves, next to West Africa. In addition, the Nile Valley, because of the opportunities for trade, bred most of the states which are known there (Trigger 1969).

There is some dispute about what happened in South Africa. Large-scale states of the Zulu type appear to be relatively modern in that area, but some scholars seem to feel that trade was not the stimulus. They maintain that certain ecological problems gave rise to opportunities to monopolize grazing and lay the basis for statehood in a high-density, cattle population area. This is a problem yet to be resolved.

Thus, during the precolonial phase of African history, the appearance of strangers on the coasts—Portuguese, British, Dutch, Danes, and others in West Africa and Portuguese at the mouth of the Zaire River and in Mozambique in Eastern Africa—created demand for new products, like ivory, or increased demand for old products, like slaves, introducing conditions for augmenting hierarchy and the rise of larger-scale states than before. However, the process, while generally leading to creation of larger kingdoms, did not invariably have that result. In some cases, the rise of a larger kingdom meant the demise, as in the case of Shambaai, of smaller kingdoms and the revolutionary reformation of some kingdoms, such as Buganda, after the introduction of firearms.

There is at least one case of a different effect. This involves the Kru of eastern Liberia and the western Ivory Coast (Massing 1977). Whether they had petty chiefs in the old days is not clear, but as a result of the appearance of European ships on their coast after 1500, they became involved in trade which led to economic growth and, apparently, egalitarianism, which continued down into colonial times.

THE COLONIAL ERA

The imposition of colonial rule had an immediate effect on most African kingdoms. In the first place, the colonial powers would not allow former chiefs and kings to exercise much authority in competition with them. At the same time, the economic basis for kingly and chiefly power was undermined or destroyed. In Central Africa this was accomplished by the abolition of slavery. In western Tanzania slavery was also abolished, and the power of the chiefs to claim ivory was curtailed.

The fundamental problem faced by chiefdoms and kingdoms was that tribute could no longer be gathered to support the hierarchical center. The colonial governments took control of taxation (which is a form of tribute) and transformed chiefs into bureaucrats. Newbury illustrates this from Rwanda (1978, 22):

> Under the European administrative yoke, transformations in the pow-
> ers of (Rwanda) chiefs represented a significant modification in the
> character of local authority. Whereas previous authorities had been
> members of a local kin group with the principal function of represent-
> ing that group to outsiders, during the European colonial period chiefs
> were appointed from above, and often from outside Kinyaga; this
> progressively removed the possibility of the local population bringing
> to bear moral or social influence. The principal function of a chief
> came to be the imposition of burdens on the people under him, while
> his major responsibility was to his political superior.

This description of what happened to the status of chiefs in Rwanda could serve for most places in Africa under colonial rule. However, the power of the colonial rulers did not extend with equal force over all areas so chieftainship survived in its precolonial form in varying degrees of magnitude where an economic basis for it was preserved.

Pastoral people, for the most part, survived the imposition of colonial rule much better. That the colonial powers had difficulty knowing how to deal with headless, egalitarian societies is suggested by the fact that the British created chiefs out of nothing and thought that they would be able to operate with at least as much efficiency as those in former state areas. In fact they did not. Pastoral populations tended to be comparatively small and remote, which was another reason colonial governments did not seem overly hasty about bringing them under control. In Kenya certain pastoral societies which lived on prime agricultural land, like the Maasai, the Nandi, the Kipsigis, and the Teso received more attention. The Nandi even fought a war with the government in the early part of the century; they sought to rebuff settlement in their area. Although all these societies had land taken from them and were manhandled in one way or another, all survive today as recognizable entities, continuing important aspects of their precolonial social forms. They resisted Europeanization the way nonpastoral people often did not, apparently because the cost to them in abandoning pastoral ways of life far exceeded the cost to agricultural-based people for whom the opportunity costs of shifts were lower (Schneider 1974).

As is the case today under national governments, the attempts by external colonial powers to manage ethnic groups within their boundaries in terms of the aims of central government suffered from insufficient understanding of socioeconomic processes in the local areas. A few examples from various parts of Africa will suffice to make the point.

In the Karamojong region of Uganda, both the former colonial government and present government have pressured the Karamojong to raise exports of beef from their area for the benefit of the nation as a whole, since the Karamojong are probably the largest cattle-raising group in Uganda. However, the government has always worked on the assumption that Karamojong raise cattle simply for "prestige" and that they have little understanding of their financial uses, as described earlier in this book. Karamojong are reluctant to sell off cattle in numbers exceeding approximately 10 percent, which would threaten herd structures as capital growth entities. Therefore, their response has been to increase raiding on the neighboring Pokot in Kenya in order to recoup losses. Here we are presented with the paradox that an apparently "modernized" pastoral society, using plows to grow crops, is now resorting more than ever to a "primitive" practice, raiding their neighbors for cattle.

Another example of unforeseen negative consequences of seemingly innocent actions by colonial governments comes from the abolition of exchange marriage among the Tiv, which was discussed earlier. As a result, there was a huge rise in the number of cases brought before the newly formed colonial court system as young men brought suits against the old and accused the old men of having used their superior tsav to bewitch them.

Examples of this kind of unforeseen reaction to apparently innocent and well-intentioned action can be multiplied many times over. They continue today in the development programs of national governments. While it is fashionable to criticize these actions of central governments, it seems reasonable

Ox plowing in Botswana—wife guiding the plow and husband directing the oxen

to argue that they are unavoidable. Even if central governments knew that such reactions might occur, they might still follow the courses of action that produce them on the grounds that if you can't bring about change in an orderly fashion, it is just as well to do it in a disorderly fashion because disruption of indigenous patterns is essential to constructing new ones that better serve national interests.

We are only now beginning to realize, however, that some of the greatest success stories in African development occurred out of sight, so to speak, among Africans long regarded by colonial powers as hidebound, who took initiative without prompting or guidance from central administration. The number of such stories is not very great because opportunities to move successfully into new types of profitable enterprises are not common. However, they are significant for what they say about the potential of Africans for change.

Probably the most famous of such incidents is the rise of cocoa production in Ghana (Hill 1970, 21ff; 1961). These Ashanti people did have experience in the last century with the production of export crops, specifically palm oil, but somehow by 1891, they began to realize that there was a market for cocoa. They had no use whatever for this crop brought in from America, but they migrated to areas suitable for its cultivation and began to produce it for export. They exported 80 lbs in 1891, 536 tons by 1900, and 40,000 tons by 1911. Since then they have always been the world's largest producers of cocoa. Hill, who has studied the history of this process most closely, describes these people as capitalists because (1) from the beginning they bought the land on which they produce cocoa specifically for cocoa production; (2) they always regarded cocoa production as a business; (3) the production system was not a sideline but a relatively large-scale enterprise; (4) they formed associations in a thoroughly commercial manner to buy blocks of land; (5) they did not let lineage obligations interfere with the conduct of the business; (6) they both saved and borrowed in order to finance the enterprises; (7) the enterprises were complex with producers setting up branches run by relatives in order to increase production; (8) they took a long view of the enterprise and responded to high world cocoa prices by buying more land and vice versa; (9) they were completely devoted to operating the enterprises, even though they still regarded their original place of orgin as home; (10) they did not depend on the colonial administration to make the businesses go, and even expended their own resources on building roads and bridges between their area of cocoa estates and their homeland.

What happened in Ghana is not unique. Berry (1975) explains that in Nigeria, cultivation of cocoa began after 1892 in the Ijebu area of Yorubaland and expanded rapidly. Berry notes that some people have claimed that both the Ghana and Nigerian cases represent mere imitations of European capitalist activities, but such a view is difficult to maintain in the light of the preceding arguments by Hill. It is probably true to say that the only thing the Africans got from the Europeans in all of this is knowledge of cocoa and the fact that there was a world market for it. From that point on, the initiative seems to have been theirs. Furthermore, the impact of this activity in Yorubaland has been large movements of population, the establishment of thousands of villages, significant modifications in patterns of rural land tenure, the decline of old methods of labor employment in favor of wage labor, and through the income earned, redistribution of power in many Yoruba communities.

The Kru people, mentioned before, are an interesting example of a contrary process, according to Massing (1977). He documents early Kru response to the appearance of European ships on the coast and the rise of trade between the Kru and these voyagers. In the early days, trade included pepper, slaves, and ivory, but by 1900 it had transformed (with the abolition of slavery and other such changes during the nineteenth century) to a trade of rubber for cloth, tobacco, salt, iron and copper bars, knives, spirits, powder, and firearms. Until European colonial control took hold about 1900, the Kru, as a result of trading with Europeans since at least 1470, had a growth economy in which production for the external European market, prompting the inflow of European goods, led to continued expansion of production enterprises and increasing wealth. However, as a result of European colonial control and the imposition of taxes and other types of economic interference, the Kru economy went into decline. Massing maintains that the home-oriented production systems in the rural Kru areas today are not a result of a lack of market orientation among the Kru but the result of a depressed internal economy caused first by colonial and later by national policies.

Shifting across the continent to coastal Kenya and the Giriama, Parkin (1972) has described how the economy of these people responded autonomously to the rise of a market for copra (coconut meat). The Giriama always appear to have been interested in developing a cash crop, but before the introduction of coconuts, they had only their labor and certain amounts of palm wine to offer to coastal Arabs and the Swahili. The latter was a commodity too perishable to constitute the foundation for an export economy. Today, as a result of the market for copra and the production demands of the crop, which unlike palm wine does not require the maintenance of extensive kinship ties, the Giriama have shifted to a more egalitarian, capitalist orientation than in the past.

Not all responses to new opportunities occurred on the coasts and among hierarchical people. Two remarkable examples of economic change occurred among the Kipsigis of Kenya and the Teso of Uganda, both formerly stateless pastoral people, living in much lusher grassland regions than most pastoralists, grasslands also suitable for economic agricultural operations. While each of these societies appeared to shift from an African to a European economic orientation, the truth is much more complicated. The Teso today are cotton growers (Uchendu and Anthony 1975). This is entirely an export crop since they did not grow cotton before Europeans came, and they do not weave today. The Kipsigis (Manners 1962), on the other hand, grow maize and tea in large quantities. Both crops are exported, the maize mainly within East Africa where it is a staple in the labor force. Both got into the export crop business after the turn of the century, and today both are for the most part committed to this type of production. Yet despite all this, the Kipsigis today continue to raise large numbers of cattle (Daniels 1975) as do the Teso. Furthermore, each seems to emphasize cattle production, despite appearances to the contrary. These cattle are not raised for the beef markets but as repositories of value, as in the past. In other words, in both the Teso and Kipsigis instances, we have people who have responded to opportunities to create wealth in external markets but who have not become Europeanized. They are using the wealth to build up herds and remain essentially Africans.

Evidence as full as that on the rise of the cocoa industry in West Africa or the maize, tea, and cotton industries in East Africa is not easy to come by, but there is still sufficient material to document many cases of widespread African responses to new opportunities which parallel the ones just reviewed. In East Africa other instances include the shift of the Chagga on Mt. Kilimanjaro from plantain to coffee production. This made the Chagga, before independence, the richest people in old Tanganyika. Similarly, the Baganda, have moved from plantain to coffee production and have become an important worldwide exporter of coffee. The Sukuma, in Tanzania, south of Lake Victoria, have become large-scale cotton producers. In Zambia, maize is raised on a large scale by people who are near enough to railroads to make transport to markets in the urban centers reasonable. This is also true of parts of the Zaire Basin. Furthermore, peanut production has become very important in such places as northern Nigeria and Senegal.

Pastoral people have been much slower to shift from indigenous modes to beef and milk production. Today in East Africa, the governments of Sudan, Somalia, Kenya, Tanzania, and Uganda are still concerned with the fact that no way to bring about a large-scale shift has been found (Schneider 1979).

In summary, during the colonial period, although government policies were often based on the assumption that Africans were naturally not economically motivated, Africans responded to new opportunities in ways that can be described as economically rational. Those who were less well off, mainly the agriculturalists, leaped at the chance to create new wealth if such was possible (cocoa, palm oil, coconuts, maize, cotton, peanuts), and those who were well off, mainly pastoralists, threw up defenses to maintain the profitable (in indigenous economic terms) pastoral mode of production acquiring, therefore, the label of conservative.

Before leaving the colonial period, a word must be said about African reaction to the imposition of colonial rule. During the discussion of life-crisis situations in Chapter 9, mention was made of the fact that revitalization movements seem endemic to the lower Zaire Basin because of the unstable socioeconomic conditions of the area. In East Africa or West Africa, where conditions seem to have been more stable in precolonial times, colonial invasions also created instability. In some cases this led to crises that manifested themselves in revitalization movements. For example, in the early days of German rule in Tanzania, around the turn of the century and after, a number of movements appeared. The Fipa on Lake Tanganyika revolted under a messianic leader, as did the Hehe, in southern Tanzania under the famous chief Mkwawa; the Turu, in central Tanzania; and the Giriama, to name only a few. The hopelessness of their situation against well-disciplined and armed European troops recalls the situation faced by the Aztecs and the Incas with the appearance of the Spaniards. Characteristic of revolutions, which are simply forms of revitalization movements, people do not revolt when the situation is hopeless, only when there is hope that action can bring freedom. The vision which derived, at the beginning of German rule, from remembrance of the free past, reappeared during the last decade of colonial rule when the colonial powers weakened. So revolutionary movements, often manifesting aspects of life-crisis rituals, sprang up all over Africa. In East Africa, again, the most famous was the Mau Mau, beginning about 1952, which laid the foundation for Kenya independence. TANU (Tanganyika African National Union) in Tanzania did the same. In West Africa, Kwame Nkrumah in Ghana (formerly the Gold Coast) symbolized the independence movement, just as the Ashanti wars of the previous century heralded the end of independence and British control. To one degree or another, every African country began colonial rule with more or less sporadic revolutionary reaction and ended with large-scale, national movements of independence.

THE NATIONALIST ERA

African nations today (see Map 1.2) are, for the most part, strange sociological phenomena. For example, they are not really nations as we understand the term. A Western nation is usually ethnically homogenous or dominated by a single ethnic group (Switzerland being a notable exception). In the United States, we nearly all speak English and subscribe to a common Christian, and some might add Jewish, tradition (even though there are minor perturbations of Islam, Hari Krishna, or whatever). The Germans speak German; the Italians, Italian. It is true that these nations are comparatively recent phenomena. However, they were built on smaller ethnic units which were much alike, speaking mutually intelligible dialects. In Africa this is seldom the case. Somalia is composed almost entirely of a single ethnic group, the Somalis; Botswana, of the Batswana; Swaziland and Sotholand, of Swazi and Sotho; Rwanda and Burundi, of Abarwanda and Abarundi. Having said this, we have

Sign of development in Botswana

nearly covered all relevant African cases of ethnic unity. Moreover, even to say this may be misleading. There is evidence that the apparent ethnic tightness of at least some of these units has been prompted by the rise of national governments, even during the colonial period, as in Burundi (Newbury 1978). Even the supposedly continuous political units are in fact greatly transformed entities, compared to the precolonial period. Other than these special cases, Tanzania, for instance, contains ethnic groups which speak every one of the major African languages: Afro-Asiatic, Bantu, Nilo-Saharan, and Click. This would be like a European country containing within its borders speakers of German, Romance, Slavic, and Arabic.

The explanation for this is complex. Left to themselves, no doubt African nations would seek to sort out ethnicity and establish homogeneity almost as an instinctive response in the way Europeans did or new nations did that arose in the last century. Some of this kind of action has in fact been attempted, notably the Somali-Ethiopian war, in which Somalia tried to integrate within its boundaries those portions of Ethiopia which contained ethnic Somalis (in the Ogaden and other parts of Ethiopia). Somalia also cast covetous glances at portions of Kenya and Djibouti which contained other Somali elements. There are two main reasons why this kind of action is not frequent. In the first place, in the interest of political practicality, the international balance of power, particularly between the United States and the Soviet Union, functions to keep Africa from bursting into flames of ethnic aggression. Thus, the boundaries established during the colonial regimes, no matter how arbitrary, have been made sacrosanct. In the second place, the leaders of these new nations have, for the most part, shed their ethnic identities and become culturally homogenized with the colonial peoples that once ruled their countries. They are no longer Africans in the full sense but are Europeans of one type or another, mainly English and French, but also Portuguese and Belgian. Their identity, like the colonial rulers before them, is with a piece of territory, not an ethnic group. Tanzania is a somewhat aberrant case in that Swahili is now the official national language—even though to many Tanzanians, Swahili is as much a foreign language as German would be to English speakers. Moreover, English is still the unofficial language of the political elite. Elsewhere, in Nigeria, Sierra Leone, Kenya, or Ghana, the language of the colonial predecessors has to serve as the official language because there is no common language, not even a lingua franca like Swahili.

Another reason for this situation is that in order to survive and prosper in the modern world, these African nations must develop some kind of a production system which will have relevance to world markets and the world economic system. The production systems of precolonial Africa are for the most part obsolete. There is no world market for African cereals, skinny African cows, cassava, yams, or many other common old products. What the world wants from Africa, and what Africa must produce in order to earn income to buy the things it wants, if only to defend itself, are things that non-Africans who have industrial products want. Thus African nations have been driven to ignore ethnicity and to try to turn African production to the world markets. Nigeria has been fortunate. With huge supplies of oil, it has found a basis for interacting with other nations and is developing the potential to hold its place. However, nearly all other nations (with the special exception of the Ivory Coast [Stryker MS]) have had troubles and continue to have them. Botswana also has important supplies of minerals in the Kalahari Desert, including diamonds, and sells cattle to the Common Market in Europe. But Tanzania has had to depend on such things as sisal, whose value has declined with the development of synthetic, petroleum-based fibers, or coffee and cotton, of which it does not produce enough. Somalia has camels to export, and there is some market for them and their products but not enough to support a place in the international economy. Zaire has had to depend on the uncertain ores of the Shaba province. Zambia depends too much on copper ore, whose price fluctuates too much. Zimbabwe, partly because of its ores, but also because of European agricultural operations, and Kenya, with agricultural products now largely produced by Africans from capitalized establishments inherited from colonial English, have somewhat better positions but are still relatively insecure.

For African leaders all this poses a serious problem. As Gamer (1976) has pointed out, a "healthy" political system is one which, like the indigenous African systems, has a rational structure of patron-client relationships. A king or chief was legitimate and accepted because he conducted an exchange, goods and services, with his subjects, which they saw as honest and the best they could do. This structure depended on the resources of the kingdom or chiefdom so that in poor regions, like western Tanzania, there were petty kingdoms and in rich areas, like Buganda, there were great kings. The present African nations did not grow rationally from the economic base they possessed. They were carved out by the colonial powers and were a rational part of each colonial nation's total political economy. In most of the African nations, the wherewithal to support a legitimate government of the size forced on them does not exist, and the failure of one governmental structure after another, to be replaced by the rule of ultimate force, the armed forces, was inevitable as was heavy dependence on foreign aid, as clients of either the Western or Communist nations. The problem today is to try to develop that basis of rational government, internally supported, a problem which in many cases may be insurmountable. Of course, as long as the great powers feel it is in their interest to prevent the total eruption of Africa into ethnic warfare, the situation will be stabilized since they provide each client nation with the wealth (or at least the arms) they need to make it possible for the rulers to give a semblance of legitimacy to their position.

The attempt to achieve a rational structure since independence has resulted in some places in great, even violent, use of force. Most mild, perhaps, is the banning of competing political parties, as was done by Kenneth Kaunda in Zambia. A step further in the use of force is the case of Tanzania. The government of Tanzania under Julius Nyerere has from the beginning of independence in 1961 planned a national society of equality, to be achieved by the combination of government support for communal private enterprise (*ujamaa* villages) and government control of all other assets, mainly land. The ideas was to prevent an elite class from rising, by stifling individual capitalist activities. However, the system has failed to produce the wealth necessary to make the nation independent of foreign influence. Corruption (patron-clientship) has become a problem, over 3000 people were reported to be under detention by 1977, and the government has resorted to force in some cases to get people into ujamaa villages. There are signs that the government's policy is changing as it seeks to raise the level of production and wealth at the expense of some of its egalitarian aims.

Burundi, Rwanda, Uganda, and Equatorial Guinea provide four of the most extreme cases of violent instability. Rwanda and Burundi are similar in that both had a Tutsi overlord caste or class ruling over Hutu peasants when the colonists took over these countries. Belgium ruled them as a single country, Ruanda-Urundi. When Belgian rule began to fade in the late 50s, the Hutu apparently sensed the possibility of a new order, different from the old caste structure. Although neither country was much developed (today they still have no railroads and poor roads as well as few export commodities), the Hutu in both countries must have perceived the possibility of links with the outside and foreign aid. Today Rwanda does have a good deal of aid from Belgium and other sources. The Rwanda Hutu rose up in 1959 and attacked the Tutsi, killing more than 100,000 and driving many others out of the country.

In Burundi, on the other hand, the Tutsi contained the situation and with an all-Tutsi army, managed in 1972 to put down a Hutu revolt. An estimated 30,000 people were killed. Today Burundi receives little outside help and probably for that reason in 1976, a military coup got rid of Tutsi President Micombero and replaced him with Colonel Jean Baptiste Bagaza, who speaks of creating national unity. In both these cases, the nations are obviously seeking a way to restructure for development, a condition of which, due to world opinion, is a removal of caste.

Uganda, or at least the area of Buganda and certain other Interlacustrine states, by contrast, has had a secure relationship with the world economy for a long time due to the fabulous growth of coffee production. It appears to have been reaction to the prosperity of Buganda and the relative poverty of development in other areas that led to the rise of General Idi Amin Dada, who is reported to have killed three hundred thousand opponents, including the Archbishop of Kampala. Although Amin was overthrown in 1978 Uganda was still very unsettled by 1979.

Equatorial Guinea is different from the Burundi and Rwanda cases but similar to Uganda in that a small detribalized class (mostly Bubis) seems to have grown up during the Spanish colonial period. This class was hated by the nonelites (mostly Fang). After independence in 1968, these outsiders rose up under Francisco Macias Nguema, President-for-Life, and began systematically killing off the elite, over 50,000 in the last 9 years. Unlike Uganda, there seemed to be an attempt by Macias and his followers to destroy development (cocoa production fell precipitously) and reinstitute a kind of indigenous African monarchical structure. While the counterrevolution had aspects of ethnic rivalry, the attempt to structure the nation in indigenous terms, failing a successful development strategy (at least for Fang), is obvious. In some respects the isolated Central African Republic under the "Emperor" Bokasso seems to have followed the same course. While Amin, Macias, and Bokasso had all been removed by 1979, there was no assurance that despotism was thereby ended once and for all.

There is a pattern here which transcends the differences of the various countries and which will also be seen in other countries of Africa. The uneven development of the national economy leads to the creation of haves and have-nots, often following tribal lines. In some cases (probably the majority) the developed tribal sector has the upper hand, allowing it to contain the have-nots. In some cases (the Hutu in Rwanda, the Kakwa [Amin's ethnic group] in Uganda, and the Fang in Equatorial Guinea), the have-nots sometimes managed to put down the ascendant group. However in the act of winning, the winners in a certain sense lose because the international community dislikes violence and so refuses to extend aid.

ZAMBIA

The peculiarities and problems of modern African nations are best illustrated by taking one case, Zambia, almost at random, although Tanzania, Kenya, Ghana or any number of other African nations would also have served.

Until independence, Zambia (see Map 6.2), was called Northern Rhodesia and was a British colony, part of the Federation of Rhodesia and Nyasaland which was dominated by the white settlers of Southern Rhodesia (later Rhodesia, then Zimbabwe-Rhodesia and presently Zimbabwe). It came into being when the scramble for African colonies was given sanction after the Berlin Conference. It was probably inevitable that it would come under British control because of its proximity to Southern Rhodesia, named after the famous British empire builder, Cecil Rhodes. Moreover, after the Boer War, the British established control of all of southern Africa including Botswana and, later, southwest Africa, now Namibia.

Zambia is smack in the center of the matrilineal belt across central Africa, and its societies, as we saw earlier, had to build on poor soil, for the most part without cattle. They economized labor more than anyplace else, so much so that large-scale indigenous systems of servitude dominated until they were abolished by the colonial government. Within the country, equivalent in size to Texas, are about sixty different ethnic groups, totaling in population in 1970 over 4,200,000 people (Morrison and others 1972). Of these people, the Bemba (Map 6.1) in the east are the largest, but they still constitute only 15 percent of the total population and the Lozi, in the west represent a powerful ethnic counterforce, who have even attempted independence. The situation here resembles Tanzania, where the largest group, Sukuma, consists of only 12 percent of the population. Thus, whatever benefits may accrue to a new nation by having at least a semblance of ethnic homogeneity are already lost. An important result of this is that Zambia, like most of the other African countries, must resort to a foreign language, English, as the language of government, commerce, and education.

Kenneth Kaunda, the leader of Zambia since independence in 1964, is typical of many African leaders in that his whole life has been extensively detached from the indigenous ways that characterized the types of Africans about whom I have talked (Hatch 1976). His father was a missionary of the Scottish mission of Livingstonia in Blantyre, Nyasaland (Malawi), and Kenneth Kaunda was born in 1924, 20 years after his father moved to Northern Rhodesia. His father served as headmaster of the mission school and later became an ordained minister. Although his father died when he was eight, and the family was very poor, Kaunda's commitment to education, one of the main roads to success before independence, sustained him. He managed to continue his education through middle school and he attended the first secondary school in the country for two years. In order to understand how all this shaped Kaunda into what was essentially a kind of black Englishman, it must be understood that school life from the earliest was on the British pattern, highly regimented with boarding away from home the rule after the most elementary grades. Even Kaunda's elementary work was done in the area of a mission station. By the time he left secondary school to become a teacher, he was thoroughly Anglicized. Nyerere of Tanzania was much the same, as were Nkrumah of Ghana or the various Frenchified leaders of the former French colonies. Since independence there have on occasion arisen to the ranks of state heads some Africans, like Mobutu of Zaire or Amin of Uganda, whose Europeanization was less thorough, but none could function without a basic working understanding of the ways and language of the former colonial masters, and none had any better chance at establishing a legitimate governmental system than the more Europeanized.

The country which Kaunda inherited from the British was dominated by copper mines in the north center of the country bordering on the mineral rich Shaba Province of Zaire, opposite the capital of Lusaka, on the main rail line to Rhodesia and South Africa. It might be thought that having a highly developed, capital-intensive ore industry within its confines was a great advantage for Zambia, in contrast to such countries as Tanzania or Kenya, which had nothing. However, it is a mixed blessing. By 1979 Zambia was in deep economic trouble, the shape of which was already apparent by 1970 (Elliott 1971). When independence came, it was accompanied by a huge rise in labor costs, mostly from the mines whose powerful labor unions, with other forces, increased the cost of producing Zambian copper by 66 percent from 1962 to 1968. As a result, of course, the demand for Zambian copper dropped. From 1964 to 1968 the consumer price index rose 40 percent forcing the government to alter drastically its policies from growth to control of inflation. This was accomplished largely by huge budget cuts. The urban dwellers, who constitute a relatively small fraction of the population (about 12 percent), were able to protect their incomes by access to the sources of power and through labor organizations, with the result that the decline in government spending mostly affected the have-nots (the rural sector). As a result, a polarization of wealth began. This pattern of polarization of new wealth accompanying a rise in national income is familiar to developmentalists all over the world and constituted the chief development problem of the 1970s. It seems almost inevitable that as new forces are introduced which raise gross national product, the product ends up in the hands of fewer and fewer people (although this is not a necessary consequence, and so reflects the malintegration of the national economic system). Tanzania, as we saw, adopted from the start a socialist regime designed to avoid just this but found by 1978 that to try to distribute income by fiat did not work because it stifles economic growth. Similarly, the Ivory Coast, a model of development success, whose economy grew from 7.5 percent to 8 percent annually over the period 1950–75 and whose per capita income rose to $550, similar to Brazil at that time, was by 1979 suffering from increasing inequality in all dimensions—between the northern and southern parts of the country, between rural and urban sectors, and between Abidjan, the capital, and the hinterland.

Those persons concerned with Third World development are in the habit of perceiving the traditional economies of Africans as noneconomies, as static, "subsistence" systems. However, this is a mistake. Africans had economies, but the goods they produced and the political systems that were based on them are irrelevant to the powerful world system that now dominates the Third World. "Development" is the breakdown of the traditional African systems and their incorporation into the world system. Commonly this means the exploitation of minerals that formerly had no value in African economies, or the cultivation of crops like cocoa, coffee, or sisal, which also had no meaning to Africans, and it means the sale of labor to enterprises which did not exist before when, as in traditional Africa, there was no labor market except that of women in marriage. As development proceeds, the pattern that emerges is a traditional sector alongside a developed sector, between which there is little interaction.

Today in Zambia the new developing sector consists of urban wage earners, copper miners, and farmers along the railroad right of way which traverses the country from north to south. Farmers specialize in growing maize for the urban markets (Schultz 1976). These developed farmers export maize and import industrial products from internal manufactories and from abroad, while the traditional farmers, farther from the railroad, continue in their old production activities. It is fair to say, therefore, that to talk of severe inflation in the Zambian economy is to speak only of the developed sector. By buying more from abroad than they can pay for with declining copper revenues, they are in a bind not felt by the indigenous rural people who are relatively untouched by the new economy.

In 1978 there was talk of a possible food shortage in Zambia because of the closure of the Rhodesian border due to the war, which prevented the importation of fertilizer for the maize crop. This assessment treats the developed sector as if it were the whole of the Zambian agricultural system. The fact is, of course, that the traditional sector provides its own fertilizer through the chitemene system discussed earlier, and it is only the developed sector's food supply that is under threat.

Statistics on the Zambian economy and society support the picture of Zambia as a dual economy (Morrison and others 1972). In 1968, 81 percent of the labor force in Zambia was engaged in agriculture, compared to 96 percent in Niger, 95 percent in Burundi, 95 percent in Tanzania or 86 percent in Ivory Coast. By 1975 (Bhagavan 1978, 34) the percentage remained about the same. All these are very high percentages, compared to industrial countries. The lower percentages of Zambia and Ivory Coast, however, reflect a higher degree of development, copper and growing manufacturing in the Zambian case. There are many more wage laborers due to the industrialized sector and the small but developed maize agricultural sector that supports them. This wage-earning sector, consisting of over 22,600 in 1963 compares with 120,000 in Zaire at that time and 53,500 in Kenya. However, both those latter countries have larger populations. While Zaire, like Zambia, is heavily dependent on the exploitation of ores (in the Shaba province, next to Zambia's copper mines), Kenya's position depends on a well-developed agricultural sector (left by white settlers) and light industry.

Up to 1966, the number of people in primary and secondary schools was relatively high, 124 per 1000 in primary schools and 63 per 10,000 in secondary schools. However, Zambia had one of the lowest percentages of people in higher education, only 0.1 percent of 20- to 24-years-olds, compared to Liberia with 8 percent or Tanzania with 1.6 percent. The amount of foreign aid received by Zambia by 1969 was not high compared to some other countries, only $10.56 per capita compared to $31.18 for Congo Brazzaville or $27.12 in Botswana. No doubt this again reflects the presence of the copper industry and Zambia's better economic position. In 1968 Zambia depended on copper for 94 percent of its export volume.

To summarize, Zambia is special in certain respects because when it became independent, it had a well-developed, highly capitalized copper mining industry which earned a good deal of money for the country and helped finance the growth of schools and other social services. However, with the rise in demand for wages by the workers in the developed sector, accompanied by increasing imports, at higher and higher prices, its copper has become uncompetitive with the rest of the world. This has placed the government in the very tenuous position of trying to force down the inflation rate and thus further threatening the stability of the main source of foreign earnings. Zambia is like many other African countries in that there is a large, one might say, huge, rural indigenous sector, touched only marginally by the developed sector. The growing differential in wealth heralds more political trouble in the future as the have-nots challenge the haves. In order to meet this problem Zambia may have to depend more and more on help from the outside, and so it will become more of a client state than it has been before because copper will not support the present level of development and the country looks like a poor bet for agricultural development.

While mining has provided the foundation for what development there has been in Zambia, this is rare. Its only parallels are such countries as Rhodesia and South Africa. Elsewhere in Africa the enclave development pattern of Zambia is duplicated, but it is more usually based on agricultural activity (excluding South Africa with its sophisticated industrial development). Beginning in West Africa and moving around the coast, but including the occasional inland development pockets, Senegal and Gambia have a peanut industry while rubber dominates around Freetown (Sierra Leone) and in western Liberia. On the Upper Niger in Mali, we find peanuts again as well as in the Kano region of upper Nigeria. Around Abidjan (the Ivory Coast), there is coffee and timber, and cocoa, in Ghana and Nigeria, although Nigeria, now, also has petroleum. Coffee is also important in coastal Cameroon, as is oil at the mouth of the Congo (actually in Cabinda, a part of Angola). Sisal is an unsteady crop in the main coastal regions of Angola, Mozambique, and Tanzania. Coffee is dominant in the Mt. Kilimanjaro region and around Lake Victoria. In addition, there are pockets of agricultural growth in Ethiopia and Sudan. This leaves most of Africa, by far, without a productive base which could serve to bring the nations into the international economic community on a large scale without appreciable foreign aid.

THE COST OF DEVELOPMENT

Lest we fall into the error of thinking that wherever development has occurred, the benefits have all been positive, we should be aware that they have always had some price in human suffering, a fact which increasingly bothers developmentalists. As we end this survey of contemporary Africa, it will be useful to look at some examples of this cost, measuring the impact of development on the people involved.

A good place to begin is right back in Zambia with studies that have been made of the effects on the Tonga people (see Map 6.2) of the construction of the Kariba Dam in 1957 and 1958. As Colson remarks (1971, 1):

> Massive technological development hurts. This is a fact largely ignored by economic planners, technicians and political leaders. In planning drastic alterations in environment that uproot populations or make old adjustments impossible, they count the engineering costs but not the social costs. After all, they do not think of themselves as paying the latter. Some people no doubt like radical change. The majority probably like variety only so long as it is an embroidery upon the reassuring familiarity of customary routines, well known paths and scenes, and the ease of accustomed relationships.

While the impact on the Tongo, who did not understand why this deed had to be done, was enormous I have chosen to look at only one segment of change, the effect on the status of wives (Colson 1971, 125ff). After the resettlement, wives found that they were at a disadvantage and in an increasingly subordinate position to the men. This was because in their previous condition, they had control of land but after the resettlement, because of the arrangements worked out by the government, husbands had control of fields. If a woman challenged her husband in such a way as to lead to divorce, she found herself without any means of creating wealth. The new fields also made possible increased production of maize for which there was often no market. So more beer was brewed, and the men were intoxicated more often during which episodes they were more inclined to abuse their wives. The women had to work harder in the new fields in order to produce a crop because the growing season was shorter. This led to a decline in the quality of cooking, augmented by the loss of certain undomesticated food plants they were used to gathering in their old habitat and culminated in more abuse by their husbands. Cruelest of all, the women did not perceive this new deteriorated situation as a general effect of the move so each decided her circumstances were exceptional and resorted to private solutions, normally short-term flights from home or divorce, which merely aggravated an already untenable situation.

Another case comes from Chad and northern Cameroon (de Garine 1978). Here people of North and South Massa, Tuburi, Kera and Mussi are mostly farmers, growing sorghum and rice but also fishing and raising cattle. By traditional African standards, they are pastoralists, relatively wealthy cattle holders. In Massa, for example, the ratio used to be 1.38 to 1, and brideprices of ten head of cattle were common. Furthermore, they raised surpluses of food providing 115 percent of their caloric needs and 132 percent of their necessary protein. As part of national policy to increase income and raise the balance of payments, the government has forced these people to grow cotton. However, this has failed to bring development to the area (although it has apparently served national development) because returns from cotton are too low. The people still put their main energies into growing millet, cassava, and peanuts. However, the cotton fields require the best soil, therefore in an area so densely populated that there is no room for expansion, growing cotton has led to a decrease in the amount of good land available for growing other crops and a consequent decline in food supply. At the same time it has meant a reduction in the amount of grazing land, leading to smaller herds. This, in turn, has led to impoverishment along with hunger, as the repositories of value have declined in numbers. Today caloric and protein levels are below needs, so there is malnutrition. In Massa the ratio of cattle to people is down to 0.5 to 1. They are forced to buy millet from the neighboring hierarchical Fulbe (Fulani) and are beginning to "mimic" them, shifting into a hierarchical system themselves. Simply put, in order to achieve national development the government has forced this formerly prosperous indigenous economy to subsidize national growth (no doubt the urban sector) at a cost of decline in living standards.

A third example of the cost of development concerns ranching schemes in East Africa, which can be dealt with on a broader scale than other cases. All over East Africa—Kenya, Tanzania, Uganda, Sudan, and Somalia—governments have, in varying degrees, proposed ranching schemes to solve the "pastoral problem" (Schneider MS). The pastoral problem is that pastoral people continue to raise very inferior beef- and milk-producing animals in terms of standards of the developed sector of the national and international market. Typically (Meyn 1970) these animals weigh about 600 lbs when full grown and produce usable slaughtered weights in meat and bone of about 300 lbs, about a half of what American beef cattle will produce. Earlier in this book, I spoke of the financial uses Africans make of cattle within their indigenous economies. For those purposes, the managing of cattle for beef production is irrelevant. As far as I know, no African governments or people involved in cattle development schemes accept this assessment. They persist in believing that the animals are raised primarily for food (an adaptation to marginal agricultural conditions) and while they now may accept that pastoralists are rational people, they tend to believe that they act irrationally (raising too much poor quality beef) because various conditions prevent them from acting rationally. One prominent theory (Livingstone 1977) claims they do this because individual pastoralists do not own their own plots of grazing land and so cannot plan rational management because others' cattle might intrude and eat up grass they had intended to use. Another common theory is that because of periodic droughts, pastoralists have to keep huge backlogs of skinny but tough cattle to tide them over when disaster strikes.

The purpose of the ranching schemes is to set aside a piece of grazing range which no one can use except members of the scheme. With control of the land, the pastoralists can now plan rationally and thus turn out large, beefy cattle for the developed market as well as for their own food. Typically these schemes fail because the participants will not, in fact, limit the number of cattle and allow them to grow beyond what the range can support. In doing so, they destroy the ranch and break up the scheme. However, the movement to allow individuals or groups of individuals to take private control of sections of the range is having an effect in some places, such as the Kajiado area of Maasailand in Kenya (Hedlund 1971). Because of certain conditions of great financial loss due to drought, some pastoralists have found it profitable to take up ranching for beef production; this compels them to cease raising cattle as repositories of value and leads to a decline in the range available to other Maasai. As a result, the indigenous economy is interrupted, and classism has arisen among these Maasai. The beef ranchers are becoming richer and more powerful while the other Maasai are gradually being turned into a peasant class. This, it will be recognized, is simply another example of how development tends to cause polarization of wealth and power.

CONCLUSION

Multiplying examples of the costs of development would serve no purpose. The three just covered are sufficient to make the point stressed by Colson, that development schemes too often emphasize the technical aspects of projects and the rewards to be gained (even if only by a few) while glossing over the "human costs." I might even add that there sometimes seems to be an unwillingness to understand the true facts about the social situations that are to be manipulated, perhaps because recognition of the human costs would cause hesitation in development.

If these human costs are taken into account, they only raise, but do not solve, the greater question of whether development should be encouraged or not. One sort of answer is implicit in the material in this chapter. There is no doubt that most, if not all, Africans would be willing to abandon traditional societies and economies if the price were right. People of the Zaire Basin are

Boy with a model of an automobile made of reeds

not wedded to cassava (in fact, as we saw, to them it is a recently introduced crop), and pastoralists are not wedded to little cows (Schneider 1974). Most of the success stories of development, where Africans willingly and gladly engaged in aspects of the developed economy (cocoa in Ghana and Nigeria, maize production in Zambia, coffee growing in East Africa) are stories of self-motivation. It was not some development agency or development-minded government that brought it about but the people themselves. In fact probably no government or development agency could possibly know enough or understand enough to determine where some development operation will succeed or fail. This implies, therefore, that development, in a perfect world, would be allowed to grow up from the people rather than down from the top.

However, that is unrealistic because, in a sense, one could say of the groups which get control of the new national governments that they are successful, regardless of the failure of particular development schemes, because they have often successfully exploited international tensions to obtain income as clients to the powerful world powers. Still, in some ways this seems obscene, and it seems realistic to suggest that to some extent, beyond what is now true, developmentalists should take account of the ability of Africans to achieve development and help lay the groundwork for that. The aim, ultimately, should be to help Africans help themselves in ways that will promote widespread economic opportunity, rather than to impose development schemes on people. Helping Africans to help themselves will in turn promote egalitarianism (democracy) which seems to be a social end most people can agree on.

BIBLIOGRAPHY

In the following titles where the ethnic group to which the publication is relevant is not obvious the group's name is indicated in parentheses.

Aberle, D. T.   1961   Matrilineal Descent in Cross-Cultural Perspective. In David M. Schneider and Kathleen Gough, *Matrilineal Kinship.* U. of California Press.

Abrahams, R. G.   1967   *The Political Organization of Unyamwezi.* Cambridge U. Press.

Alagoa, E. J.   1970   Long-Distance Trade and States in the Niger Delta, *J. of African History,* 11, 319–329.

Allan, W.   1965   *The African Husbandmen.* Barnes and Noble; N. Y.

Ames, D. W.   1955   The Use of a Transitional Cloth-Money Token among the Wolof. *American Anthropologist;* 57, 5, 1016–1024.

Austen, R. A.   1969   Ntemiship, Trade, and State-Building: Political Developments among the Western Bantu of Tanzania, in D. F. McCall and others (eds.), *East African History.* Praeger; N. Y.

Balandier, G.   1970   *Political Anthropology.* Penguin Press; London.

Barnes, J. A.   1951   The Fort Jameson Ngoni, in E. Colson and M. Gluckman (eds.), *Seven Tribes of British Central Africa.* Manchester U. Press, Manchester.

Barth, F.   1966   *Models of Social Organization.* Royal Anthropological Institute; London.

———.   1967   On the Study of Social Change, *American Anthropologist* 69, 661–669.

Bascom, W. R.   1969   *The Yoruba of Southwestern Nigeria.* Holt, Rinehart and Winston; N. Y.

———.   1977   Some Yoruba Ways with Yams, in J. Kuper (ed.), *The Anthropologists' Cookbook.* Routledge and Kegan Paul; London.

Bascom, W. R. and M. J. Herskovits (eds.)   1959   *Continuity and Change in African Cultures.* U. of Chicago Press; Chicago.

Baxter, P. T. W.   1972   Absence Makes the Heart Grow Fonder: Some Suggestions Why Witchcraft Accusations Are Rare among East African Pastoralists, in M. Gluckman (ed.), *The Allocation of Responsibility.* Manchester U. Press; Manchester.

Baxter, P. T. W. and U. Almagor   1978   *Age, Generation and Time; Some Features of East African Age Organization.* C. Hurst and Co.; London.

Beck, C. S.   1974   *Explorations in Bantu Phenomenology.* MA Thesis, Bryn Mawr College.

Beidelman, T.   1961   Right and Left Hand among the Kaguru: A note on Symbolic Classification, *Africa,* 35, 250–256.

————. 1967   *The Matrilineal People of Eastern Tanzania.* International African Institute; London.

————. 1971   *The Kaguru, A Matrilineal People of Eastern Tanzania.* International African Institute; London.

Bennett, M. K.   1962   *An Agroclimatic Mapping of Africa,* Food Research Institute Studies, 3: 195–216.

Berry, S.   1975   *Cocoa, Custom, and Socio-Economic Change in Rural Western Nigeria.* Clarendon Press; Oxford.

Bhagavan, M. R.   1978   *Zambia: Impact of Industrial Strategy on Regional Imbalance and Social Inequality.* The Scandanavian Institute of African Studies; Uppsala.

Black, D.   1976   *The Behavior of Law.* Academic Press; N. Y.

Bledsoe, C.   1976   Women's Marital Strategies Among the Kpelle of Liberia, *J. of Anthropological Research,* 32, 372–389.

Bohannan P.   1957   *Justice and Judgement among the Tiv.* Oxford U. Press; London.

————. 1964   *Africa and Africans.* Natural History Press; Garden City, N. Y.

Bohannan, P. and L.   1968   *Tiv Economy.* Northwestern U. Press; Evanston.

Bohannan P. and P. Curtin   1971   *Africa and Africans (rev. ed.).* Natural History Press; Garden City, N. Y.

Bohannan, P. and G. Dalton   1962   *Markets in Africa.* Northwestern U. Press; Evanston.

Buxton, J.   1963   Mandari Witchcraft, in J. Middleton and E. H. Winter (eds.), *Witchcraft and Sorcery in East Africa.* Routledge and Kegan Paul; London.

Clark, G.   1971   *World Prehistory: A New Outline.* Cambridge U. Press; Cambridge.

Clark, J. D.   1970   *The Prehistory of Africa.* Praeger; N. Y.

Colson, E.   1962   *The Plateau Tonga of Northern Rhodesia.* Manchester U. Press; Manchester.

————. 1971   *The Social Consequences of Resettlement: The Impact of the Kariba Resettlement upon the Gwembe Tonga.* Manchester U. Press; Manchester.

Colson, E. and M. Gluckman (eds.)   1951   *Seven Tribes of British Central Africa.* Manchester U. Press; Manchester.

Coursey, D. G.   1977   The Cultivation and Use of Yams in West Africa, in A. A. Konczacki and J. M. Konczacki (eds.), *An Economic History of Tropical Africa.* Frank Cass; London.

Cunnison, I.   1960   Headmanship and the Ritual of Luapula Villages, in S. Ottenberg and P. Ottenberg (eds.), *Cultures and Societies of Africa.* Random House; N. Y.

————. 1966   *Bagarra Arabs.* Clarendon Press; Oxford.

Dahl, G. and A. Hjort   1976   Having Herds: Pastoral Herd Growth and Household Economy. *Stockholm Studies in Social Anthropology,* 2, Department of Social Anthropology, U. of Stockholm; Stockholm.

Daniels, R. E.   1975   Pastoralists with Plows: Cultural Continuities among the Kipsigis of Kenya. Paper presented at the 74th Annual Meeting of the American Anthropological Association; San Francisco.

Davis, A. J.   1973   Coptic Christianity, in E. P. Skinner, *Peoples and Cultures of Africa.* Natural History Press; Garden City, N. Y.

De Craemer, W., J. Vansina, and R. C. Fox   1976   Religious Movements in Central Africa: A Theoretical Study. *Comparative Studies in Society and History,* 18, 458–475.

De Garine, I.   1978   Population, Production, and Culture in the Plains Societies of Northern Cameroon and Chad: The Anthropologist in Development Projects, *Current Anthropology,* 19, 42–57.

De Heusch, L.   1975   What Shall We Do With the Drunken King? *Africa,* 45, 363–372.

Douglas, M.   1963   *The Lele of Kasai.* Oxford U. Press; Oxford.

———.   1964   Matriliny and Pawnship in Central Africa. *Africa,* 34, 301–313.

———.   1966   *Purity and Danger.* Penguin; Harmondsworth.

Drachoussoff, V.   1947   Essai sur L'agriculture Indigene au Bas-Congo, *Bull. Agriculture du Congo Belge,* 798–806.

Driberg, J. H.   1929   *The Savage as He Really Is.* Routledge and Kegan Paul; London.

Einzig, P.   1966   *Primitive Money* (rev. ed.). Pergamon Press; N. Y.

Elliott, C.   1971   *Constraints on the Economic Development of Zambia.* Oxford U. Press; Oxford

Evans-Pritchard, E. E.   1937, 1950   *Witchcraft, Oracles and Magic Among the Azande.* Clarendon Press; Oxford.

———.   1940   *The Nuer.* Oxford U. Press; Oxford.

———.   1960   A selection from Nuer Religion, in C. Leslie, *Anthropology and Folk Religion.* Vintage; N. Y.

Fallers, L.   1964   *The King's Men* (Baganda). Oxford U. Press; Oxford.

———.   1965   *Bantu Bureaucracy* (Basoga). U. of Chicago Press; Chicago.

Feierman, S.   1974   *The Shambaa Kingdom.* U. of Wisconsin Press; Madison.

Fernandez, J. W.   1978   African Religious Movements, *Annual Review of Anthropology,* 7, 195–234.

Fielder, R. J.   1973   The Role of Cattle in Ila Economy, African Social Research, 15, 327–361.

Forde, D.   1954   *African Worlds.* Oxford U. Press; Oxford.

———.   1963   *Habitat, Economy and Society.* Dutton; N. Y.

———.   1964   *Yako Studies.* Oxford U. Press; Oxford.

Forde, D. and G. I. Jones   1950   *The Ibo and Ibibio-Speaking Peoples of South-Eastern Nigeria.* International African Institute; London.

Fortes, M.   1945   *The Dynamics of Clanship among the Tallensi.* Oxford U. Press; Oxford.

———.   1960   Oedipus and Job in West Africa, in C. Leslie, *Anthropology of Folk Religion.* Vintage; N. Y.

———.   1965   Some Reflections on Ancestor Worship in Africa, in M. Fortes and G. Dieterlan (eds.), *African Systems of Thought.* Oxford U. Press; Oxford.

Fortes, M. and G. Dieterlan (eds.)   1965   *African Systems of Thought.* Oxford U. Press; Oxford.

Gamer, R. E.   1976   *The Developing Nations.* Allyn and Bacon; Boston.

Gibbs, J. L., Jr.   1965   *Peoples of Africa.* Holt, Rinehart and Winston; N. Y.

Gluckman, M.   1950   Kinship and Marriage among the Lozi of Northern Rhodesia and the Zulu of Natal, in A. R. Radcliffe-Brown and D. Forde (eds.), *African Systems of Kinship and Marriage.* Oxford U. Press; Oxford.

———.   1951   The Lozi of Barotseland in North-Western Rhodesia, in E. Colson and M. Gluckman (eds.), *Seven Tribes of British Central Africa.* Manchester U. Press; Manchester.

———.   1955   *The Judicial Process among the Barotse of Northern Rhodesia,* Manchester U. Press; Manchester.

Godelier, M.   1977   Anthropology and Economics, in M. Godelier (ed.), *Perspectives in Marxist Anthropology.* Cambridge U. Press; Cambridge.

Goldschmidt, W.   1967   *Sebei Law.* U. of California Press; Berkeley.

———.   1976   *Culture and Behavior of the Sebei.* U. of California Press; Berkeley.

Goody, J.   1971   *Technology, Tradition and the State in Africa.* Oxford U. Press; Oxford.

———.   1973   Bridewealth and Dowry in Africa and Eurasia, in J. Goody and S. J. Tambiah, *Bridewealth and Dowry,* Cambridge U. Press; Cambridge.

Gray, R. F.   N. D.   *The Mbugwe.*

———.   1963   *The Sonjo of Tanganyika.* Oxford U. Press; Oxford.

Greenberg, J. H.   1963   The Languages of Africa, *International Journal of American Linguistics,* 29.

Griaule, M.   1965   *Conversations with Ogotemmeli.* Oxford U. Press; Oxford.

Gulliver, P. H.   1955   *The Family Herds, A Study of Two Pastoral Tribes in East Africa, the Jie and Turkana.* Routledge and Kegan Paul; London.

———.   1963   *Social Control in an African Society, A Study of the Arusha: Agricultural Masai of Northern Tanganyika.* Routledge and Kegan Paul; London.

Hartwig, G.   1976   *The Art of Survival in East Africa: The Kerebe and Long-Distance Trade.* Africana Publishing Co.; N. Y.

Hatch, J.   1976   *Two African Statesmen.* Secker and Warburg; London.

Hedlund, G. B.   1971   The Impact of Group Ranches on a Pastoral Society. Institute of Development Studies, Staff Paper 100, U. of Nairobi.

Herskovits, M. J.   1926   The Cattle Complex in East Africa, *American Anthropologist,* 28, 230–272, 361–388, 494–528, 633–664.

———.   1938   *Dahomey, An Ancient African Kingdom* (2 vols.). J. J. Augustin; N. Y.

———.   1962   *The Human Factor in Changing Africa.* Knopf; N. Y.

Heyer, J.   1971   *A Linear Programming Analysis of Constraints on Peasant Farms in Kenya,* Food Research Institute Studies, 10, Stanford University, 55–67.

Hill, P.   1961   The Migrant Cocoa Farmers of Southern Ghana, *Africa,* 31, 209–230.

———.   1970   *Studies in Rural Capitalism in West Africa.* Cambridge U. Press; Cambridge.

———.   1972   *Rural Hausa.* Cambridge U. Press; Cambridge.

Hoebel, E. A.   1961   Three Studies in African Law, *Stanford U. Law Review,* 13, 418–442.

Hopkins, A.   1973   *An Economic History of West Africa.* Longman; London.

Horton, R.   1964   Ritual Man in Africa. *Africa,* 34, 85–104.

Huntingford, G. W. B.   1953   *The Southern Nilo-Hamites.* International African Institute; London.

Johnston, B. F.   1958   *The Staple Food Economies of Western Tropical Africa.* Stanford U. Press; Palo Alto.

Jones, G. I.   1977   Native and Trade Currencies in Southern Nigeria during the Eighteenth and Nineteenth Centuries, In A. A. Konczacki and J. M. Konczacki (eds.), *An Economic History of Tropical Africa.* Frank Cass; London.

Karp, P. and I.   1979   Right and Left in American Society, in W. Arens (ed.), *The American Dimension,* 2nd edition.

Klima, G. J.   1970   *The Barabaig, East African Cattle-Herders.* Holt, Rinehart and Winston; N. Y.

Konczacki, A. A. and J. M. Konczacki (eds.)   1977   *An Economic History of Tropical Africa.* Frank Cass; London.

Konnerup, N. M.   1966   The Outlook for Animal Agriculture in Africa, Proceedings of the Agricultural Research Institute; Washington, D. C.

Kopytoff, I.   1964   Family and Lineage among the Suku of the Congo, in R. F. Gray and P. H. Gulliver (eds.), *The Family Estate in Africa.* Routledge and Kegan Paul; London.

Kottack, C.   1979   *Cultural Anthropology.* Random House; N. Y.

Kriege, E. J.   1936   *The Social System of the Zulus.* Longman; London.

Kriege, E. J. and J. D.   1943   *The Realm of the Rain Queen.* Oxford U. Press; Oxford.

Kuper, A.   1975   The Social Structure of the Sotho-Speaking Peoples of Southern Africa, *Africa,* 45, 67–81, 139–149.

Kuper, H.   1963   *The Swazi, A South African Kingdom.* Holt, Rinehart and Winston; N. Y.

Kuper, H., A. J. B. Hughes, and J. van Velsen   1955   *The Shona and Ndebele of Southern Rhodesia.* International African Institute; London.

Laughlin, C. D., Jr.   1974   Deprivation and Reciprocity, *Man,* 9, 380–396.

Lee, R.   1969   !Kung Bushman Subsistence: An Input-Output Analysis, in D. Damas (ed.), *Contributions to Anthropology: Ecological Essays.* Queen's Printer; Ottawa.

Legesse, A.   1973   *Gada: Three Approaches to the Study of African Society* (Borana Galla). Free Press; N. Y.

Lemarchand, R.   1977   *African Kingship in Perspective.* Frank Cass; London

Levi-Strauss, C.   1962   *The Savage Mind.* U. of Chicago Press; Chicago

Levine, D. N.   1965   *Wax and Gold* (Amhara). U. of Chicago Press; Chicago.

Lewis, H. S.   1965   *A Galla Monarchy, Jimma Abba Jifar, Ethiopia 1830–1932.* U. of Wisconsin Press; Madison.

Lewis, I. M.   1961   *Pastoral Democracy.* Oxford U. Press; Oxford.

———.   1976   *Social Anthropology in Perspective.* Penguin Books; Harmondsworth.

Lienhardt, G.   1961   *Divinity and Experience, the Religion of the Dinka.* Clarendon Press; Oxford.

Linton, R.   1937   One Hundred Per Cent American, *The American Mercury,* 40: 427–429.

Little, K.   1960   The Role of the Secret Society in Cultural Specialization, in Ottenberg and Ottenberg, 1960.

Little, P.   N. D.   The Plantain in East Africa: An Exchange Theory Approach to the Political History of East African Plantain Societies. Paper Delivered at Annual Meeting of Central States Anthropological Society, Notre Dame, 1978.

Livingstone, D.   1857   Missionary Travels and Researches in South Africa. J. Murray; London.

Livingstone, I.   1977   Economic Irrationality among Pastoral Peoples in East Africa: Myth or Reality? Institute of Development Studies, U. of Nairobi, Discussion Paper No. 245.

Lloyd, P.   1965   The Political Structure of African Kingdoms: An Exploratory Model, in *Association of Social Anthropology, Political Systems and the Distribution of Power.* Praeger; N. Y.

Lystad, R.   1958   *The Ashanti, A Proud People.* Rutgers U. Press; New Brunswick.

MacGaffey, W.   1970   *Custom and Government in the Lower Congo.* U. of California Press; Berkeley.

————.   1978   Review of C. Meillassoux, L'Esclavage en Afrique Précolonial, *African Economic History.* 50–53.

Mair, L.   1977a   *African Kingdoms.* Clarendon Press; Oxford.

————.   1977b   *Primitive Government* (rev. ed.). Indiana U. Press; Bloomington.

Malcolm, D. W.   1953   *Sukumaland.* Oxford U. Press, Oxford.

Manners, R. A.   1962   Land Use, Trade and Growth of Market Economy in Kipsigis Country, in P. Bohannan and G. Dalton (eds.), *Markets in Africa.* Northwestern U. Press; Evanston.

Maquet, J.   1964   Objectivity in Anthropology, *Current Anthropology,* 5, 47–55.

————.   1971   *Power and Society in Africa.* World U. Library; London.

————.   1972   *Civilizations of Black Africa.* Oxford U. Press; Oxford.

Marriott, M.   1955   Little Communities in an Indigenous Civilization, in M. Marriott (ed.), *Village India.* American Anthropologist Memoir No. 83, 171–222.

Marwick, M. G.   1965   *Sorcery in its Social Setting, A Study of the Northern Rhodesian Cêwa.* Manchester U. Press; Manchester.

Massing, A.   1977   Economic Development in the Kru Culture Area. Ph.D. Dissertation, Indiana University.

Mead, M.   1955   *Cultural Patterns and Technical Change.* Mentor Books; N. Y.

Meillassoux, C.   1972   From Reproduction to Production; A Marxist Approach to Economic Anthropology. *Economy and Society,* 1, 93–104.

Merriam, A. P.   1974   *An African World, The Basongye Village of Lupupu Ngye.* Indiana U. Press; Bloomington.

Meyn, K.   1970   *Beef Production in East Africa.* Institute fur Wirtschaftforshung, Weltforum Verlag; Munich.

Middleton, J.   1963   Witchcraft and Sorcery in Lugbara, in Middleton and Winter, 1963.

———.   1965   *The Lugbara of Uganda.* Holt, Rinehart and Winston; N. Y.

Middleton, J. and D. Tait.   1958   *Tribes without Rulers.* Routledge and Kegan Paul; London.

Middleton, J. and E. H. Winter   1963   *Witchcraft and Sorcery in East Africa.* Routledge and Kegan Paul; London.

Miers, S. and I. Kopytoff (eds.)   1977   *Slavery in Africa.* U. of Wisconsin Press; Madison.

Miller, J. G.   1970   Cokwe Trade and Conquest in the Nineteenth Century, in R. Gray and D. Birmingham, *Pre-Colonial African Trade.* Oxford U. Press; Oxford.

Miracle, M.   1966   *Maize in Tropical Africa.* U. of Wisconsin Press; Madison.

———.   1967   *Agriculture in the Congo Basin.* U. of Wisconsin Press; Madison.

Mitchell, J. C.   1951   The Yao of Southern Nyasaland, in E. Colson and M. Gluckman (eds.), *Seven Tribes of British Central Africa.* Manchester U. Press; Manchester.

Moore, S. F.   1976   The Secret of Men: A Fiction of Chagga Initiation and its Relation to the Logic of Chagga Symbolism, *Africa,* 46, 357–370.

———.   1978   *Law as Process: An Anthropological Approach.* Routledge and Kegan Paul; London.

Morgan, W. B. and J. C. Pugh   1973   *West Africa.* Methuen and Co.; London.

Morrison, D. G. and others   1972   *Black Africa, A Comparative Handbook.* Free Press; N. Y.

Murdock, G. P.   1949   *Social Structure.* Macmillan; N. Y.

———.   1959   *Africa, Its Peoples and Their Culture History.* McGraw-Hill; N. Y.

———.   1967   Ethnographic Atlas: A Summary, *Ethnology,* VI. 109–236.

Nadel, S. F.   1942   *Black Byzantium* (Nupe). Oxford U. Press; Oxford.

Needham, R.   1960   The Left Hand of the Mugwe: An Analytical Note on the Structure of Meru Symbolism. *Africa,* 30, 20–33.

Newbury, M. C.   1978   Ethnicity in Rwanda: The Case of Kinyaga, *Africa,* 48.

Onwuejeogwu, M.   1975   *The Social Anthropology of Africa.* Heinemann; London.

Ottenberg, P.   1965   The Afikpo Ibo of Eastern Nigeria, in Gibbs 1965.

Ottenberg, S. and P.   1960   *Cultures and Societies of Africa.* Random House; New York

Parkin, D. J.   1972   *Palms, Wine and Witnesses.* Chandler; San Francisco.

Phillipson, D. W.   1977   The Spread of the Bantu Language, *Scientific American,* 106–114.

Radcliffe-Brown, A. R.   1952   The Mother's Brother in South Africa, in A. R. Radcliffe-Brown (ed.), *Structure and Function in Primitive Society.* Free Press; Glencoe.

Radcliffe-Brown, A. R. and D. Forde.   1950   *African Systems of Kinship and Marriage.* Oxford U. Press; Oxford.

Ray, B. C.   1976   *African Religions.* Prentice-Hall; Englewood Cliffs, N. J.

Richards, A. I.   1939   *Land, Labour and Diet in Northern Rhodesia* (Bemba). Oxford U. Press; Oxford.

————.   1950   Some Types of Family Structure amongst the Central Bantu, in A. R. Radcliffe-Brown and D. Forde (eds.), *African Systems of Kinship and Marriage.* Oxford U. Press; Oxford.

————.   1967   African Systems of Thought: An Anglo-French Dialogue, *Man,* 2, 286–298.

Rigby, P.   1966   Dual Symbolic Classification among the Gogo of Central Tanzania, *Africa,* 36, 1–17.

————.   1969   *Cattle and Kinship among the Gogo.* Cornell U. Press; Ithaca.

Sahlins, M.   1962   Poor Man, Rich Man, Big Man, Chief: Political Types in Melanesia and Polynesia, *Comparative Studies in Society and History,* 5, 285–303.

Sangree, W.   1966   *Age, Prayer and Politics in Tiriki, Kenya.* Oxford U. Press; Oxford.

Schapera, I.   1938   *A Handbook of Tswana Law and Custom.* Oxford U. Press; Oxford.

————.   1950   Kinship and Marriage among the Tswana, in A. R. Radcliffe-Brown and D. Forde (eds.), *African Systems of Kinship and Marriage.* Oxford U. Press; Oxford.

————.   1953   *The Tswana.* International African Institute; London.

Schapera, I. and S. Roberts   1975   Rampedi Revisited: Another Look at a Kgatla Ward, *Africa,* 45, 258–280.

Schneider, H. K.   1953   The Pokot (Suk) of Kenya with Special Reference to the Role of Livestock in their Subsistence Economy. University Microfilms; Ann Arbor.

————.   1964a   Economics in East African Aboriginal Societies, in M. J. Herskovits and M. Harwitz, *Economic Transition in Africa.* Northwestern U. Press; Evanston.

————.   1964b   A Model of African Indigenous Economy and Society, *Comparative Studies in Society and History,* 7, 37–55.

————.   1969   A Statistical Study of Brideprice in Africa. Paper Delivered at Annual Meeting of American Anthropological Assn., New Orleans.

————.   1970   *The Wahi Wanyaturu, Economics in an African Society.* Aldine; Chicago.

————.   1974   Economic Development and Economic Change: The Case of East African Cattle, *Current Anthropology,* 15, 259–276.

————.   1977   Prehistoric Transpacific Contact and the Theory of Culture Change, *American Anthropologist,* 79, 9–25.

————.   1978   Development and the Pastoralists of East Africa." Paper delivered at meeting of Nomad Commission, London.

————.   1979   *Livestock and Equality in East Africa, the Economic Basis for Social Structure.* Indiana U. Press; Bloomington.

Schultz, J.   1976   *Land Use in Zambia.* Weltforum Verlag; Munich.

Scudder, T.   1971   *Gathering among African Woodland Savannah Cultivators: A Case Study—the Gwembe Tonga.* Institute for African Studies, U. of Zambia.

Shorter, A.   1972   *Chiefship in Western Tanzania; A Political History of the Kimbu.* Clarendon Press; Oxford.

Skinner, E. P.   1962   Trade and Markets among the Mossi People, in P. Bohannan and G. Dalton (eds.), *Markets in Africa*. Northwestern U. Press; Evanston.

————.   1973   *Peoples and Cultures of Africa*. Natural History Press; Garden City, N. Y.

Smith, C.   1976   Exchange systems and the Spatial Distribution of Elites: The Organization of Stratification in Agrarian Societies, in C. Smith (ed.), *Regional Analysis*, Vol. II. Academic Press, N. Y.

Smith, M. G.   1966   The Hausa of Northern Nigeria, in J. L. Gibbs, Jr., *Peoples of Africa*. Holt, Rinehart and Winston; N. Y.

Smith, R. H. T.   1971   West African Market-places: Temporal Periodicity and Locational Spacing, in C. Meillassoux (ed.), *The Development of Indigenous Trade and Markets in West Africa*. Oxford U. Press; Oxford.

Southall, A. W.   c1954   *Alur Society*. W. Heffer and Sons; Cambridge.

Stanley, H. M.   1891   *In Darkest Africa*. Vol. II. Scribners; N. Y.

Stenning, D.   1960   *Savannah Nomads* (Fulani). Oxford U. Press; Oxford.

Stevenson, R. F.   1968   *Population and Political Systems in Tropical Africa*. Columbia U. Press; N. Y.

Stryker, R. E.   MS   Neocolonialism and Development: A Study of the Ivory Coast Political Economy.

Sumner, C.   1973   The Ethiopic Liturgy: An Analysis, in E. P. Skinner, *Peoples and Cultures of Africa*. Natural History Press; Garden City, N. Y.

Tait, D.   1958   The Territorial Pattern and Lineage System of Konkomba, in J. Middleton and E. H. Winter (eds.), *Witchcraft and Sorcery in East Africa*. Routledge and Kegan Paul; London.

Tempels, P.   1959   *Bantu Philosophy*. Presence Africaine; Paris.

Trigger, R. G.   1969   The Personality of the Sudan, in D. McCall and others, *Eastern African History*. Praeger; N. Y.

Turnbull, C.   1972   *The Mountain People* (Ik). Jonathan Cape; London.

Turner, V. W.   1961   *Ndembu Divination: Its Symbols and Techniques*. Manchester U. Press; Manchester.

————.   1966   Colour Classification in Ndembu Ritual, in M. Banton (ed.), *Anthropological Approaches to the Study of Religion*. Tavistock; London.

————.   1967   *The Forest of Symbols*. Cornell U. Press; Ithaca.

————.   1968   *Drums of Afflication*. Clarendon Press; Oxford.

————.   1969   *The Ritual Process*. Aldine; Chicago.

————.   1973   Symbols in African Ritual, *Science,* Vol. 179, pp. 1100–1105, March 16, 1973.

Uchendu, V.   1965   *The Igbo of Southeast Nigeria*. Holt, Rinehart and Winston; N. Y.

Uchendu, V. C. and K. R. M. Anthony.   1975   *Agricultural change in Teso District, Uganda*. East African Literature Bureau; Nairobi.

Vansina, J.   1954   *Les Tribus Ba-Kuba et les Peuplades Apparentees*. International African Institute; London.

————.   1962   Trade and Markets among the Kuba, in P. Bohannan and G. Dalton (eds.), *Markets in Africa*. Northwestern U. Press; Evanston.

————. c1965 *Introduction a l'Ethnographie du Congo.* Editions Universitaires du Congo; Brussels.

————. 1968 Long-Distance Trade in Central Africa, in R. O. Collins (ed.), *Problems in African History.* Prentice-Hall; Englewood Cliffs, N. J.

Vaughn, J. H. 1977 The Slave as Institutionalized Outsider, in S. Miers and I. Kopytoff (eds.), *Slavery in Africa.* U. of Wisconsin Press; Madison.

Von Sick, E. 1916 Die Waniaturu (Walimi). Baessler-Archiv, 1–42.

Wagner, G. 1954 The Abaluyia of Kavirondo (Kenya), in D. Forde, *African Worlds.* Oxford U. Press; Oxford.

————. 1956 *The Bantu of North Kavirondo.* Oxford U. Press; Oxford.

Wallace, A. F. C. 1956 Revitalization Movements, *American Anthropologist,* 58, 264–281.

Wilson, M. 1951 *Good Company, a Study of Nyakyusa Age-Villages.* Oxford U. Press; Oxford.

Winans, E. 1962 *Shambala.* U. of California Press; Berkeley.

Winter, E. 1958 The Aboriginal Political Structure of Bwamba, in J. Middleton and D. Tait (eds.), *Tribes without Rulers.* Routledge and Kegan Paul; London.

Woodburn, J. 1970 *Hunters and Gatherers: The Material Culture of the Nomadic Hadza.* British Museum; London.

INDEX